Napa & Sonoma

Courtesy Benziger, Kent Hansen

Napa &
Sonoma

A Great Destination

Peg Melnik with Tim Fish

The Countryman Press   Woodstock, Vermont

We dedicate this book to our beloved,
adventuresome children,
Sophie and Tucker.

Watching you grow up in this amazing place
called Wine Country
has been a delight.

Napa & Sonoma: A Great Destination

ISBN 978-1-58157-136-3
Ninth Edition

Interior photographs by the author unless otherwise specified
Photograph on page 32–33 by © g01xm, iStockphoto.com.
Photograph on page 230–31 by © Chuck Place, iStockphoto.com.
Maps by Erin Greb Cartography, © The Countryman Press
Book design and composition by Eugenie S. Delaney

Published by The Countryman Press, P.O. Box 748, Woodstock, VT 05091

Distributed by W. W. Norton & Company, Inc., 500 Fifth Avenue, New York, NY 10110

Printed in the United States of America

10 9 8 7 6 5 4 3 2 1

Acknowledgments

MANY PEOPLE made this book possible. We want to thank all the wineries, restaurants, inns, and other businesses that put up with our phone calls, e-mail inquiries, and spontaneous visits. Numerous organizations proved to be great resources.

We would also like to acknowledge the smart and devoted team at W. W. Norton's The Countryman Press, particularly Kermit Hummel, Lisa Sacks, and Melissa Dobson. Closer to home, we'd like to thank Jenny Kaplan for her brilliant vision and ingenuity, and Meena Ruybalid for her outstanding contribution, her dedication, and her excellent work. We'd also like to thank two publications that are dear to us: the *Santa Rosa Press Democrat* and *Wine Spectator*. While this book is produced independently of both, we are grateful to them for providing us gainful employment while we pursue this project in our off hours.

Finally, we want to thank our children, Sophie and Tucker, for their patience with us over the years. Sophie was born the week of our very first deadline in 1991 and has grown up with this book. Tucker followed eight years later, and as long as we bribed him with ice cream, he tagged along willingly as we traveled the trails of Napa and Sonoma.

Now we would like to hear from you. What do you like about this book, and how do you think it might be improved? Also, let us know about your experiences in Wine Country—both good and bad. We hope the inns, restaurants, wineries, and other businesses that are mentioned here live up to their recommendations. If they don't, let us know. Contact Tim Fish and Peg Melnik directly via e-mail at TimFish@comcast.net and PegMelnik@gmail.com, or through the website www.napasonomainsider.com.

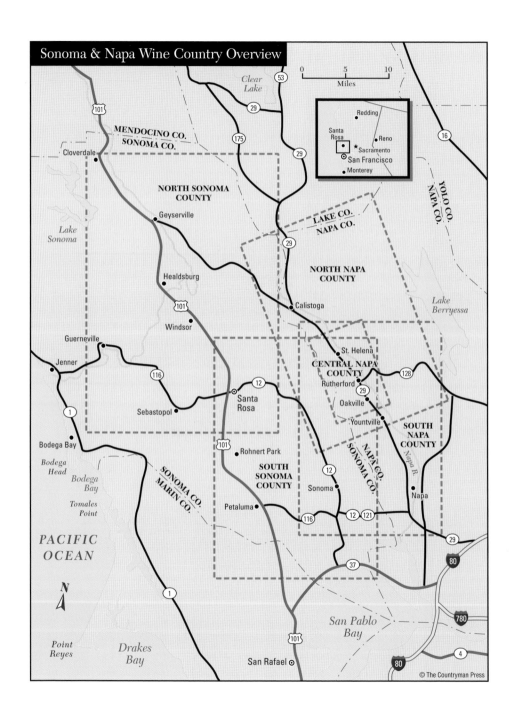

Sonoma & Napa Wine Country Overview

Clear Lake

MENDOCINO CO.
SONOMA CO.

Cloverdale

NORTH SONOMA
COUNTY

Geyserville

Lake
Sonoma

Healdsburg

LAKE CO.
NAPA CO.

NORTH NAPA
COUNTY

Calistoga

Lake
Berryessa

Windsor

Guerneville

Jenner

St. Helena

CENTRAL NAPA
COUNTY

Rutherford

Sebastopol

Santa
Rosa

Oakville

Yountville

SOUTH
NAPA
COUNTY

Bodega Bay

Rohnert Park

Bodega
Head

Bodega
Bay

SONOMA CO.
MARIN CO.

SOUTH
SONOMA
COUNTY

NAPA CO.
SONOMA CO.

Tomales
Point

Napa R.

Sonoma

Napa

PACIFIC
OCEAN

Petaluma

N

Point
Reyes

Drakes
Bay

San Pablo
Bay

San Rafael

YOLO CO.
NAPA CO.

0   5   10
Miles

Redding

Santa
Rosa

Reno

Sacramento

San Francisco

Monterey

© The Countryman Press

6

Contents

Introduction

WELCOME TO THE NINTH EDITION of *Napa & Sonoma: A Great Destination,* the definitive guide to this lovely area and all the things to see and do in it. Our guide has been endorsed by the esteemed wine critics Harvey Steiman, who praised its lack of "stuffiness or pomposity," and Robert Parker Jr., who called it "essential reading for any visitor."

This thoroughly revised and updated edition, personally researched by the authors, has a number of exciting new features. As always, you can trust your tour guides: Tim Fish is associate editor of the international magazine *Wine Spectator.* Peg Melnik is a veteran columnist, wine blogger, and tasting coordinator for the New York Times–owned *Santa Rosa Press Democrat,* the premier daily newspaper in Wine Country.

If you follow their lead, you'll sidestep tourist traps to experience the region at its most authentic. (For updated reports on all things Wine Country, check out our website www.napasonomainsider.com and follow our blog.)

Get ready to tour Napa & Sonoma like a genuine insider. See you in Wine Country!

—Tim Fish and Peg Melnik, Santa Rosa, California

LEFT: Vineyards are the backdrop of Wine Country. Tim Fish

The Way This Book Works

THIS EDITION of *Napa & Sonoma: A Great Destination,* is divided into three parts. Part I orients you to the region, with "How to Travel Like an Insider" providing everything you'll need to be in the know. Here you'll learn about the latest developments in Wine Country. Find out why, for example, the city of Napa now has more than enough appeal to attract droves of tourists; and learn what's behind the family-oriented resort approach at the Francis Ford Coppola Winery in Geyserville. Next, take our crash course in wine tasting, get step-by-step tasting advice, and, if you're interested in taking your wine education to the next level, find information about wine classes in the Napa & Sonoma area.

"A Brief History of Nappa & Sonoma" provides a brief historical overview, where you'll learn how and why wine became the organizing principle of the region.

Part II covers the major cities in Wine Country, providing detailed listings for lodging, restaurants, and wineries, and covering special attractions as well as the retail, cultural, and recreational scenes. You'll also find a segment we call "Palate Adventures," which includes a number of establishments of culinary interest, including eateries, food markets, wine shops, and breweries.

Pay close attention to the Top 10 Picks for each city in Chapters 1 through 9, and the Insider Secrets dispersed throughout the book. Here's an example of an Insider Secret, from "Bodega Bay & West County" (see sidebar, this page).

Insider Secrets are here to give you an advantage over travelers following other guides, and the information they impart is solid gold . . .

Don't miss the themed escapes you'll find throughout this book. The suggested

> *Insider Secret:*
> One of the most stunning (and undiscovered) drives in Wine Country is the stretch from **Occidental to Bodega Bay on Coleman Valley Road.** (The locals would prefer to keep this hush hush, so don't tell them we sent you.) This route is the most scenic approach to the bay; you'll see sheep, cows, and the occasional llama. (Take Coleman Valley Road from Occidental to Bodega Bay.)

outings there will suit a range of interests; foodies, romantics, outdoor enthusiasts, art lovers, and others will find recommendations catered to their personal obsessions. See also regional highlights in our Best Day in San Francisco (Chapter 1), Best Day in Napa Valley (Chapter 3), and Best Day in Sonoma County (Chapter 6).

Finally, in Part III of this guide you'll find all the logistical information to make your trip to Wine Country as seamless as possible, including information on transportation to and around the region, climate considerations, and a list of helpful resources to guide your travel plans.

A note on the lodging and dining listings: We use price codes to convey a general understanding of cost (since specific prices are prone to change). Here are the corresponding rates for the price codes you will find throughout.

Lodging Price Codes
Inexpensive:	Up to $100
Moderate:	$100 to $150
Expensive:	$150 to $250
Very Expensive:	Over $250

Dining Price Codes
Inexpensive:	Up to $20
Moderate:	$20 to $30
Expensive:	$30 to $40
Very Expensive:	$40 or more

Dining price codes reflect the cost of a single meal, including appetizer, entrée, and dessert, but not including cocktails, wine, tax, or tip.

PART I

How to Travel
Like an Insider

WHAT'S THE ADVANTAGE of being an insider in Wine Country? You get the authentic Napa & Sonoma experience and can take full advantage of all that this beautiful area has to offer. Follow our lead, and soon you'll be touring Wine Country like a genuine insider.

ACQUAINT YOURSELF WITH THE LATEST DEVELOPMENTS

Things have been changing rapidly in Napa and Sonoma since the last edition of this guidebook was published. Here are some of the most interesting happenings, trends, and plans for the future.

"Wine Country" refers to the California wine-growing region north of San Francisco, most famously Napa Valley and Sonoma County. Napa Valley includes the cities of Napa, Yountville and the Stag's Leap District, Oakville & Rutherford, St. Helena, and Calistoga. Sonoma County is home to Healdsburg, Bodega Bay & West County (short for West Sonoma County), the city of Sonoma, and Santa Rosa. Sonoma Valley is a subset of Sonoma County, and its base is the city of Sonoma.

- Napa is evolving faster than any other city in Wine Country, and with the development of the riverfront at the south end of downtown, it now has the sex appeal to attract tourists in droves. Getting everyone's attention are the Japanese restaurant Morimoto Napa, the trendy AVIA Napa hotel, and the hot wine bar Carpe Diem, among others. What's more, there are 20-plus tasting rooms within walking distance of downtown Napa. (See Chapter 1 for details.)

LEFT: Wine tasting can be quite atmospheric in Wine Country, as here, by candlelight in a cave.

Inside the wine caves at Jarvis in Napa Valley.

- The millennials have arrived. This generation of wine drinkers, the offspring of the baby boomers, range in age from 21 to 31. If you are in this age group, expect to be courted in Wine Country. Vintners are well aware of marketing studies that reveal millennials have plenty of disposable income to tour and shop.

- The Francis Ford Coppola Winery in Geyserville is experimenting with a new family-oriented resort approach, with a pool near the tasting room, boccie courts, a movie gallery, and more. Coppola, the Academy Award–winning director best known for *The Godfather* trilogy and *Apocalypse Now*, envisions it as "a wine wonderland . . . where people of all ages can enjoy the best things in life—food, wine, music, dancing, games, swimming, and performances . . ." (Check out the listing in Chapter 6, p. 154.)

- This is Wine Country, but it's also a place where highbrow microbreweries and brewpubs flourish. Here people are quite fussy about their wine *and* their beer, don't you know. Vinnie Cilurzo of Russian River Brewing Company in Santa Rosa is among the region's serious brewmasters. This being Wine Country, Cilurzo is, in fact, experimenting with beer aged in used wine barrels, imparting complex and distinctive flavors (see Chapter 9, p. 222, for full listing).

- Wine Country is part of the "true wine" movement. The "natural" or "true wine" trend that started in Italy and took hold in France in recent years has reached California, where a growing number of wineries are using plants instead of chemicals to keep pests at bay. Some wineries even boast they're vegan. Wineries that follow the movement's precepts might also eschew the practice of adding sugar or acid to aid fermentation and fix a wine's flavor balance during fermentation. Some reject filtering their wine, believing that true wine is truly a product of the place it was grown and pressed—conveying "terroir," or the unique qualities derived from geology, geography, and climate. True wine is clearly a growing trend in Wine Country. Check out the doings of industry leader Benziger Family Winery in Glen Ellen (Chapter 7, p. 172).

TAKE OUR CRASH COURSE IN WINE TASTING

There's nothing snooty to it—simply swirl and sniff; sip and swish; and spit. And in the end, trust your palate. Whether you're an experienced wine taster or a novice, it's all about what *you* like.

1. Swirl and sniff
When you swirl the wine in your glass (gently, in small circles, for 10 seconds or so), you release the molecules that produce the aromas. *Insider tip:* To get the full effect of the aromas released, put one hand over the glass while swirling it with the other.

Did you know that 75 percent of taste comes from one's sense of smell? Jot down the aromas you detect—fruit, herbs, spice, etc.

2. Sip and swish
The tongue plays a major role in wine tasting because it holds the taste buds that recognize sour, sweet, and salty. Let the wine make an impression on you. Is the

The true wine movement takes root at Benziger Family Winery.

wine rich or light? Is it harsh or smooth? Does it have an aftertaste? Is it dry? Sour? Sweet? Salty? Jot down what you taste.

3. Spit
In tasting rooms you'll see a spit bucket on the counter. Use it, especially if you're touring by automobile and don't have a designated driver. Visiting tasting room after tasting room, your wine intake can quickly catch up with you if you consume every sample.

That's all there is to it! Now that you know the ropes, maybe you'd like to take your wine knowledge to the next level. There are plenty of learning opportunities out there.

The Aroma Wheel

The Aroma Wheel was created by Ann Noble, professor emerita of viticulture and enology at the University of California at Davis, as a guide in helping people describe aromas they detect in wine. To learn more, visit her website at www.winearomawheel.com. Noble has also filmed a presentation available on YouTube: http://www.youtube.com/watch?v=2skRww R5Nbk.

FURTHER YOUR WINE EDUCATION

For those who consider learning an adventure, a great wine education can be had at the Culinary Institute of America (CIA) the West Coast campus at Greystone in St. Helena. Programs range from two-hour Wine Exploration courses for the traveler, offered on Saturdays, to two- to five-day continuing-education courses, a one-month Wine Immersion course, and an Advanced Wine and Beverage program.

CIA Greystone's faculty is the best and the brightest in Wine Country. Its director is Karen MacNeil, author of *The Wine Bible,* and among the many noted faculty members is celebrity chef John Ash, an award-winning cookbook author.

In addition to choice instructors, the program has a state-of-the-art facility at the Rudd Center. Once the distillery of the old Christian Brothers winery, the remodeled center has two tasting theaters, an air-filtration system, spit sinks at each tasting area, and inset lighting. Each seat is also so equipped that a computer can quickly tally votes in blind tastings. Wine education has gone high-tech! (To find out more about class offerings, visit www.ciaprochef.com/winestudies or call 800-888-7850.)

KNOW THE BACK STORY: THE PARIS TASTING OF 1976

California and French wine lovers have a long-standing love-hate relationship—California loves French wine and France hates California's. We exaggerate—but only somewhat. California winemakers have always aspired to the quality and reputation of Bordeaux and Burgundy wines, while French enthusiasts ignored the wines of California. That is, until May 24, 1976.

It began with British wine merchant Steven Spurrier, who had a taste for California wine but had a difficult time convincing his English and European customers. Spurrier hit on the idea of staging a blind tasting of California and French wines, using the nine greatest palates of France. It was unheard of. California had

You may never want to leave your room at Milliken Creek Inn.

beaten French wines in past tastings, but the judges were always American, and what did they know?

The French judges were aware that they were sampling both French and American wines, though the identities of the individual wines were concealed. As the tasting progressed, the tasters began pointing out the wines they believed were from California, and their comments about them grew increasingly patronizing. When the bottles were unmasked, however, the judges were mortified: the wines they thought were classic Bordeaux or Burgundy were in reality from California. Six of the 11 highest-rated wines were, in fact, from California—almost entirely from Napa. The 1973 Stag's Leap Wine Cellars cabernet sauvignon beat 1970 vintages of Château Mouton-Rothschild and Château Haut-Brion, and a 1973 Chateau Montelena chardonnay bested Burgundy's finest whites. France contested the findings, of course, but it was too late. California, particularly Napa, had earned its place on the international wine map.

> The 2008 feature film *Bottle Shock,* directed by Randall Miller and starring Alan Rickman and Bill Pullman, centers on the Paris Tasting of 1976, the event that marked Napa Valley's arrival on the international wine scene.

Good food, good wine, beautiful setting: it's all here.   Tim Fish

BROADEN YOUR ENOLOGICAL VOCABULARY

A quick rundown of the top wine varietals . . .

CABERNET FRANC (cab-ehr-NAY FRAHN): Red wine of Bordeaux, similar to cabernet sauvignon, but lighter in color and body. Often used in blends.

CABERNET SAUVIGNON (cab-ehr-NAY so-vihn-YOHN): Red, fragrant, and full-bodied wine of Bordeaux. Dry and usually tannic. Can age in the bottle 5 to 10 years. Also referred to simply as "cabernet" or "cab."

CHARDONNAY (shar-doe-NAY): California's most popular white grape, famed in France as the essence of white burgundy. Produces wine that's fruity, with hints of citrus or butter.

CHENIN BLANC (SHEH-nin BLAHNK): A white grape that produces a wine that's more delicate and less complex than chardonnay. Slightly sweet.

FUMÉ BLANC (FOO-may BLAHNK): Same as sauvignon blanc. The name has traditionally been used to describe a dry-style sauvignon blanc.

GEWÜRZTRAMINER (geh-VURZ-trah-MEE-ner): A white grape that yields a medium-bodied, semisweet, and lightly spicy wine.

MERLOT (mehr-LOW): Increasingly popular red grape from Bordeaux. Similar to cabernet sauvignon, but softer and more opulent.

PETITE SIRAH (peh-TEET ser-AH): Dark, rich, intense red wine.

PINOT BLANC (PEA-no BLAHNK): In America it's best known as a less complex version of chardonnay. In France's Alsace region, the grape is used to make dry crisp white wines.

PINOT NOIR (PEA-no NWAHR): Silky, fruity, dry red grape that is also used to produce French Burgundy.

RIESLING (REEZ-ling): A white grape that produces a delicate wine, medium bodied and semisweet, with a melony fruit taste. Many of the best hail from Germany.

SANGIOVESE (san-joh-VEY-zeh): The sturdy and often spicy red grape used in Chianti.

SAUVIGNON BLANC (SOH-vihn-yohn BLAHNK): A crisp, light white wine with hints of grass and apples.

SÉMILLON (say-mee-YAWN): A cousin to sauvignon blanc; the two are often blended together.

SYRAH (ser-AH): Ruby-colored grape of the Rhone region in France. Smooth, yet with rich and massive fruit.

VIOGNIER (vee-oh-NYAY): This highly perfumed white wine is surprisingly dry on the palate. Native to the Rhone area of France, it's increasingly chic in California.

ZINFANDEL (ZIN-fan-dell): A spicy and jamlike red wine. A California specialty. Used also to make a blush wine called white zinfandel.

In Napa & Sonoma, the mighty grape rules.   © Michael Norwood Photography, iStockphoto.com

A WINE GLOSSARY

No one expects you to be an expert at wine tasting, but here's a crash course in the words of wine, how to pronounce them, and what they mean, should you want to impress the locals.

APPELLATION: A legally defined grape-growing region. Alexander Valley, for example, is an appellation.

BLANC DE BLANCS (blahnk deh BLAHNK): A sparkling wine made from white grapes, usually chardonnay. Delicate and dry.

BLANC DE NOIRS (blahnk deh NWAHR): A sparkling wine made from red grapes, usually pinot noir. Sometimes faintly pink. Fruity but dry.

BLUSH: A pink or salmon-colored wine made from red grapes. Juice from red grapes is actually white. Red wine derives its color from juice left in contact with the grape skin. The longer the contact, the darker the wine.

BRUT (BROOT): The most popular style of sparkling wine. Typically a blend of chardonnay and pinot noir. Dry.

CRUSH: Harvesting and pressing of grapes. The beginning of the winemaking process.

ESTATE BOTTLED: Wines made from vineyards owned or controlled by the winery.

FERMENTATION: The conversion of grape juice into wine, using yeast to change sugar into alcohol.

LATE HARVEST: Sweet dessert wine made from grapes left on the vine longer than usual. *Botrytis cinerea* mold forms, dehydrating the grapes and intensifying the sugar content.

MALOLACTIC FERMENTATION: A second fermentation that converts malic acids (which have a tart-apple quality) to softer lactic acids (which lend a buttery quality).

MÉTHODE CHAMPENOISE (meh-TUD sham-pen-WAHZ): Traditional French champagne-making process. Still wine is placed with sugar and yeast into a bottle, which is then sealed. The yeast devours the sugar, creating bubbles. The wine then "sits on the yeast," or ages in the bottle, several years. Finally, the yeast is extracted, and the sparkling wine—never once removed from its original bottle—is ready to drink.

OAK: Wine aged in oak barrels picks up some of the smell and taste of the wood. Also contributes to tannins and long aging. Example: "That chardonnay has too much oak for my taste."

RESERVE: A term traditionally used to mean wine held back, or reserved, for the winery owners, but the meaning has become vague in recent years. It's now sometimes used to mean better-quality grapes or wine aged longer in oak barrels.

RESIDUAL SUGAR: Unfermented sugar that remains in the wine. Wine is considered sweet if it contains more than 0.5 percent residual sugar by weight.

RIDDLING: Process used to extract yeast from sparkling wine. A laborious process that slowly shakes deposits to the neck of the bottle, where they can be removed without disturbing the wine.

SPARKLING WINE: Generic term for champagne. Technically, real champagne can come only from the Champagne region of France.

TANNINS: Thought to further a wine's ability to age, tannins derive from the skin and stalk of the grapes as well as oak barrels. Wines containing an abundance of tannins (typically young reds) produce a puckery sensation in the mouth and are described as "tannic."

TERROIR (teh-RWAHR): Literally "soil" in French, refers to the unique quality that locale—geography and climate—imparts to the wine.

VARIETAL: A wine named for the grape variety from which it's made. Example: Chardonnay is a varietal; Bordeaux is not. (Bordeaux is a region in France—but Bordeaux wine can contain a number of varietals: cabernet sauvignon, merlot, etc.)

VINTAGE: The year the grapes for a particular wine are harvested. Nonvintage wines can be blends of different years.

VITICULTURAL AREA: A wine-growing region. The Russian River Valley, for example, is a viticultural area of Sonoma County.

A Brief History
of Napa & Sonoma

History repeats itself;
that's the one thing that's wrong with history.

—Clarence Darrow

WHY WAS IT, back in school, that the worst, most monotonous teachers taught history? It didn't take long before all those dates and wars and proclamations made your brain glaze over like an Easter ham. Well, that kind of history won't repeat itself here. It helps, of course, that Napa and Sonoma counties have a lively past, busy with fascinating people and place—and, yes, dates and wars and proclamations, too. From the thunderous tremors that raised the land out of a prehistoric sea to the chic winery life of today, Napa and Sonoma counties have been twins— fraternal rather than identical. They share similar origins but have grown into distinctly different siblings.

NATURAL HISTORY

A vast inland sea once spanned Napa and Sonoma counties, the salt water nourishing the soil over millennia. The Mayacamas Mountains as well as coastal and other mountain ranges attest to the land's violent origins. Continental plates have fought for elbow room here for millions of years, colliding and complaining, creating a tectonic furnace of magma and spewing forth volcanoes and towering mountain spines that now divide and surround the two counties.

At 4,344 feet, Mount St. Helena is the area's tallest remnant of the volcanic era. Magma still simmers below the hills, producing the area's powerful geysers and Calistoga's soothing mineral water. Other vivid reminders occur on occasion: earthquakes. The San Andreas Fault runs up the center of Bodega Head on the

LEFT: The first public tour of Beringer Vineyards in 1934.   Courtesy Beringer Vineyards

coast, and the more timid Rodger's Creek Fault sits beneath Santa Rosa and Healdsburg.

When the ancient sea receded, it left bays and lagoons that became fertile valleys. The Napa and Russian rivers formed and for eons roamed back and forth over the face of the Napa and Santa Rosa plains, mixing the soil and volcanic ash. It's hard to imagine a land more made to order for wine. The soil is rich with minerals and the rocky nature of the land creates excellent drainage. Cool air masses from the Pacific meet the dry desert air from the east, creating a unique climate. Fog chills the mornings, then burns off as the days turn ideally warm; as the sun sets, the crisp air returns. And perhaps most important: rain. Typically, Napa and Sonoma counties are drenched from December through April; then things dry up until November.

FIRST INHABITANTS

Brave the occasionally harrowing California freeway system, and you'll inevitably see this bumper sticker: California native. How natives do moan about newcomers! It's rather silly, of course, since people are such a recent addition to Northern California—5,000 years, in the grand scheme of things, is hardly enough time to unpack.

The earliest "newcomers" crossed the land bridge that once connected Asia and Alaska, then wandered south. The first known inhabitants were the Pomo and Miwok tribes in Sonoma, and the Wappo, who lived in Napa Valley and eastern Sonoma County. It was a plentiful place and allowed for an unhurried way of life, the men hunting and the women gathering berries, mussels, and other foods. Communities thrived. Most were small, but some villages had populations of 1,000 or more.

These early inhabitants gave special names to this land of theirs, names that remain today. Not that historians particularly agree on what the words mean. *Mayacamas* is a Spanish adaptation of a Native American word that meant "howl of the mountain lion." *Napa,* depending on which story you believe, is Wappo for "grizzly bear," "fish," or "bountiful place." The first European arrivals were heavily outnumbered. As many as 12,000 Wappo lived between Napa and Clear Lake to the north, and 8,000 Pomo prospered in what are now Sonoma, Lake, and Mendocino counties. That would quickly change.

The Spanish naval officer and explorer Francisco de Bodega y Cuadra stumbled on present-day Sonoma County somewhat by accident in 1775 while piloting his ship the *Sonora* along the coast in search of San Francisco Bay. Rough seas and a damaged skiff prevented Bodega y Cuadra and crew from actually coming ashore, but Bodega's name nonetheless stuck: Bodega Bay. Russians, however, not the Spanish, were the first to establish an outpost in the area.

By the early 1800s the Russian-American Company, a private entity supported largely by imperial Russia, was expanding south after the Alaskan fur trade began to play out. In 1812 a colony was established on the Sonoma coast. Exploring the coastline farther, the Russian-American Company's Ivan Kuskov selected a bluff a few miles to the north and established Fort Ross the following year. The fort became the hub of Russian activity in the region.

The Spanish were determined that their presidio in San Francisco would be the dominant force in the area. Even Mexico declaring independence from Spain in 1822 didn't lessen the importance of the land north of San Francisco. California had been explored and established largely through the mission system, which began in 1769 as a way to civilize the "heathen" Natives and convert them to Catholicism. It was also a way to establish a Spanish presence and, if a mission was successful, add greatly to the wealth and power of the church.

In 1823 Father José Altimira, an ambitious young priest at San Francisco's Mission Dolores, became convinced that a new mission was needed in the northern territory. But church authorities—cautiously considering their waning influence with the new Mexican government—balked, so Altimira turned to the Mexican governor of California, Don Luis Arguello. Seeing an opportunity to thwart the Russians, Arguello approved the idea. Altimira set out that year with a party of 14 soldiers to explore the land north of the San Francisco Bay.

On July 4, 1823, with a makeshift redwood cross, Altimira blessed the mission site in what is now the city of Sonoma, and the Mission San Francisco Solano was founded. It was California's last mission and the only one established under Mexican rule. In the early years the mission was a great success, and despite having the reputation of being a harsh taskmaster, Altimira converted more than 700 Native Americans. In the fall of 1826 Native laborers staged a violent uprising after bringing in a bountiful harvest. The mission was partially burned, and Father Altimira fled for his life. The mission was rebuilt under another priest's leadership, and by 1834 was at the height of its prosperity when the Mexican Congress secularized the mission system and returned the acquired wealth to the people. It was the beginning of a new era.

Some swear harvest is the only season in Wine Country.

Sonoma's historic City Hall on the Plaza, dedicated in 1908.   Tim Fish

Lieutenant Mariano Guadelupe Vallejo was an enterprising 28-year-old officer given the opportunity of a lifetime. The Mexican government sent him to Sonoma to replace the padres and also to establish a presidio and thereby thwart Russian expansion. Vallejo's ambitions were far greater than even that; he soon became one of the most powerful and wealthy men in California. As commandant general, Vallejo ruled the territory north of San Francisco and eventually set aside more than 100,000 acres for himself. He laid out the town of Sonoma around an 8-acre plaza—the largest in California—and for himself built the imposing Petaluma

Adobe in 1836. It would be the largest adobe structure in Northern California and the first crop-producing rancho in the area.

It was Vallejo who pushed for the settlement of Napa and Sonoma counties. He found an ally in frontiersman George Yount. Others had been exploring Napa Valley since 1831, but Yount was the first to explore with the notion of settlement. Befriending the already powerful Vallejo, Yount established the 11,814-acre Rancho Caymus in 1836, now the Yountville area of central Napa County. About that same time, Vallejo was giving Sonoma land grants to family members, who established the rancho predecessors of Santa Rosa, Kenwood, and Healdsburg. Mexican influence continued to expand, particularly after 1839, when the Russians, having wiped out the otter population that was the source of their trading operation, sold Fort Ross.

Otters weren't the only inhabitants facing annihilation. Indian uprisings were not uncommon, and Yount's house in Napa Valley was half home, half fortress. Vallejo occasionally led campaigns against rebellious Indians, but perhaps the most devastating blow came in 1837 when a Mexican corporal inadvertently brought smallpox to Sonoma Valley. This disease all but wiped out Sonoma County's Native population, which had no immunity to the virus.

BEAR FLAG REVOLT

Throughout the 1830s and early 1840s, American settlers streamed into California, lured by stories of free land. Mexican rule, however, denied Americans land ownership, and this led to confrontations. Tensions peaked in 1846 when rumors spread that Mexico was about to order all Americans out of California. At dawn on June 14, some 30 armed horsemen from Sacramento Valley and Napa Valley rode into Sonoma. So began the Bear Flag Revolt, 25 eventful days when Sonoma was the capital of the independent Republic of California. Few soldiers still guarded the Sonoma outpost when the riders arrived, and the insurrectionists captured Sonoma without a single shot. A new republic was declared and a makeshift flag was hoisted to the top of a pole in the plaza. Saddle maker Ben Dewel crafted this flag for the new government, using a grizzly bear as the chief symbol. (Some said it looked more like a prized pig.) The Bear Flag Republic had a short reign. In July, an American navy vessel captured the Mexican stronghold of Monterey and claimed California for itself. The Bear Flag boys immediately threw in with the Americans, and four years later, in 1850, California became a state. Eventually, in 1911, the Bear Flag was adopted as the state flag.

A FIRST GLASS OF WINE

Initially oats and wheat were the primary crops of Napa and Sonoma counties, and sheep and cattle were also dominant. Father Altimira planted 1,000 vines of mission grapes, a rather coarse variety brought north from Mexico for sacramental wine. Napa's first vineyard was planted in 1838 by Napa's first Euro-American settler, George Yount. He brought mission vines east from Sonoma and made wine for his own use. It wasn't until 1856, when a Hungarian aristocrat named Agoston Haraszthy arrived in Sonoma, that the idea of a wine industry first took root. Haraszthy had attempted vineyards in San Diego and San Mateo and immediately recognized potential in the soil and climate of Sonoma and Napa valleys. Purchasing land and a winery northeast of the plaza, Haraszthy established Buena Vista—which means "beautiful view."

Wineries began to spring up throughout Napa and Sonoma counties, the beginnings of wine dynasties such as Beringer and Inglenook that still exist today. The wine industry was small but growing in the late 1800s, though it shared the land with other important crops: hops, timber, and apples in Sonoma, and wheat in Napa. Winemaking and drinking in those days was anything but the chic activity it is today. Wine was sold almost exclusively in bulk and often wasn't even blended until it reached its selling point. It was vended from barrels in saloons and stores, with customers usually bringing their own containers. Gustave Niebaum of Inglenook and the old Fountaingrove Winery in Santa Rosa were among the first to bottle their own wines. Niebaum was also the first to use vintage dates on his wine and promote "Napa Valley" on his labels.

Winemaking received a major blow late in the century in the form of phylloxera. A voracious microscopic aphid that infests vine roots, phylloxera first appeared in Europe in the 1860s, devastating the vineyards of Chateau Margaux, Chateau Lafite, and others. Only by grafting their vines to American rootstock were the Europeans able to save their classic wines. While the European wine industry recovered, California wine began to receive its first world notice. Sonoma County —not Napa—had been the undisputed capital of California wine, but fate and phylloxera would change all that. Phylloxera surfaced first in Sonoma Valley in 1875, and it slowly spread north to the Russian River. By 1889 Sonoma County's vineyards were in ruins when the French invited American wines to compete in the World's Fair in Paris. Napa Valley's wines scored well, raising Napa from obscurity to fame. The crown had been snatched by the time phylloxera finally invaded Napa. Growers tried everything to kill the pest, from chemicals to flooding their fields, but nothing worked. Eventually most were forced to pull out their vines. Some planted again, using resistant stock. Others gave up and planted fruit trees.

Grapes eventually became the default crop in Napa & Sonoma.   Tim Fish

Looming even larger on the horizon of the wine industry was Prohibition. The temperance movement in the United States had been gaining steam since the turn of the century, and by 1917 a majority of states had outlawed alcohol. The US Congress cinched it with the Volstead Act, which

Road signs testitfy to the proliferation of wineries in Napa & Sonoma today.   Tim Fish

prohibited the manufacture, sale, and transportation of alcoholic beverages except those used for medicinal and sacramental purposes. When Prohibition began, on January 1, 1920, in Sonoma County alone three million useless gallons of wine were left to age in vats. Sebastiani in Sonoma, Beaulieu in Rutherford, and a handful of other wineries survived by making religious wine and "medicinal spirits." But most wineries closed—almost 200 alone in Sonoma County and more than 120 in Napa Valley. By the time Prohibition was repealed in 1933, the Great Depression was on, followed by World War II. It would be some time before the California wine industry recovered. But when it did, it took the world by storm (See "Know the Back Story: The Paris Tasting of 1976," p. 18).

WINE COUNTRY TODAY

Today Napa and Sonoma counties continue to grow, much to the chagrin of long-standing residents. Tourism bureaus report that each year about 4.7 million people travel to Napa Valley, and 7.2 million visit Sonoma County, drawn increasingly by wine, landscape, and climate. Santa Rosa is a small but blossoming metropolis. Highway 29, the main road through Napa Valley, pulses with activity. How different it is from the days of grizzly bears and the Wappo Natives.

As the designation "Wine Country" implies, the wine industry has grown exponentially in the region since the mid-20th century. Consider this fact: in 1976 there were 65 wineries in Napa Valley alone, and today there are roughly 400. Despite this growth, Napa and Sonoma remain strikingly beautiful places.

PART II

1

City of Napa

THE CITY OF NAPA is no longer a drive-by city. Long groomed by investors, Napa has arrived. The Japanese restaurant Morimoto Napa was said to be a game-changer when it debuted in 2010 under the ownership of quirky celebrity chef Masaharu Morimoto. The wine bar Carpe Diem and the AVIA Napa hotel are among the other new establishments marking Napa's transformation to world-class destination city.

Napa, a city of 76,000 at the southern end of Napa Valley, has truly become a cosmopolitan oasis for highbrow food and drink. One local boasts that there are 20 tasting rooms within walking distance, the largest concentration of such venues in the country. As for restaurants, Napa is a citizen of the world, with downtown eats ranging from Italian to Thai, Vietnamese to French, and everything in between . . .

Insider Secret:
Vintner Donald Hess created a winery called the **Hess Collection,** and the collectables? Fine wine and fine art. When it comes to art, his procurement strategy typically involves a sleepless night. If he loses sleep over a piece, he's apt to buy it, because he knows that it has moved him. (www.hesscollection.com)

Checking In

Best places to stay in and around Napa.

When traveling, it's key to find your base so you can plan day trips accordingly. Do you thrive in the bustle of downtown or would you prefer a more bucolic setting? Napa offers both. The choice is yours.

AVIA NAPA HOTEL (www.aviahotels.com, 707-224-3900, 1450 1st St., Napa, CA 94559; Price: Expensive to Very Expensive) This hotel in the heart of downtown

LEFT: The evolving city of Napa.

Travel Like an Insider:

*Our Top 10 Picks for
the City of Napa*

1. Morimoto Napa (www.morimoto
napa.com) The specialties at this contemporary Japanese restaurant are
seafood and Wagyu (marbled) beef.
The spendy Morimoto Napa has outdoor dining, but it's not always visible
through the crowd in the lounge.
Inside there's a tasty sushi bar.

2. Carpe Diem Wine Bar (www
.carpediemwinebar.com) This trendy
bar has a California-focused wine list
and good eats like artisanal cheeses
and charcuterie, grilled flatbreads, and
light signature dishes. Carpe diem
means "seize the day," and here, people seize it to sip.

3. AVIA Napa Hotel (www.avia
hotels.com) This urban hotel in downtown Napa is a great place to stay if
you want to explore the nearby tasting
rooms and restaurants on foot. The
concierge gives guests the skinny on

Napa's AVIA Hotel is urban chic.

the best places to go, eat, and sip. For those who prefer to stay put, a wine bar,
the Riddling Rack, is in the lobby.

4. Uptown Theatre (www.uptowntheatrenapa.com) Recent performers have
included musicians B.B. King, Jackie Greene, Cat Power, and Aimee Mann, and

Napa is an ambassador to Wine Country, giving guests valuable advice on the
best places to go, eat, and sip. It is
close to tasting rooms and not far from
the Oxbow Public Market. For ease
and comfort, there's a restaurant on the
premises—the AVIA Kitchen & Wine
Bar, which serves American cuisine.
There are 141 guest rooms and suites
on five floors, and the hotel has some
great perks: On the second floor,
there's a terrace with cabanas and a fire
pit. And intrepid explorers can unwind
by means of a complimentary chair
massage, offered daily in the lobby.

A soak in the tub, Wine Country style, at
AVIA Napa Hotel.

comedians Lewis Black, Ron White, and Margaret Cho. The iconic theater was restored to its original art deco splendor in 1994.

5. Oxbow Public Market (www.oxbowpublicmarket.com) This market offers one-stop shopping, with delectable seafood, desserts, spices, and more. It's a treat for the palate, with popular eats including Kara's Cupcakes, Oxbow Cheese Merchant, and Kanaloa Seafood Market, among others. Looking for scrumptious gourmet goodies? Come here.

6. The Hess Collection (www.hesscollection.com) Both a winery and a museum, the Hess has the most impressive collection of modern art north of San Francisco. The museum features the works of Francis Bacon and Robert Motherwell. The winery concentrates on cabernet sauvignon and chardonnay.

7. Ubuntu (www.ubuntunapa.com) What sets this restaurant apart is its unique vegetarian-only menu. Ubuntu is an African concept that stresses interconnectedness and generosity toward others, and this place walks the walk.

8. Di Rosa Preserve (www.dirosapreserve.org) Located in the scenic Carneros District of southern Napa Valley, Di Rosa is both an art gallery and a nature preserve. The nationally known collection, which includes more than two thousand works of San Francisco Bay Area art, is on display in a former stone winery, with large-scale sculptures outdoors amid 35 acres of rolling meadows.

9. Milliken Creek Inn & Spa (www.millikencreekinn.com) The inn, nestled between the Silverado Trail and the Napa River, combines the amenities of a large resort with the intimacy of a B&B. A great spot for a romantic getaway, the rooms beckon you to relax and unwind. This place is set up to pamper: spa and massage services, yoga, jazz, private wine tastings, breakfast in bed, Italian linens, and Napa River views.

10. Azzurro Pizzeria e Enoteca (www.azzurropizzeria.com) If only more casual Italian restaurants had food this tasty at a price so right. Azzurro is a good idea for lunch or for those much-needed come-as-you-are dinners during your Wine Country vacation. The menu includes salads and pastas and a tantalizing selection of gourmet pizzas.

BEAZLEY HOUSE (www.beazley house.com, 707-257-1649, 800-559-1649, 1910 1st St., Napa, CA 94559; Price: Expensive to Very Expensive) One of Napa's first B&Bs, this shingled, circa 1902 mansion has six charming and cozy rooms. Even more desirable is the carriage house, built in 1983, with a fireplace and two-person spa standard in each of its 11 guest rooms. The main house is a beauty; the dining and common rooms have coved ceilings and oak floors with mahogany inlays. The Beazleys offer a warm welcome at breakfast, and Carol—a

A scrumptious breakfast at the Beazley House.

The Beazley House has great curb appeal.

former nurse—concocts healthful, tasty fare served buffet-style. The Beazleys also run the nearby Daughter's Inn.

CANDLELIGHT INN OF THE DUNN LEE MANOR (www.candle lightinn.com, 707-257-3717, 800-624-0395, 1045 Easum Dr., Napa, CA 94558; Price: Expensive to Very Expensive) This 1929 English Tudor–style mansion is in the heart of suburbia, but the 1-acre grounds along Napa Creek are beautifully parklike. The inn has a total of 10 rooms—six of them romantic suites with two-person whirlpool baths, private balconies or decks, and fireplaces—and the decor is comfortable but not overly fussy. One suite has a cathedral ceiling and a stained-glass window. A three-course breakfast is served overlooking the lovely gardens that surround the house.

CARNEROS INN (www.thecarneros inn.com, 707-299-4900, 800-400-9000,

4048 Sonoma Hwy., Napa, CA 94559; Price: Very Expensive) Situated on the beautiful rolling hills of the Carneros grape-growing region just outside the city of Napa, this luxury Plumpjack resort opened in 2004 and includes 86 individual cottages that range in size from 975 to 1,800 square feet. The inn also has 10 suites and 12 vacation homes, popular for travelers staying two or more nights. The decor is rustic-meets-chic, with corrugated metal roofs, Brazilian cherry floors, and wood-burning fireplaces in stone hearths. The inn has 3 full-service restaurants, a spa, two pools, and a hot tub.

COTTAGES OF NAPA VALLEY (www.napacottages.com, 707-252-7810, 866-900-7810, 1012 Darms Ln., Napa, CA 94558; Price: Expensive to Very Expensive) These cozy cottages are the ultimate in private getaways. Each of the eight master-suite cottages' 450 to

600 square feet of space has a fireplace, a whirlpool tub, a kitchenette, a deck, and an outdoor fireplace. Spa services include a relaxing, in-room massage. Breakfast—delivered to your front porch—is in a basket featuring pastries from Yountville's Bouchon Bakery (see listing under Palate Adventures in Chapter 2). Sweet.

CHURCHILL MANOR (www .churchillmanor.com, 707-253-7733, 800-799-7733, 485 Brown St., Napa, CA 94559; Price: Expensive to Very Expensive) From the moment you spy Churchill Manor, you'll know it's special. A National Historic Landmark, the inn was built in 1889 on a lush acre, and it has the Greek Revival columns, wraparound verandas, and grand parlors of days gone by. If you like antiques, this is your place. Hand-painted delft tiles, 24-carat-gold trim, and an antique beaded opera gown are among the rich details in the rooms. A generous, gourmet buffet-style breakfast is served in the marble-tiled solarium, where wine and cheese are offered in the evening.

ELM HOUSE INN, BEST WESTERN (http://bit.ly/aPohoF, 707-255-1831, 888-849-1997, 800 California Blvd., Napa, CA 94559; Price: Moderate to Expensive) This wood-shingled inn is modern but done in the style of an old European village. Italian marble fireplaces adorn some of the 22 rooms (all with private baths), and each has a TV, phone, and stocked refrigerator. An elevator makes the inn wheelchair-accessible. A complimentary breakfast buffet is served in the courtyard when weather permits. The inn is located at a busy intersection.

EMBASSY SUITES NAPA VALLEY (www.embassynapa.com, 707-253-9540, 1075 California Blvd., Napa, CA 94559; Price: Expensive to Very Expensive) All 205 rooms in this hotel are two-room suites with French country furnishings, equipped for light cooking with mini-refrigerators, coffeemakers, and microwave ovens. A daily complimentary full breakfast is cooked to order, and complimentary cocktails are served for two hours each evening. Small pets are allowed for a fee in certain rooms. This is an elegant, business-class hotel that's also ideal for leisure travelers. A $6.2 million renovation was completed in 2007.

HENNESSEY HOUSE (www.hen nesseyhouse.com, 707-226-3774, 1727 Main St., Napa, CA 94559; Price: Moderate to Very Expensive) This home—on the National Register of Historic Places—is a stunning example of a perfectly restored 1889 Eastlake-style Queen Anne. The main house has six rooms, all appointed with antiques and private baths. A full breakfast is served in the dining room, with its restored, hand-painted stamped-tin ceiling. The neighborhood is urban but quiet and is a short walk to downtown Napa.

LA BELLE EPOQUE (www.labellee poque.com, 707-257-2161, 800-238-8070, 1386 Calistoga Ave., Napa, CA 94559; Price: Expensive to Very Expensive) The stained-glass windows and fine Victorian furniture in this nine-room inn will transport you to another time and place. Built in 1893, this gingerbread beauty is near downtown, with its abundance of new restaurants and activities. Rates include gourmet breakfast served in the dining room or on the sunporch or delivered to the room, a private wine cellar, hosted wine reception, and tasting passes to wineries. And if you're so inclined, enjoy a massage in the inn's secluded garden or your own guestroom.

The picturesque La Belle Epoque.   innlight marketing

LA RESIDENCE COUNTRY INN

(www.laresidence.com, 707-253-0337, 800-253-9203, 4066 St. Helena Hwy., Napa, CA 94558; Price: Expensive to Very Expensive) Built in 1870 by a New Orleans riverboat pilot who arrived in San Francisco during the Gold Rush, this Gothic Revival inn still has the flavor of the Old South, with its plantation shutters and parklike setting. The pace is slow and easy, with lots of porches and decks and a jogging and bicycling trail. A full breakfast is served in the dining room, where guests dine privately at small tables near a fireplace.

MERITAGE RESORT AND SPA

(www.themeritageresort.com, 707-259-0633, 875 Bordeaux Way, Napa, CA 94558; Price: Expensive to Very Expensive) The most unique feature of the Meritage, situated on 8 acres of private vineyards, is its 22,000-square-foot underground cave, which includes a spa, banquet facility, and a wine tasting bar. Aboveground, the Meritage has 158 rooms, a vineyard with walking trails, and even a wedding chapel that seats 60. The business center offers high-speed Internet and conference and banquet rooms. An on-premises award-winning gourmet restaurant, Siena, with its Tuscan-inspired decor, features California cuisine with an Italian twist—great pastas and pizzas.

MILLIKEN CREEK INN & SPA

(www.millikencreekinn.com, 707-255-1197, 800-835-6117, 1815 Silverado Tr., Napa, CA 94558; Price: Expensive to Very Expensive) Milliken Creek is located at the base of Wine Country. Nestled between the Silverado Trail and the Napa River, the 12 rooms of this boutique luxury inn, which combines the amenities of a large resort and the intimacy of a B&B, beckon you to relax and unwind. This place is set up to pamper: spa and massage services, yoga, jazz, private wine tastings, breakfast in bed, Italian linens, and Napa River views. Great for a romantic getaway.

NAPA RIVER INN (www.napariver inn.com, 707-251-8500, 877-251-8504, 500 Main St., Napa, CA 94559; Price: Expensive to Very Expensive) Once a mill, later a warehouse, this lovely old brick building right on the Napa River is now a luxury boutique hotel. The inn was built in the 1800s, and has the charm of a fine B&B but the privacy of a hotel. It's also pet friendly. Located in the heart of Napa's downtown, which is now bustling with new shops and restaurants, the inn is not far from the historic Napa Valley Opera House and two of the city's top restaurants— Angele and Celadon. Guests receive a complimentary breakfast at Sweetie Pie Pastries, and the hotel also offers personalized complimentary breakfast delivery.

NAPA VALLEY MARRIOTT (www .marriotthotels.com/sfonp, 707-253-8600, 800-228-9290, 3425 Solano Ave., Napa, CA 94558; Price: Expensive to Very Expensive) With 274 rooms and suites, the Marriott is one of the largest inns in the valley. Nicer than a motel, it's not quite a hotel, either, but it's comfortably appointed and has the usual services you would expect from a chain hotel. On the north edge of the city, it's convenient to most of the valley. There is a spa, a heated outdoor

> **Insider Secret:**
> **Milliken Creek Inn & Spa** offers a classy alternative to a Vegas wedding: its Elopement Package includes an on-site ceremony, complete with officiant. You supply the bride or groom.

A massage in a cave?

The underground spa at **Spa Terra** of the Meritage Resort (www.spa terra.com) is undeniably unique. Treatment rooms, some reserved for couples, are in "the hushed serenity of the cave," with a wine tasting bar within reach. Men's and women's private lounges feature steam grottos and water walls. Services include massages and body treatments, facials, and manicures. Perhaps the most decadent offering is the Solo Vino package, which begins with a grape seed scrub, followed by a jet shower, and then application of a wine mud mask before a 50-minute Swedish massage. The pricey treatment includes a cheese tray and a glass of red or white wine.

pool and whirlpool, and complimentary daily wine tasting.

OLD WORLD INN (www.oldworld inn.com, 707-257-0112, 800-966-6624, 1301 Jefferson St., Napa, CA 94559; Price: Expensive to Very Expensive) A charming 1906 Victorian, this inn received a facelift in recent years, and it's more beautiful than ever. The interior is impeccably designed, done in tastefully dramatic pastels and draped fabrics. The dining and common rooms on the first floor have gorgeous redwood woodwork and polished wood floors. The Old World Inn's main house has 21 rooms consisting of an air, earth, or water theme and is located just across the street from the original inn. A two-course gourmet breakfast is served at the inn. Though located on a busy street, the inn is surprisingly quiet.

RIVER TERRACE INN (www.river terraceinn.com, 707-320-9000, 866-627-2386, 1600 Soscol Ave., Napa, CA 94559; Price: Moderate to Very Expensive) Opened in 2003, this is the latest addition to the burgeoning tourist scene along the river in downtown Napa, with its wave of new hotels and restaurants. This three-story hotel, with an exterior design that's both stylish and rustic, appeals to vacationers and business travelers alike. The 106 rooms and 28 junior suites all have a touch of luxury, with crown moldings, ceiling fans, and granite bathrooms with whirlpool tubs. Most of the rooms have balconies, many of which overlook the river.

SILVERADO RESORT (www.silver adoresort.com, 707-257-0200, 800-532-0500, 1600 Atlas Peak Rd., Napa, CA 94558; Price: Very Expensive) Golf is king at Silverado. Its two courses—which underwent a $3.5 million facelift in 2003—are considered the best in Napa Valley. With more than 750 regular members, the resort is constantly bustling with activity. The main house, an imposing mansion built just after the Civil War, was remodeled in 1992. Today, there are 280 rooms scattered over the 1,200-acre estate. All rooms are comfortably furnished to feel like home, and the kitchenettes contain just about everything you need for light cooking. The concierge staff is perhaps the best in the valley.

STAHLECKER HOUSE (www.stahleckerhouse.com, 707-257-1588, 800-799-1588, 1042 Easum Dr., Napa, CA 94558; Price: Expensive) This 1948 ranch-style house seems more like a private home than a B&B, situated on 1.5 acres of landscaped grounds embellished with a creek and mature trees. It has four appealing guest rooms with canopy beds, antique furniture, fireplaces, and private baths. The hosts serve a gourmet candlelight breakfast in the dining room and complimentary beverages around the clock.

WESTIN VERASA NAPA (www .westin.com/verasanapa, 800-937-8461, 1314 McKinstry St., Napa, CA 94559; Price: Expensive) The hotel has 180 spacious guest rooms and suites—studios, one-bedroom, and two-bedroom—with kitchenettes. This kind of condo hotel has been around for decades in resort towns, but visitors are just starting to see more of them in Northern California. The Westin provides views of the Napa River or historic downtown Napa. There is an outdoor heated pool and a gym.

> ## Especially for the big spender in Napa Valley
>
> When price is no object, book a table at **Morimoto Napa** (p. 46) for contemporary Japanese fare, and experience a hotel that pampers with style at **Meadowood Napa Valley** (p. 97).

Local Flavors

Taste of the town—local restaurants, cafés, bars, bistros, etc.

RESTAURANTS

Downtown Napa sets an international table, offering a wide range of cuisines, including French, Japanese, Italian, and Mexican. Bon appétit! Buon appetito! *Enjoy.*

ANGELE (www.angelerestaurant.com, 707-252-8115, 540 Main St., Napa, CA 94558; Price: Expensive; Cuisine:

French) This French-style bistro, located in a former boathouse on Napa's booming riverfront, has an elegant but unstuffy atmosphere, with concrete floors and walls and rough-hewn wood rafters. There are some serious players behind it; owners include Claudia Rouas, who built Auberge du Soleil, and Bettina Rouas, the former manager of the French Laundry. The menu is classic to a tee, with petrale sole, duck, roasted boneless quail, and veal loin with sweetbread ravioli. The wine list is modest but deftly selected, with a fine grouping of French and Napa wines.

AZZURRO PIZZERIA E ENOTECA (www.azzurropizzeria.com, 707-255-5552, 1260 Main St.; Price: Inexpensive; Cuisine: Italian) This restaurant offers tasty Italian food at a great price. Azzurro is a good idea for lunch or for those much-needed casual dinners during your Wine Country vacation. Located in a storefront in downtown Napa, Azzurro has a smart, functional atmosphere and limited sidewalk dining. There's a short list of salads, pasta, and pizzas, and so far, we haven't found a dud on the menu. The roasted mush-

room pizza with taleggio cheese and thyme is addictive, and salads such as Caesar and spinach with goat cheese and dried fruit vinaigrette are light but flavorful. The wine list is small but well suited to the menu.

BISTRO DON GIOVANNI (www .bistrodongiovanni.com, 707-224-3300, 4110 St. Helena Hwy., Napa, CA 94558; Price: Moderate to Expensive; Cuisine: Italian) The seduction begins the moment you approach Bistro Don Giovanni. Inside, the setting is romantic, a high-ceilinged room done in warm tones, white linen, and modern art with vineyard views through tall windows. Bistro Don Giovanni is Napa's most popular Italian restaurant, and the menu includes the requisite salads, pasta, and risotto as well as pizza from a wood-burning oven. Salads are first-rate, and the antipasto is a generous and flavorful plate. House specialties include silk handkerchiefs (thin sheets of pasta with pesto), a robust braised lamb shank, and fillet of salmon pan-seared with a thin crust to protect its moist and flaky heart. The wine list is mostly Napa and Italian and

Seize the Day . . . and Sip Away

A recent arrival on the Napa scene, **Carpe Diem Wine Bar** (www.carpe diemwinebar.com, 707-224-0800, 1001 2nd St., Napa, CA 94559) is a hip and friendly sipping and dining environment that gets great reviews from locals and visitors alike. The wine list is weighted to California offerings, and the menu features light fare: artisanal cheeses and charcuterie, soups and salads, grilled flatbreads, and a selection of signature dishes.

Fine end to a great day in Napa Valley: a nightcap at Carpe Diem Wine Bar.

Nightlife at Carpe Diem Wine Bar.

rather pricey. Service is attentive. This place is a find. Don't miss it!

BISTRO SABOR (www.bistrosabor .com, 707-252-0555, 1126 First St., Napa, CA 94558; Price: Inexpensive; Cuisine: Latin American; Special Features: salsa dancing on Saturday nights) "Street food" is the theme at this bistro, and it has the best prices in all of Wine Country with Latin American dishes from $4 to $12, including hot-from-the-fryer churros and savory pupusas, salmon ceviche tostadas,

Insider Secret:
Red-hot lovers find themselves on the dance floor at **Bistro Sabor** on Saturday nights for salsa dancing, and they linger until 2 AM. The restaurant spins the hottest merengue, cumbia, bachata, and reggaeton hits. You game?

chorizo quesadillas, and fresh tropical fruit salads. The people behind Ceja Vineyards in Napa own this restaurant, and authenticity is the goal.

BOON FLY CAFÉ, AT THE CARNEROS INN (www.thecarneros inn.com, 707-299-4900, 4048 Sonoma Hwy., Napa, CA 94559; Price: Moderate to Expensive; Cuisine: California) Location is this café's major appeal— it's in the heart of rural Carneros Wine Country—but the food is stylish and hearty, perfect for a wine-tasting lunch or dinner in shorts or jeans. The interior is high-tech-meets-retro-California, a barn setting with towering ceiling, exposed metal beams, tin tabletops, and wood floors. The food shares similar sensibilities: modern yet full of comfort, stocked with artsy BLTs, Kobe burgers, grilled mahimahi, and towering stacks of French fries and onion rings. Breakfast is rich enough to feed a farmhand, with eggs Benedict, "Green Eggs and Ham" (special ingredient: lemon leek cream), breakfast flatbread, and the like. The wine list is modest and focused largely on wines from the surrounding Carneros region, and the prices are generally a steal.

BOUNTY HUNTER WINE BAR (www.bountyhunterwine.com, 707-226-3976, 975 1st St., Napa, CA 94559; Price: Moderate to Expensive; Cuisine: California) This wine bar has a comfortably eccentric atmosphere, with exposed brick walls, a towering, tin-covered ceiling, and various bear and ram heads decorating the walls. Wine is the key player here, but the food hardly plays second fiddle. There are more than 50 wines available by the glass, and many come in themed flights of three. The wine list is both international and domestic, and there are about four hundred selections, ranging from bargains to major investments. The menu is wine friendly, as you might expect, ranging from small plates of olives and charcuterie to Kobe beef sliders and ribs.

CELADON (www.celadonnapa.com, 707-254-9690, 500 Main St., Napa, CA 94559, Price: Expensive; Cuisine: California) Celadon masters the art of balance better than most restaurants. Its food is top rate, its service is intelligent and well paced, and its décor is refreshing. Most impressive at Celadon is the food. Recommended dishes include the Maine crab cake and the Moroccan-inspired braised lamb shank. The wine list has a good selection by the glass, and prices across the board are reasonable. The restaurant's name refers to a type of pottery with a pale green glaze, and throughout this smart restaurant there are touches of pale green, pleasing and subtle.

COLE'S CHOP HOUSE (www.coles chophouse.com, 707-224-6328, 1122 Main St., Napa, CA 94559; Price: Very Expensive; Cuisine: Steakhouse) Cole's Chop House is slick. A quiet storefront from the outside, inside it's a bustling, cosmopolitan nightclub with a jazz trio playing in the balcony. This place has a pulse. Located inside a circa 1886 building with loftlike 35-foot ceilings, it's a big restaurant with lots of tables and lots of people, but the service is seamless. Besides, Napa is cabernet country, and that's a wine that demands a slab o' meat. The New York and porterhouse steaks are all top-of-the-line, dry-aged Chicago. The à la carte side dishes are family-style huge, so two people can share. The wine list has a good selection of half bottles and more than a dozen offerings by the glass. There's a good showing of French wines and some older California library wines.

FARM, AT THE CARNEROS INN (www.thecarnerosinn.com, 707-299-4880, 4048 Sonoma Highway Napa, CA 94559; Price: Very Expensive; Cuisine: American) Farm, the restaurant at the Carneros Inn, is rustic chic. The building is barnlike, with a high-pitched ceiling and exposed rafters, but it also has a contemporary feel, with clean lines, numerous windows, and dramatic lighting. As for the food, it's quite good. Impressive are the wood-fired stone oven pizza, the halibut, and the suckling pig. Farm also has a decent wine list, focusing on Napa and Sonoma bottlings, and it has 21 wines by the glass. The bar is upscale with an urban feel. Best of all, the inn offers a place to stay after dinner (see listing under *Checking In*).

LA TOQUE (www.latoque.com, 707-257-5157, 1314 McKinstry St., Napa, CA.; Price: Expensive; Cuisine: French) La Toque is a popular restaurant because it's more accessible than the French Laundry and easier on the wallet, and yet the experience is sublime. Chef Ken Frank learned to cook in France, and he's a genius in the kitchen. Tasty entrées include the Colorado range–fed buffalo, the Pacific king salmon, and the braised veal cheek. The wine list is smart and the service is nimble. Located in the upscale Westin Verasa Napa (see listing under *Checking In*), La Toque has patio seating and a chef's table for six in the kitchen. In the hotel lobby, you'll experience the casual side of Frank's cooking at Bank Café & Bar.

MORIMOTO NAPA (www.mori motonapa.com, 707-252-1600, 610 Main St., Napa, CA 94559; Price: Very Expensive; Cuisine: Contemporary Japanese) Morimoto Napa is a hot spot. The celebrity chef Masaharu Morimoto is known to millions as the star of TV's *Iron Chef* and *Iron Chef America*, and he has garnered critical acclaim for his seamless integration of Western and Japanese ingredients. The restaurant serves contemporary Japanese cuisine and includes a sushi bar, a lounge, and outdoor dining overlooking the River Walk. Do not miss this spot, even though it's spendy.

NORMAN ROSE TAVERN (www .normanrosetavern.com, 707-258-1516, 1401 1st Street, Napa, CA. 94559; Price: Moderate; Cuisine: American) Here you'll find highbrow tavern food with specialties that include lamb burgers and spinach and goat cheese dip. The burger is also a house favorite. There's also plenty to sip, with microbrews from Northern California as well as Oregon and Alaska. The wine focuses almost entirely on local bottlings, with 98 percent from California. The decor, with plenty of old barn wood, is comfort-driven and yet has a modern appeal.

Ubuntu, a vegetarian restaurant in Napa, is a hit. Elijah Woolery

OENOTRI (www.oenotri.com, 707-252-1022, 1425 1st Street, Napa, CA 94559; Price: Expensive; Cuisine: Italian) Here you can travel to Italy by palate rather than passport. The menu features artisanal pizza Napoletana (compliments of a wood-fueled Acino oven imported from Naples), and pasta and handcrafted salumi are among the dishes taking their inspiration from Campania, Calabria, Basilicata, and Puglia. The wine list highlights the southern Italian region, and the restaurant also has a full bar and features unique cocktails.

UBUNTU RESTAURANT AND YOGA STUDIO (www.ubuntunapa.com, 707-251-5656, 1140 Main St., Napa CA 94559; Price: Moderate; Cuisine: Garden-Inspired Vegetarian) This unique restaurant focuses on biodynamic dishes, drawing from its own gardens and the labors of local farmers in the spirit of *ubuntu*, an African concept that recognizes all life as interconnected. In the loft above the restaurant, with soundproofed doors, is the yoga studio, and Ubuntu has a calendar with scheduled lectures, films, and music. Chef Jeremy Fox, who's worked at Rubican and the four-star Charles Nob Hill in San Francisco, makes highly spiced dishes that appeal to both omnivores and herbivores. Popular entrées include the cauliflower in an iron pot, roasted, pureed, and raw, and the fig pizza.

WINERIES

Cabernet sauvignon is king in Napa Valley, and yet there's plenty to explore in our lineup of Napa wineries, including Domaine Carneros, a house of sparkling wine that's also well known for its sleek pinot noir. Check out our entries and set out to *drink in* Napa.

ACACIA WINERY (www.acaciawinery.com, 707-226-9991, 2750 Las Amigas Rd., Napa, CA 94559; Tasting: By appointment Mon.–Sat. 10–4:30 and noon–4:30 Sun.) Named for a tree that grows throughout the area, Acacia specializes in chardonnay and pinot noir, and it's now owned by international beverage giant Diageo. The winery is a modern California barn that sits on the slopes of the Carneros District, which shoulders the top of San Pablo Bay. Acacia uses grapes from surrounding vineyards, a region suited to Burgundian grapes.

ARTESA VINEYARDS & WINERY (www.artesawinery.com, 707-224-1668, 1345 Henry Rd., Napa, CA 94559; Tasting: Daily 10–5) Artesa began life in 1991 as sparkling-wine specialist Codorniu Napa. Spain's Codorniu has been making bubbly since 1872 but couldn't make a go of it in California. The winery eventually changed its name and switched to still wine: pinot noir, chardonnay, merlot, sauvignon blanc, and Syrah. So far, the wines are quite promising. The mystery of the winery begins to unravel as you approach the entrance, a long staircase with a waterfall cascading down the center. Inside, it seems anything but a bunker, with elegant decor, a sunbaked atrium, and spectacular views through grand windows. It's a must for any student of architecture.

BOUCHAINE VINEYARDS (www.bouchaine.com, 707-252-9065, 800-654-WINE, www.bouchaine.com, 1075 Buchli Station Rd., Napa, CA 94559; Tasting: Daily 10:30–4) Well off the tourist path, on the windswept hills of southern Carneros, sits this modern, redwood winery. Built on the vestiges of a winery that dates to the turn of the 20th century, Bouchaine is a grand redwood barn that sits alone on rolling

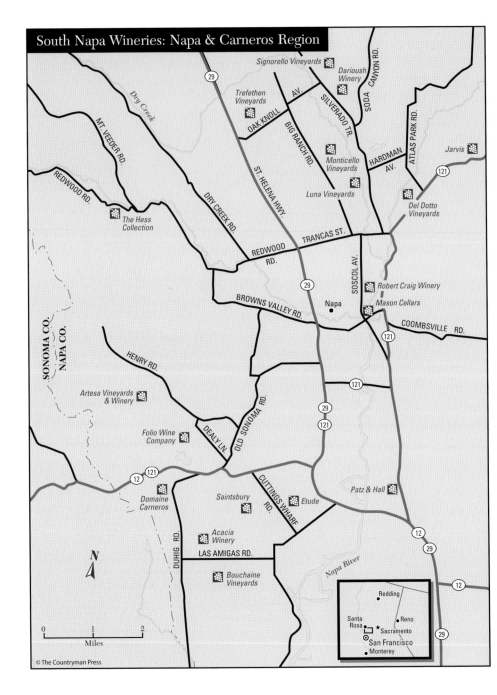

South Napa Wineries: Napa & Carneros Region

Signorello Vineyards

Darioush Winery

Trefethen Vineyards

Monticello Vineyards

Luna Vineyards

Jarvis

Del Dotto Vineyards

The Hess Collection

TRANCAS ST.

Robert Craig Winery

Mason Cellars

Napa

COOMBSVILLE RD.

HENRY RD.

Artesa Vineyards & Winery

Folio Wine Company

Domaine Carneros

Saintsbury

Etude

Patz & Hall

Acacia Winery

LAS AMIGAS RD.

Napa River

Bouchaine Vineyards

Redding

Santa Rosa

Reno

Sacramento

San Francisco

Monterey

0   1   2
Miles

© The Countryman Press

hills that lead to San Pablo Bay. A fire warms the tasting room on cool Carneros days. Chardonnay and pinot noir are specialties, but try the crisp and spicy gewürztraminer.

DARIOUSH WINERY (www.darioush .com, 707-257-2345, 4240 Silverado Tr., Napa, CA 94558; Tasting: Daily 10:30–5) Darioush Khaledi grew up in Iran's Shiraz region and immigrated to the United States in the late 1970s. The passionate wine lover spent the early 1990s searching for a vineyard estate and founded Darioush Winery in 1997. Darioush, which opened in the summer of 2004, is unique in Wine Country: East meets West. The winery has classic Persian elements blended with modern European touches, and 90 percent of the stone used in building the winery came from the ancient quarries used by King Darius of ancient Persia. Darioush focuses on the Bordeaux varietals, with small lots of chardonnay, viognier, and Shiraz.

DEL DOTTO VINEYARDS (www.deldottovineyards.com, 707-256-3332, 707-963-2134, 1055 Atlas Peak Rd., Napa, CA 94558; Tasting: By appointment) Dave Del Dotto, a pop culture icon of sorts, is best known for his real estate infomercials that aired in the 1980s. He came to Napa Valley in 1989 to create a new image, and in 1998 he opened a winery with an Italian ambience. Though varietals here include cabernet franc, merlot, and pinot noir, the winery is best known for cabernet sauvignon. The tours take you through 120-year-old caves, with opera music piped in.

DOMAINE CARNEROS (www .domainecarneros.com, 707-257-0101, 800-716-2788, 1240 Duhig Rd., Napa, CA 94581; Tasting: Daily 10–6) The Domaine Carneros winery is an exclamation point along Highway 12, towering on a hilltop surrounded by vineyards. Built in the style of an 18th-century French chateau, Domaine Carneros is no everyday winery. Owned in part by champagne giant Taittinger, Domaine Carneros makes a $14 million statement about its French heritage. The terrace of this cream-and-terra-cotta chateau overlooks the lovely rolling hills of the

Carneros District. Inside are marble floors and a maple interior crowned with ornate chandeliers.

ETUDE (www.etudewines.com, 707-257-5300, 1250 Cuttings Wharf Rd., Napa, CA 94559; Tasting: Daily 10–4:30; reserve tasting by appointment) The winery and tasting room were inaugurated with the 2003 vintage. The masonry buildings, which total about 40,000 square feet, was the former home of a brandy distillery. Founder and winemaker Tony Soter sold the winery to Foster's Group and is no longer involved. Etude produces a full range of wines, from cabernet sauvignon to pinot gris, but it gets the most attention for its class-act pinot noir.

FOLIO WINEMAKERS' STUDIO (www.foliowinemakersstudio.com, 707-256-2757, 1285 Dealy Ln., Napa, CA 94559; Tasting: Daily 10–5) Michael Mondavi spent most of his career at the house his father built: Robert Mondavi Winery. Now on his own, Michael took over the former Carneros Creek Winery and is in the process of sprucing it up considerably. He has also launched a number of new labels—including I'M Wines, Oberon, Hangtime, Spellbound, and Medusa, all of which can be sampled in the "taste gallery." The winery is off the beaten path, but worth checking out.

HESS COLLECTION (www.hess collection.com, 707-255-1144, ext. 226, 4411 Redwood Rd., Napa, CA 94558; Tasting: Daily 10–5:30) If there's a gallery in Wine Country that deserves the title museum, it's the Hess Collection. Swiss entrepreneur Donald Hess transformed the old Mont La Salle Winery into an ultramodern showcase for his two great passions: art and wine. The art collection spans the upper two

The striking art at the Hess Collection.

floors and features the works of internationally known artists such as Francis Bacon, Robert Motherwell, and Frank Stella. A mix of paintings and sculpture, the works are provocative and often haunting, though humor plays a role too. Stop in at the tasting room to explore Hess's other passion. Hess concentrates on two wines: cabernet sauvignon and chardonnay. The chardonnays are stylish and oaky; the cabernets are well made.

JARVIS (www.jarviswines.com, 707-255-5280, 800-255-5280 ext. 150, 2970 Monticello Rd., Napa, CA 94559; Tasting and Tours: By appointment) Jarvis boasts that it was the first winery in the world to put the entire facility underground. That's right—the winery is housed amid 46,000 square feet of roaming caves, complete with an underground waterfall. When digging the cave, workers found a spring, which they decided to incorporate into

the design to ensure an adequate level of humidity. If that isn't enough to pique your interest, another interesting aspect of Jarvis is that its winemaker, Dimitri Tchelistcheff, is the son of the legendary winemaker Andre Tchelistcheff, who revolutionized Napa Valley cabernet. The winery produces a full slate of wines, including mainstream cabernet as well as lesser-known petit verdot, but its best efforts are cab and chardonnay.

LUNA VINEYARDS (www.lunavineyards.com, 707-255-5862, 2921 Silverado Tr., Napa, CA 94558; Tasting: Daily 10–5) In 1995 George Vare and Mike Moon launched Luna, which means "moon" in Italian, with an intent to focus on Italian varietals such as pinot grigio and Sangiovese. In keeping with their Italian theme, they built their winery in the California style of Craftsman architecture, with hints of Tuscan influence. Luna also produces merlot and cabernet. Don't miss the pinot grigio; it's as tasty as pinot grigios that hail from Italy.

MASON CELLARS (www.mason cellars.com, 707-255-0658, Tasting Room: 714 First St., Napa, CA 94559; Tasting: Thurs.–Mon. 11–5) Randy Mason has been making wine in Napa Valley for years but finally struck out on his own in 1993. The house specialty is sauvignon blanc, and Mason has a genuine gift for it. His style is lush yet crisp, emphasizing fresh and lively grapefruit and fig flavors. Mason makes his wine miles away from this tasting room, which is a smart-looking storefront in the burgeoning Oxbow District in downtown Napa.

MONTICELLO VINEYARDS (www.monticellovineyards.com, 707-253-2802, ext. 18, 800-743-6668, 4242 Big Ranch Rd., Napa, CA 94558; Tasting: Daily 10–4:30) If the visitors' center of this winery looks familiar, check the nickel in your pocket. It's modeled after Thomas Jefferson's Virginia home,

Jarvis's unique cave setting.

Monticello. A Jefferson scholar, owner Jay Corley paid tribute to one of America's first wine buffs. Corley began as a grape grower in the early 1970s and started making wine in 1980. Cabernet sauvignon has of late superseded chardonnay as the winery's specialty. The cabernet is generally well structured and elegant.

PATZ & HALL (www.patzhall.com, 707-265-7700, 877-265-6700, Tasting Room: 851 Napa Valley Corporate Way, Suite A, Napa, CA 94558; Tasting: By appointment) One of the true stars of California wine, Patz & Hall specializes in chardonnay and pinot noir. The winery harvests grapes from top vineyards around Northern California—such as Hyde and Pisoni—and the wines aren't cheap, but they're astounding for their plush and rich flavors and deep aromas. While the wines are made in Sonoma, the tasting salon was established in Napa to provide an accessible showcase. It's a sit-down tasting, and the atmosphere is sophisticated, like the art-filled den of an Upper West Side apartment in New York.

ROBERT CRAIG WINE CELLARS (www.robertcraigwine.com, 707-252-2250 ext. 1, Tasting Room: 625 Imperial Way Napa, CA 94559; Tasting: By appointment Mon.–Sat.) For most wine fans, visiting this boutique cabernet sauvignon producer was out of the question until Craig opened this tasting room in downtown Napa. Craig is a Napa veteran who launched his own label in 1992, and he makes three cabernets: a Bordeaux-style blend called Affinity and two wines made from the rocky slopes above the valley, Howell Mountain and Mount Veeder. The mountain wines are intense, concentrated, and rich. The tasting room is an intimate storefront.

SAINTSBURY (www.saintsbury.com, 707-252-0592, 1500 Los Carneros Ave., Napa, CA 94559; Tasting: By appointment Mon.–Sat.) David Graves and Richard Ward came to Carneros in search of Burgundy. Enthused by the district's potential for Burgundian grapes chardonnay and pinot noir, in 1981 the duo formed Saintsbury, named for the author of the classic *Notes on a Cellar-Book*. With its unassuming design, weathered redwood siding, and steeply sloped roof, the winery fits snugly amid the grapevines in this rural area. We have a soft spot for Saintsbury's moderately priced Garnet pinot noir, and its Carneros pinot and chardonnay are typically lush and complex.

SIGNORELLO VINEYARDS (www.signorellovineyards.com, 707-255-5990, 800-982-4229, 4500 Silverado Tr., Napa, CA 94558; Tasting: By appointment weekdays; Fri.–Sun. 10–5) This small winery built in 1985 is a stylish but low-key affair that has garnered attention for its vibrant chardonnay and sémillon, a cousin of sauvignon blanc. Its stable of red wines includes a powerful cabernet sauvignon as well as merlot and pinot noir. Ray Signorello's first vintage was 1985, and he prefers a low-tech, natural approach to winemaking.

TREFETHEN VINEYARDS (www.trefethen.com, 707-255-7700, 866-895-7696, 1160 Oak Knoll Ave., Napa, CA 94558; Tasting: Daily 10–4:30) Shaded by a 100-year-old oak, this winery was built in 1886 by Hamden W. McIntyre, the architect behind Inglenook and Greystone Cellars. The Trefethen family bought the winery in 1968 and restored it, painting the redwood beauty a pumpkin orange. Tours highlight the McIntyre-designed, three-level gravity-flow system in which grapes are crushed on the third floor, juice is fermented on the second, and wine is aged in barrels on the ground level. Since its first vintage in 1973, Trefethen has made its name with chardonnay.

WINERY COLLECTIVES

These tasting rooms allow guests "one-stop sipping," pouring brands from several wineries.

Gustavo Thrace (www.gustavo thrace.com, 707-257-6796, 1021 McKinstry, Napa, CA 94559) Partners Thrace Bromberger and Gustavo Brambila bring you their signature '06 Barbera, which is an Italian varietal, as well as offerings from several other small producers. Thrace runs sales and marketing; Gustavo serves as winemaker. Gustavo is one of the characters in the 2008 film *Bottle Shock*, set during the famous Judgment of Paris tasting in 1976. He is portrayed by the actor Freddy Rodriguez.

Napa Wine Merchants (707-257-6796, 1146 1st St., Napa, CA 94559) This collective, in the historic Gordon Building, has about 75 different offerings. You typically come across these wines on restaurant wine lists. Wineries include Mandolin and Waterstone.

Vintners Collective (www.vintners collective.com, 707-255-7150, 1245 Main St., Napa, CA 94559) This is the crème de la crème of collectives. It's housed in a historic building and offers a range of sought-after wines, including those by Showket, Mi Sueño Winery, and Philippe Melka.

Wineries of Napa Valley (www .napavintages.com, 707-253-9450, 1285 Napa Town Center, Napa, CA 94559) This tasting room is next door to Napa's visitors' center and includes Goosecross Cellars, Girard Winery, and Burgess Cellars.

Palate Adventures

Gastronomical highlights in the city of Napa.

• Go gourmet

Oxbow Public Market (www.oxbow publicmarket.com, 707-226-6529, 610 & 644 1st St., Napa, CA., 94559) The spot for highbrow eats. Specialty merchants include Kara's Cupcakes, Model Bakery, Oxbow Cheese Merchant, and Kanaloa Seafood Market, among others. You'll also find farmstands with local produce, culinary gifts, and restaurants.

Chefs' Market (Napa Downtown Association, www.napadowntown.com, 707-257-0322, 1310 Napa Town Center, Napa, CA., 94559) This free event, open to the public, is held every Thursday from 5 PM to 9 PM from the end of May through mid-August. Spanning 1st to Main to Franklin streets, the market features food and wine tastings from Napa Valley restaurants and wineries, cooking demonstrations, dozens of food vendors, produce from 25 of the region's top farmers, three musical stages, and a block of children's entertainment.

Insider Secret:

Who knew spices had such a repertoire? **Whole Spice,** at the Oxbow Market, offers 300 different spices, along with a broad range of salts and mushroom powders. It's literally a sea of spice. (www.wholespice.com)

Countless artisanal cheeses at Oxbow Public Market.   Frankie Frankeny

Especially for the art lover in Napa Valley

Napa Valley offers modern art, sculpture gardens, galleries, and more, alone or paired with wine at a winery. These suggestions for art and wine lovers are sure to please . . .

Hess Collection (p. 49)

Di Rosa Preserve (p. 56)

I Wolk Gallery (p. 112)

Clos Pegase (p. 124)

Cliff Lede Vineyards (p. 71)

This happy pup is on display at the Di Rosa Preserve in Napa Valley.

- *Sample and savor*

Napa Valley Wine & Cigar (www.napavalleywineandcigar.com, 707-253-8696, 161 Silverado Trail, Napa, CA 94559) This place is a treat for smoking palates. Cult cabs in the $700 range and highbrow stogies can be found here, along with, you guessed it, humidors. Sample in the lounges (one for wine, one for smokes), then purchase to savor later.

Downtown Joe's Microbrewery (www.downtownjoes.com, 707-258-2337, or 707-258-BEER, 902 Main St., Napa, CA 94559) Some great beer—plus a comfortable wooden bar and a patio along the Napa River—can be found at this stylish and historic storefront in downtown Napa. The copper brew kettles are in plain sight, so you can watch the brewmaster do his stuff. The food is solid pub fare.

- *Take a Wine Country train ride*

Napa Valley Wine Train (www.winetrain.com, 707-253-2111, 800-427-4124, 1275 McKinstry St., Napa, CA 94559) The train itself is a gloriously restored vintage beauty, and the trip through Napa Valley is a charming and scenic adventure. The food isn't the best in Wine Country, but the ride makes up for it. If money is an object, it's best to take the midday excursion and have lunch.

To Do

Check out these great attractions and activities . . .

SHOPPING

While the restaurant scene is heating up, the shopping in Napa lags behind. Most tourists looking to browse and buy still find their way to St. Helena or Calistoga. That said, the retail scene has picked up somewhat in Napa from years past. Our top picks:

Oxbow Public Market (707-266-6529, 644 1st. St., Napa CA 94559) is the place for gourmet fare. Like San Francisco's Ferry Building Marketplace, its

Beyond Wine Country

The sights farther afield . . .

TO THE SOUTH

The striking countryside and tony hamlets of Marin County are directly south of Wine Country. In San Rafael, just east of Highway 101, don't miss the dramatic **Marin Civic Center,** one of the last buildings designed by Frank Lloyd Wright. If you're not in a hurry, consider trekking north or south on Highway 1, the winding two-lane road that hugs the rugged coastline. It will take you by **Muir Woods,** home to some of the tallest redwoods north of the Bay, and also to the majestic **Mount Tamalpais.** Drive to its 3,000-foot summit for a spectacular view of San Francisco (clear weather permitting, that is). **Point Reyes Lighthouse** is also worth a stop along Highway 1, as are the many oyster farms near Marshall.

Farther south—just a one-hour drive from Wine Country—is one of the most intriguing, romantic, and ethnically diverse cities in America: **San Francisco.** (Check out our "Best Day in San Francisco" for the full tour.) Across the Bay are **Oakland** and the ever-eclectic **Berkeley,** both stops worth making.

TO THE EAST

While motoring your way to Sacramento along I-80, your thoughts may turn to . . . onions. The aroma of onions and other commercially grown produce fills the air in fertile Sacramento Valley, where fruits and vegetables are tended in endless flat fields. The city of **Sacramento,** the state capital and once a major hub for rail and river transportation, is proud of its historic center: **Old Town,** a faithful re-creation of the city's original town center, with a multitude of shops, restaurants, and museums.

TO THE NORTH

Not to be outdone by Napa and Sonoma counties, Mendocino County is also a major player in the game of fine wine, with several premium wineries along Highway 101 and in beautiful Anderson Valley. The coastal hamlet of **Mendocino,** one of Hollywood's favorite movie locations, is also a treasure trove for shoppers. Its art galleries, antiques shops, and fine dining, and its New England–like atmosphere, make it a popular second destination for Wine Country visitors.

appealing range of food purveyors includes Model Bakery and Three Twins Organic Ice Cream. At The Beaded Nomad (707-258-8004, 1238 1st. St., Napa, CA 94559) you don't have to be a child of the '60s to relish the wares. This shop features jewelry and imported items such as masks and bronze statues. Copperfield's (707-252-8002, 3900 Bel Aire Plaza, Napa, CA 94558) is an all-purpose bookstore and a fun stop for readers. The Napa Valley Emporium (707-253-7177, 1260 Napa Town Center, Napa, CA 94559) sells customized apparel, from T-shirts and aprons to caps, as well as grape-related gifts such as wine racks and corkscrews. Finally, at Napa Premium Outlets (707-226-9876, 629 Factory Stores Dr., Napa, CA 94558) there's a maze of 40 stores including Mikasa, Kenneth Cole, Cole Haan, J. Crew, Liz Claiborne, Tommy Hilfiger, Jones New York, Ann Taylor, Timberland, Nine West, Book Warehouse, and Levi's.

• *Check out the live music and theater*

Uptown Theatre (uptowntheatrenapa.com, 707-259-0123, 1350 3rd St., Napa, CA 95449) The Uptown, with its classic art deco design, was revived with a $15 million remodel in 1994. Today it's versatile, with a large auditorium for concerts, live music and comedy, fund-raisers, and corporate parties.

Napa Valley Opera House (www.nvoh.org, 707-226-7372, 1030 Main St., Napa, CA 94559) Built in 1879, this Italianate beauty is a solid structure that reels in theater and musical performances, from pop to classical.

• *Go gallery hopping*

Di Rosa Preserve (www.dirosapreserve.org, www.dirosaart.org, 707-226-5991, 5200 Sonoma Hwy., Napa, CA 94559; Open Wed.–Fri. 9:30–3, Sat. by appt.; free admission to Gatehouse Gallery; tours are $10 and $15; children under 12 free; discounts for seniors, students, and the handicapped) Di Rosa Preserve is both an art gallery and a nature preserve. The nationally known collection includes more than 2,000 works of San Francisco Bay Area art, on display in a former stone

A front-row seat at Uptown Theatre.

Best Day in San Francisco

The opening of the **Golden Gate Bridge** in 1937 made Napa and Sonoma counties easily accessible to and from San Francisco, and today many Wine Country travelers visit this celebrated city at some time during their stay. Our tour de San Francisco offers its share of culinary delights, while immersing you in the culture of what's been called the Paris of the West.

1. First stop: the **Ferry Building Marketplace** (www.ferrybuildingmarketplace .com, 1 Ferry Building at the Embarcadero & Market Sts.) If possible, come on a Tuesday, Thursday, or Saturday, when you'll find the **Ferry Plaza Farmers Market** in full swing. A great variety of fresh fruits and vegetables is on offer, as well as artisanal creations.

2. Next stop, lunch at **Ton Kiang** (www.tonkiang.net, 415-387-8273, 5821 Geary Blvd., San Francisco, CA 94121). The highlight here is dim sum, which literally means "to touch your heart" and comes in the form of dumplings, steamed dishes, and other goodies served in small portions. Favorites include barbeque pork buns and shrimp & spinach dumplings.

3. Now it's time to play tourist. Ride the **Powell-Hyde Cable Car** (at Powell & Market Sts., the Powell-Hyde line). Visit **Lombard Street** (Lombard St. between Hyde & Leavenworth Sts.), known as the "crookedest street in San Francisco." Go for a sundae at **Ghirardelli Soda Fountain & Chocolate Shop** (415-474-3938, Ghirardelli Square, 900 N. Point St., San Francisco CA 94109).

4. Next up, be a culture vulture and explore the city's museums. Top picks include the cutting-edge **San Francisco Museum of Modern Art** (www.sfmoma.org, 415-357-4000, 151 3rd St., San Francisco, CA 94103) and the graceful palace of the **Legion of Honor** (www.legionofhonor.org, 415-750-3600, 100 34th Ave., San Francisco, CA 94122; at Clermont St., in Lincoln Park).

5. Time for good eats. Here are two great options: **Greens** (www.greens restaurant.com, 415-771-6222, Building A., Fort Mason Center, San Francisco, CA 94123) is a destination for the health conscious, with some of the most inspired vegetarian cooking around. The decor is warm and inviting, the views are stunning, and the wine list is smart, worldly but playing to a local strength—California wine. **Michael Mina** (www.michaelmina.net, 415-397-9222, 252 California St., San Francisco, CA 94111) offers the signature dishes of the eponymous celebrity chef, including black mussel soufflé and Maine lobster pot pie. Great Union Square location.

6. Rest your head at the **Westin St. Francis** (www.westin.com, 415-397-7000, 335 Powell St. at Geary St., San Francisco, CA), a prized property that is both luxurious and well situated right on Union Square. The revolving flags outside give you a clue as to what dignitary is currently a guest.

winery and outdoors, amid 35 acres of rolling meadows in the scenic Carneros District of southern Napa Valley.

Hess Collection (www.hesscollection.com, 707-255-1144, ext. 226, 4411 Redwood Rd., Napa, CA 94558) This multitasking winery houses the most impressive collection of modern art north of San Francisco.

Artesa Vineyards & Winery (www.artesawinery.com, 707-224-1668, 1345 Henry Rd., Napa, CA 94559) Artesa is a work of art in itself: built into a hillside, the winery looks like a lost tomb. Contemporary art is on display throughout the building.

> **Insider Secret:**
> The Uptown Theatre is a vintage venue with some interesting history. Back in 1928 a then-unknown comic named Bob Hope performed his act there for a week.

• *Ignite your interest in history*
Napa Firefighters Museum (www
.napafirefightersmuseum.org, 1201 Main Street, Napa, CA. 94669, 707-259-0609) is a place where firefighting-related memorabilia and artifacts from the 19th and 20th centuries are preserved for future generations. *Tip:* Kids and aspiring heroes of all ages love this place.

RECREATIONAL FUN

• *Explore the great outdoors*
Ballooning with Napa Valley Aloft (www.nvaloft.com, 800-627-2759, 707-944-4400, 6525 Washington St., Yountville, CA 94599) In 1995 owners Carol Ann and Nielsen Rogers combined three historic ballooning companies into one larger company. Napa Valley Aloft offers champagne flights daily, shuttle service, and a minister who's available for in-flight weddings. Sunrise launches daily from parking lot of V Marketplace in Yountville.

Gallery hopping in Napa Valley's Di Rosa Preserve.

The old stone winery at the Di Rosa Preserve.

Golfing at Silverado Country Club and Resort (www.silverado resort.com, 707-257-5460, 800-362-4727, 1600 Atlas Peak Rd., Napa, CA 94558) This club is private to members and guests. It offers two 18-hole championship courses, par 72; a pro; and a shop. Many consider it to be the best course in Northern California. Price: expensive.

Horseback riding with a perk—tent camping, at Northbay Natural Horsemanship (www.northbaynaturalhorsemanship.com, 707-479-8031, Napa, CA 94559) These stables offer training and lessons. Organized camping excursions involve riding by day and tent camping by night. Work on horsemanship while enjoying nature.

Tennis at Silverado Country Club and Resort (www.silveradoresort.com, 707-257-0200, 1600 Atlas Peak Rd., Napa, CA 94558) The courts are open to members and guests. Altogether, there are 14 courts, three of them lit, and there's a pro on-site.

2

Yountville & Stag's Leap

IN ALL OF WINE COUNTRY, this is the cradle of cuisine. It's home to the world-renowned French Laundry, and the lineup of other restaurants—from Bouchon to Bistro Jaunty to Bottega—confirms that this is a foodie's paradise.

The name of this food haven is derived from the early pioneer George Calvert Yount, who planted the first vineyard in the Napa Valley.

This chapter includes wineries from the nearby Stag's Leap District, a region that garnered international recognition when a cabernet sauvignon from Stag's Leap Wine Cellars outscored French producers Mouton-Rothschild and Haut-Brion, among others, in the Paris Tasting of 1976. A Who's Who of French wine cognoscenti selected cabernet in a blind tasting over the best of Bordeaux, and this win jolted the wine world.

> **Insider Secret:**
> The White House usher, the president's food and wine point person, is Daniel Shanks. But few know that Shanks was the long-time manager of the restaurant at **Domaine Chandon** winery before he was hired at the White House in 1995 after an extensive FBI check. (www.chandon.com)

Checking In

Best places to stay in and around Yountville.

Accommodations in the region serve both seekers of chic and the value-oriented. All will provide a welcome place to hang your hat, and some are destinations unto themselves.

BARDESSONO (www.bardessono.com, 707-204-6000, 6526 Yount St., Yountville, CA 94599; Price: Moderate to Very Expensive) This 62-room hotel courts eco-

LEFT: Sculpture at Cliff Lede Vineyards.

"Twin Venuses from Thunder" by Jim Dine courtesy of © 2007 Jenn Farrington Studios

conscious travelers with its earth-friendly design: the architecture, the heating and cooling systems, the lighting and landscaping: all are certifiably "green." But this doesn't mean that guests forgo luxury. Quite the opposite, in fact. Among the low-impact indulgences are luxurious suites with organic bed linens and robes, and champagne bubble baths for two. The Bardessono Restaurant & Bar is on the premises, as is the Spa at Bardessono. Oh yes, and man's best friend is also welcome here. Of course, there's a cleaning fee of $125 per stay. But isn't your four-legged beast worth it?

BORDEAUX HOUSE (www.bordeaux house.com, 707-944-2855, 800-677-6370, 6600 Washington St., Yountville, CA 94599; Price: Moderate to Expensive) The inn—a modern, distinctive redbrick building—is a far cry from the usual cozy Victorian. Likewise, the furnishings have an eclectic style, with a mix of antiques and modern pieces. A full breakfast is served in the common room. Close to all of Yountville's shops and restaurants, it's a good choice for those on a budget.

LAVENDER (www.lavendernapa.com, 707-944-1388, 800-522-4140, 2020 Webber St., Yountville, CA 94599; Price: Moderate to Very Expensive) A little bit of Provence in the heart of Napa Valley. Surrounded by its name-sake flowering herb, the inn has eight guest rooms in all, including two in the main house—a lovely old farmhouse with a wide porch—and the others in three cottages. The decor is done in French country furnishings and fabrics, and all rooms have fireplaces. In the breakfast room a Parisian-style bistro breakfast is served. Guests have pool privileges at nearby sister inn Maison Fleurie. The innkeepers are exceptionally friendly.

Insider Secret:
Bardessono has many perks, one being its complimentary daily yoga class for guests. The green traveler, it turns out, likes to breathe deep.

MAISON FLEURIE (www.maison fleurienapa.com, 707-944-2056, 800-788-0369, 6529 Yount St., Yountville, CA 94599; Price: Moderate to Very Expensive) French for "flowering house," Maison Fleurie is a lovely complex of vine-covered buildings blessed with a colorful past—built in 1873, it was a bordello and a speakeasy. Today, it is a 13-room inn in the heart of the increasingly chic burg of Yountville, but it has the feel of a French country inn, featuring provincial antiques and reproductions. A full breakfast is served family-style in the fireside dining room.

NAPA VALLEY LODGE (www .napavalleylodge.com, 707-944-2468, 888-944-3545, 2230 Madison St., Yountville, CA 94599; Price: Very Expensive) This delightful lodge has 55 well-appointed and spacious rooms and suites—33 with fireplaces—decorated with wicker and tropical plants and offering postcard views of the valley. It is styled as a Spanish hacienda, with a red-tile roof and balconies or terraces off every room. This is a restful location surrounded by ripening grapes in the vineyards, and it's an easy walk to Yountville's shops. Special golf packages are also available. The inn underwent a $6 million remodel in 2007.

OAK KNOLL INN (www.oakknoll inn.com, 707-255-2200, 2200 E. Oak Knoll Ave., Napa, CA 94558; Price: Very Expensive) Oak Knoll Inn is a

Travel Like an Insider:

Our Top 10 Picks for Yountville and Stag's Leap District

1. French Laundry (www.frenchlaundry.com) Not only is the French Laundry the best restaurant in Wine Country, it's arguably the best in the country—period. Owner-chef Thomas Keller has become a celebrity, and there's a two-month waiting list for reservations (if you can get them to answer the phone!).

2. Bardessono (www.bardessono.com) This "green" hotel has a simple message: being eco-conscious doesn't mean you have to forgo luxury. Bardessono is true to its earth-friendly initiatives and yet offers plenty of low-impact indulgences— luxurious suites and champagne bubble baths for two, to name a couple.

3. Bottega (www.michaelchiarello.com) This restaurant owes its hotness to chef Michael Chiarello, the Emmy-winning host of the Food Network's *Easy Entertaining* and vintner of Chiarello Family Vineyards. Bottega shines a light on Chiarello's signature bold Italian flavors and elegant style. The menu highlights artisanal and house-made ingredients, as well as local produce.

4. Domaine Chandon (www.chandon.com) When the famed French Champagne house Moët Hennessy built this ultramodern winery in the hills west of Yountville in 1973, it was clear that California winemaking had come of age. Thus began the influx of European sparkling-wine firms to Northern California.

5. Ad Hoc (www.adhocrestaurant.com) Celebrity chef Thomas Keller (of the French Laundry fame) is also behind this first-rate eatery. Here, comfort food reigns—favorites from Keller's childhood. Irresistible dishes served in generous portions include fried chicken, spiced hanger steak, and braised beef short ribs. The menu changes daily.

6. Cliff Lede Vineyards (www.cliffledevineyards.com) When Canadian Cliff Lede bought the old S. Anderson Winery, where sparkling wine had been the focus, he began producing cabernet sauvignon and sauvignon blanc practically from scratch; right out of the gate the wines were competing with the Valley's best.

7. Redd (www.reddnapavalley.com) Acclaimed chef Richard Reddington opened this classy restaurant in 2005. From the atmosphere to the food to the service and the wine list, there isn't a false note.

8. Stag's Leap Wine Cellars (www.cask23.com) Stag's Leap Wine Cellars falls into the select pilgrimage category. It achieved instant fame when its 1973 cabernet won the famous Paris Tasting of 1976, which changed the way the world looked at California wine.

9. Bouchon Bakery (www.bouchonbakery.com) Expect sweet Parisian treats from this bakery, yet another venture of celebrity chef Thomas Keller. Keller opened the restaurant Bouchon in 2003, and it's now one of the most popular and flashy in Napa Valley—so why not open a bakery to boot?

10. Villagio Inn & Spa (www.villagio.com) At the Tuscan-inspired Villagio Inn & Spa guests can lounge by the 40-foot lap pool and enjoy complimentary access to the facilities at Spa Villagio, including outdoor soaking tubs, steam room, and sauna. Add a complimentary bottle of wine and you've got pampering, Wine Country style.

A room with a view at the Poetry Inn.

treasure, perhaps our favorite B&B in Napa Valley. It's intimate—only four guest suites—but the rooms are spacious and luxurious, with tall French windows, rustic fieldstone walls, and vaulted ceilings. The innkeepers are gracious and unstuffy. The phrase "gourmet breakfast" is used loosely at many B&Bs, but not here: Barbara Passino creates truly magnificent fare, including poached eggs in puff pastry and an indulgence called a chocolate taco stuffed with fresh sorbet. There's also quite a spread set out for the nightly wine-and-cheese hour.

PETIT LOGIS INN
(www.petitlogis.com, 877-944-2332, 6527 Yount St., Yountville, CA 94599; Price: Moderate to Expensive) This inn has a culinary edge. It's within walking distance of the French Laundry—by many accounts the best restaurant in America—and it's also near some other top-rated restaurants, including Bouchon and Bistro Jeanty. All five guest rooms feature a fireplace and a 6-foot double Jacuzzi. The shingled lodge

with a trellis of vines has a French country, minimalist feel. The inn is simple and lovely, and the price is right. Wireless Internet is available.

POETRY INN (www.poetryinn.com, 707-944-0646, 6380 Silverado Trail, Stag's Leap District, Napa, CA 94558; Price: Very Expensive) Cliff Lede, a Canadian businessman, established Cliff Lede Vineyards in 2002 and opened the nearby Poetry Inn in 2005. The inn, on a hillside in the Stag's Leap District, has stunning views of the Napa Valley. The three rooms have king-sized beds, private balconies, and wood-burning fireplaces. A popular spa treatment is a massage in the open air. Breakfasts include Brie-and-strawberry-stuffed French toast—decadence at its best.

VILLAGIO INN & SPA (www.villagio .com, 707-944-8877, 800-351-1133, 6481 Washington St., Yountville, CA 94599; Price: Very Expensive) Villagio Inn & Spa has 112 spacious guest rooms, and each features a wood-burning fireplace, a patio or balcony, a refrigerator, and a bottle of chilled chardonnay. Of course, the drawing card here is the 13,000-square-foot Spa Villagio, with 16 treatment rooms and five private spa suites that include oversized infinity tubs, fireplaces, and wet bars. Yet another plus is the nearby V Marketplace, featuring upscale specialty shops, galleries, cafés, a complete wine cellar, and a hot-air balloon company—all housed within a 130-year-old restored brick winery.

VINTAGE INN (www.vintageinn.com, 707-944-1112, 800-351-1133, 6541 Washington St., Yountville, CA 94599; Price: Very Expensive) This is an exceptional inn designed with villa-style units clustered around a common waterway. The 80 spacious and beautifully decorated rooms have oversized beds, whirlpool-spa tubs, ceiling fans, in-room coffeemakers and refrigerators, private verandas, and wood-burning fireplaces. Second-story rooms cost a little more but are worth it for the vaulted ceilings and, especially, the views. California bubbly is served with the breakfast buffet. The V Marketplace shopping complex is next door.

YOUNTVILLE INN (www.yountvilleinn.com, 707-944-5600, 6462 Washington St., Yountville, CA 94599; Price: Expensive to Very Expensive) Prefer a full-service hotel but can't afford the sky-high rates of some of the nearby lodgings? This inn is a good alternative. Set on a peaceful creek and featuring mature landscaping, the hotel has an elegantly rustic feel to it. There are 51 rooms, each featuring a fieldstone fireplace. Many of the top rooms have vaulted ceilings and private patios. A continental breakfast is served.

Villagio Inn & Spa. Tim Fish

Local Flavors

Taste of the town—local restaurants, cafés, bars, bistros, etc.

RESTAURANTS

This is a place where food is sheer genius. Snagging a spot is not easy. Best to make a reservation (months ahead of time, in some cases) and say a prayer. Here chefs like Thomas Keller (the French Laundry, Bouchon, Ad Hoc) and Michael Chiarello (Bottega) are revered. Americans are not a patient people by nature, but they know great food is worth the wait.

AD HOC (www.adhocrestaurant.com, 707-944-2487, 6476 Washington St., Yountville, CA 94599; Price: Expensive, Prix Fixe $49; Cuisine: Traditional American Comfort Food) Celebrity chef Thomas Keller, best known for his award-winning restaurant the French Laundry, is also behind this first-rate eatery. Here, comfort food reigns. Irresistible dishes, served in generous portions, include fried chicken, spiced hanger steak, and braised beef short ribs. The menu, which changes daily, is limited to a single four-course meal (no-stress ordering!), and food is served family style. The wine list includes imports but focuses on Napa Valley labels, with a few bottlings from Sonoma. This is a great spot in Wine Country—and it may be as close as you can get to Thomas Keller's ingenuity, given that the French Laundry requires a two-month wait.

BISTRO JEANTY (www.bistrojeanty .com, 707-944-0103, 6510 Washington St., Yountville, CA 94599; Price: Expensive; Cuisine: French) Having for years prepared the meticulously elaborate creations at Domaine Chandon, chef Philippe Jeanty returned to his roots in 1998 and opened this delightful bistro. The idea, he said, was to create the French country comfort food he grew up with in Champagne. It's hard not to be won over by Jeanty's menu, which is ripe with classics such as cassoulet, *daube de boeuf*, and escargots. A favorite is coq au vin, a hearty red wine stew of moist chicken and mushrooms: delicious. The wine list won't impress stuffy collectors; it's a small and impeccable list selected strictly with the menu in mind.

BOTTEGA (www.botteganapavalley .com, 707-945-1050, 6525 Washington St., Yountville, CA., Price: Expensive; Cuisine: Italian) This place is hot hot hot. Celebrity chef Michael Chiarello, the Emmy Award–winning host of the Food Network's *Easy Entertaining* and vintner of Chiarello Family Vineyards, is doing something very right with Bottega. The restaurant shines a light on Chiarello's signature bold Italian flavors and elegant style.

Especially for Napa Valley travelers with canine companions

There are more wineries, restaurants, and shops welcoming dogs (and their drivers) than ever before in Wine Country. Here are some of the best bets:

Bardessono (p. 61) This luxury hotel charges an additional $125 cleaning fee for pets, and you can dine with your dog on the restaurant's patio.

Fideaux (p. 111) This fun shop carries pet items both practical and decadent.

Chef Thomas Keller of the French Laundry is behind this restaurant. Tim Fish

The menu highlights artisanal and house-made ingredients, as well as local produce. The ambiance is vintage Napa Valley, rustic and elegant; the restaurant is located in one of the oldest wineries in the region, the Groezinger Estate.

Insider Secret:

Star chef Thomas Keller read a touching letter he received from Julia Child at her 90th birthday celebration in Napa in 2002. In the letter, Child encouraged Keller to follow his passion and persevere despite any obstacles.

BOUCHON (www.bouchonbistro.com, 707-944-8037, 6534 Washington St., Yountville, CA 94599; Price: Expensive; Cuisine: French) If Bistro Jeanty down the road is trying to corner the market on French country bistros, then Bouchon has Paris in mind. The mood is distinctly urban. Noted New York designer Adam Tihany—famous for Cirque 2000, among others—has created a chic den with burgundy, velvet, bold mosaics, and a zinc raw bar handcrafted in France. If this sounds elaborate even by Napa Valley standards, there's good reason: the man behind it is Thomas Keller of the French Laundry in Yountville and Per Se in New York. Bouchon is truly one of the best dining experiences in Wine

Insider Secret:
There is something sinfully delicious at Bouchon—the terrine of duck foie gras. It's ridiculous even to *try* to resist this indulgence. It's also impossible.

Country. If Bouchon has the authentic feel of an upscale brasserie, it has a menu to match. Specialties include an incredible *steak frites* (French for "steak with fries"); equally delectable is the *poulet rôti* (roasted chicken with polenta, garden squash, wild mushrooms, and sweet corn with chasseur sauce). To begin, why not sample from the raw bar? The oysters are impeccable. The wine list is sharply focused on wines that bring out the menu's best, and prices are average. Service is first-rate, and Bouchon stays open late; the bar is one of the busiest and classiest in the valley.

BRIX (www.brix.com, 707-944-2749, 7377 St. Helena Hwy., Yountville, CA 94599; Price: Expensive; Cuisine: California) The food here is reliable if a bit unexciting compared with the valley's top kitchens, but the atmosphere is soothing, and wine is taken seriously—a wine shop is just inside the front door. With its peaked wood ceiling and warm, earthy tones, the dining room recalls a private ski lodge. The service—professional, experienced, and attentive—is so skilled that it's almost inconspicuous. The menu is a bit too vast for our taste, and it shows: everything is good, never great. We prefer a kitchen that focuses on a few entrées and does them well.

ETOILE AT DOMAINE CHANDON (www.chandon.com /etoile-restaurant.html, 707-204-7529,

800-736-2892, 1 California Dr., Yountville, CA 94599; Price: Very Expensive; Cuisine: California French) Domaine Chandon is not the consummate experience it once was—the French Laundry has stolen its thunder—and in fact it's downright disappointing at times, particularly for the price. Housed in a modern, curved-concrete building with terrace views of the landscaped grounds, the restaurant is elegant but not pretentious. Servers dote over the table; we don't mind being pampered. Being part of the Domaine Chandon winery, the emphasis here is naturally on sparkling wine. The superb wine list covers America and France with a surprisingly modest markup. The menu, which changes with the seasons, combines California creativity with the great traditions of French cooking. The kitchen is generally more successful with seafood dishes—not surprising because bubbly plays such a crucial role at Chandon.

Belly up to the oyster bar at Bouchon.

The French Laundry is worth the price and the wait.

FRENCH LAUNDRY (www.french laundry.com, 707-944-2380, 6640 Washington St., Yountville, CA 94599; Price: Very Expensive, Prix Fixe $240; Cuisine: California French) The French Laundry is internationally renowned, perennially appearing on lists of the top restaurants in the country and even the world. Owner-chef Thomas Keller has become a celebrity, and the rich and famous flock here; Robert Redford is a regular. This place is hot. Is it worth all the fuss? Yes, if you can afford it. It's easily the most expensive restaurant in Wine Country—a dinner for two with a bottle of wine, tax, and tip can exceed $600. The grand stone house, which was built in 1900, was a bar and brothel before becoming a French-style laundry. It was a restaurant of considerable distinction even before Keller took over in 1994. He expanded the gardens and the kitchen. The atmosphere is formal–OK, frankly it's a little stuffy. You're there to worship the food quietly, and we can live with that. You might call Keller's cuisine "California labor-intensive." Every dish is an artistic feat as well as a culinary joy, and when it comes to butter, the kitchen's motto is: No fear. The pace is unhurried, although service is attentive. Allow at least two or three hours for the meal. There isn't a false step on the menu, and it's impossible to recommend a particular dish because we've seldom had the same thing twice. That's just how creative this kitchen is. And while the food is serious, Keller reveals his sense of humor in naming certain dishes. You might find macaroni and cheese on the menu, but it won't be like anything your mom or Kraft ever made. Then there's the signature dessert, coffee and doughnuts: you've never had cinnamon-sugared doughnuts so good, and they're served with a cup of coffee—cappuccino-flavored mousse complete with foam. (Note: The doughnuts are not on the menu but are available on request.) The wine list is impressive and expensive, with a superb offering of California and French wines. Wines by the glass are lacking. Save up your allowance, and make a reservation well in advance (there's a two-month wait).

MUSTARDS GRILL (www.mustards grill.com, 707-944-2424, 7399 St. Helena Hwy., Napa, CA 94599; Price: Moderate; Cuisine: California) After all these years, Mustards Grill still lives up to its reputation. The secret of Mustards isn't actually a secret at all: hearty bistro food prepared with style, at a moderate price and in a lively atmosphere. "Truck-stop deluxe," they call it. The open kitchen takes center stage, dominating an intimate dining room. The tables are packed in close, but trust us: the resulting din lends an air of privacy. While servers seem harried, they're efficient and friendly. Chef-owner Cindy Pawlcyn, who also runs Cindy's Backstreet Kitchen and Go Fish up the road, creates comfort food with flair. House specialties include a juicy Mongolian pork chop, pan-roasted liver (yes, liver!), plus braised lamb shanks and grilled rabbit. A must are the onion rings, a heaping pile that comes thinly sliced and highly seasoned. The wine list is well focused and priced fairly. The wine-by-the-glass selection is also first-rate.

REDD (www.reddnapavalley.com, 707-944-2222, 6480 Washington St., Yountville CA 94599; Price: Very Expensive; Cuisine: California) Richard Reddington made a name for himself at Masa's and Jardinière in San Francisco and Auberge du Soleil in Napa Valley, and then stepped out on his own with this classy restaurant. The interior is sleekly urban, with polished wood and aqua-blue highlights. The menu shows Asian and French influences and showcases Reddington's passion for putting a high polish on what's ordinarily considered rustic comfort food. Excellent signature dishes include glazed pork belly with apple purée, burdock, and soy caramel, as well as Liberty Farms duck breast cassoulet with thyme jus. The wine list is on the expensive side, but it's loaded with old- and new-world collectibles (California and French), and the wine service is first rate. If you're in the mood to splurge, Redd is an excellent choice.

Insider Secret:
Arrive at the French Laundry with sufficient time before your reservation so that you can stroll across Washington Street and see the restaurant's two-and-a-half-acre garden. It's farmed year-round, and depending on the season, you'll see edible blossoms, tomatoes, greens, and squash, among other items destined for the dinner table. The garden also supplies fresh fare to Thomas Keller's other restaurants in Yountville: Ad Hoc and Bouchon.

WINERIES

Some describe cabernet from Stag's Leap District as "an iron fist in a velvet glove." The best are good on two counts: they're tasty when released, and they're capable of aging well. As for Yountville, the first vines were planted in 1836 and the appellation is best known for cabernet, even though the biggest winery, Domaine Chandon, is a house of sparkling wine.

CHIMNEY ROCK WINERY (www .chimneyrock.com, 707-257-2641, 800-257-2641, 5350 Silverado Trail, Napa, CA 94558; Tasting: Daily 10–5) The design of this winery is Cape Dutch–inspired; South Africa was once home to the winery's founder, the late Sheldon "Hack" Wilson. Today, Chimney Rock is owned by wine importer Tony Terlato, who has invested millions

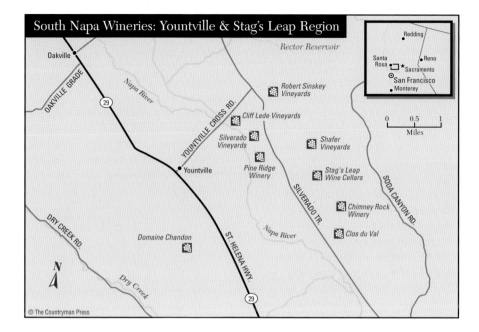

South Napa Wineries: Yountville & Stag's Leap Region

in upgrading the facility. The emphasis here is on cabernet sauvignon, which prospers in the Stag's Leap District. The winery's best cabernets are sleekly structured yet age beautifully.

CLIFF LEDE VINEYARDS (www .cliffledevineyards.com, 800-428-2259, 707-944-8642, 1473 Yountville Cross Rd., Yountville, CA 94599; Tasting: Daily 10–4) Canadian Cliff Lede has made a major impact on Napa Valley. He bought the old S. Anderson Winery, where sparkling wine had been the focus, and began producing cabernet sauvignon and sauvignon blanc, and right out of the gate the wines were competing with the valley's best. Lede added a gracefully elegant California bungalow-style visitors' center and art gallery. In the hills east of the winery, Lede opened the Poetry Inn, a small, upscale, and exclusive inn that just may be the best in the valley (see entry under *Checking In*).

CLOS DU VAL (www.closduval.com, 707-261-5200, 800-993-9463, 5330 Silverado Tr., Napa, CA 94558; Tasting: Daily 10–5) Bernard Portet was raised among the casks and vines of Château Lafite-Rothschild, where his father was cellar master. The Bordeaux influence is strong here, in both the wines and the winery. An elegant and understated building surrounded by vineyards, Clos du Val evokes a small country winery, with red roses marking the end of each vine row, in typical French fashion.

Listen up, Romeo wannabes!

Try these Napa Valley gems when you want to impress.
Domaine Chandon (www.chan don.com) What's more romantic than sipping sparkling wine with someone special?
Bouchon (www.bouchonbistro .com) offers one of the best dining experiences in Wine Country.

The tasting room has a vaulted ceiling and windows that open into the cellar. Established in 1972, Clos du Val was an early Napa pioneer, and the cabernets are typically elegant and complex. The winery's roster includes a wonderfully fleshy zinfandel, but the merlot and pinot noir can be inconsistent.

DOMAINE CHANDON (www .chandon.com, 707-944-2280, 888-242-6366, 1 California Dr., Yountville, CA 94599; Tasting: Daily 10–6) The turning point for California sparkling wine came in 1973, when the famed French Champagne house Moët Hennessy built this ultramodern winery in the hills west of Yountville. Domaine Chandon is a museum of sorts, with artifacts and explanations of *méthode champenoise,* the classic French process of making bubbly. The winery tour is thorough, and takes visitors past the mechanized riddling racks and the bottling line. "Sensory tours" include tasting. Domaine Chandon makes a variety of sparkling wines, from a round and refreshing brut to the expensive and intense Etoile.

PINE RIDGE WINERY (www.pine ridgewine.com, 707-253-7500, 800-486-0503, 5901 Silverado Tr., Napa, CA 94558; Tasting: Daily 10:30–4) Pine Ridge is an unassuming winery sequestered among the hills along the Silverado Trail. From the tasting room, take your glass onto the patio or explore the shady grounds. Tours begin in the vineyard and trek through the aging caves; on some tours, samples from oak barrels are offered. The winery's cabernet sauvignon is rich and focused.

ROBERT SINSKEY VINEYARDS (www.robertsinskey.com, 707-944-9090, 800-869-2030, 6320 Silverado Tr., Napa, CA 94558; Tasting: Daily 10–4:30) On a rise overlooking the Silverado Trail, this winery blends a modern design with the warmth of stone and redwood. The ceiling of the tasting room stretches 35 feet high, wisteria entwines courtyard columns, and through a huge glass window you can get a good view of the winery at work. There are a number of tours offered, but visitors generally get an extensive trip through the cave dug into the hillside behind the winery as well as a hike through the winery's culinary garden. The pinot noir is among the best in Napa.

SHAFER VINEYARDS (www.shafer vineyards.com, 707-944-2877, 6154 Silverado Tr., Napa, CA 94558; Tasting: By appointment Mon.–Fri.) Dynamite is not often required to plant vineyards, but back in 1972, John Shafer was convinced that hillsides were the best place to grow cabernet sauvignon. Mountain vineyards may be the rage now, but they weren't then. The soil is shallow on the hills below the Stag's Leap palisades, so dynamite was required to terrace the vineyards. The vines struggle against the bedrock to find water and nourishment, and these stressed and scrawny vines produce intense wines. Shafer's winery is a classic California ranch. The tasting room opens through French doors onto a second-floor veranda with an expansive view of lower Napa Valley. Under the vine-covered hill behind the winery is an 8,000-square-foot cave, carved out of solid rock. The cave—cool and immaculately clean—is the high point of the tour. Shafer makes two Napa Valley cabernet sauvignons—One Point Five and the Hillside Select. Both cabernets hail from the Stag's Leap District, with the Hillside the top of the line. Merlot is also bottled separately, along with chardonnay.

SILVERADO VINEYARDS (www .silveradovineyards.com, 707-257-1770, 800-997-1770, 6121 Silverado Tr., Napa,

CA 94558, Tasting: Daily 10–5) Built by the Walt Disney family in 1981, Silverado offers a dramatic view from its perch atop a Silverado Trail knoll. The tasting den is a welcoming spot, with a high-pitched, raftered ceiling and plenty of seats outside to enjoy the landscape. Here the focus is on cabernet sauvignon, but the winery also makes merlot, sangiovese, chardonnay, and sauvignon blanc, along with some less mainstream varietals.

STAG'S LEAP WINE CELLARS (www.cask23.com, 707-944-2020, 5766 Silverado Tr., Napa, CA 94558, Tasting: Daily 10–4:30 by appointment) Founded by the Winiarski family in 1972, the winery has an unassuming charm despite its fame. This is the place, after all, responsible for the cabernet that stunned the French judges at the Paris Tasting of 1976,

Insider Secret:
A bottle of the Stag's Leap cab that won the Paris Tasting of 1976, impressing the French judges, who were certain it was a Bordeaux, is in the Smithsonian, a testament to the moment the world discovered California wine.

putting California wine on the map. The tasting room is merely a table tucked among towering wooden casks in one of the aging cellars. Don't expect to sample the winery's premier bottling, Cask 23, referred to as "liquid art" and priced accordingly. The winery was purchased in late 2007 by Washington-based Ste. Michelle Estate and Italian vintner Piero Antinori.

Palate Adventures

Experience Paris in Northern California, and snag a great wine.

• *Score Parisian treats*
Bouchon Bakery (707-944-2253, www.bouchonbakery.com, 6528 Washington St., Yountville, CA 94599) Expect delectable offerings from this bakery. Thomas Keller, of the French Laundry fame, is behind it. Breads, muffins, pastry, cookies, chocolates. Also sandwiches, which Bouchon describes as "the French version of fast food—delicious ingredients between excellent bread." *Merci beaucoup!*

• *Scope out sips, smokes, and artisanal oils*
Groezinger Wine Merchants (www.groezingers.com, 707-944-2331, 6484 Washington St., Yountville, CA 94599) One of the oldest boutique shops in Napa Valley, Groezinger offers a great selection of standards as well as collectibles and offbeat wines, in a very hip atmosphere.

V Wine Cellar (www.vwinecellar.com, 707-531-7053, 6525 Washington St., Yountville, CA, 94599) This shop focuses on cult offerings: high-scoring wines that are hard to find. It has about 2,500 labels and 40 different types of cigars. If you want to sit and sip, there's a comfortable lounge area.

St. Helena Olive Oil Company (www.sholiveoil.com; 707-967-1003, 8576 St. Helena Hwy., Napa, CA 94558) One tasty stop up the road in Rutherford, this shop showcases local artisans, and carries Napa Valley–bottled extra-virgin olive oils, balsamic vinegars, mustards, and jams.

To Do

Check out these great attractions and activities . . .

SHOPPING

Our top picks in Yountville: Hansel & Gretel Clothes Loft (707-944-2954, 6525 Washington St., Yountville, CA 95499) outfits babies, girls up to 16, and boys up to 12. The toys are inventive, and the service is friendly. Domain Home & Garden (707-945-0222, 6525 Washington St., Yountville, CA 94599) has everything from fountains and furniture to wine racks. Antique Fair (707-944-8440, 6512 Washington St., Yountville, CA 94599) has large, stately French walnut pieces: huge armoires, tables, bookcases, carved bed frames, and more. Overland Sheepskin Co. (707-944-0778, 6505 Washington St., Yountville, CA 94599) is devoted to fighting Mother Nature's cool winters in Wine Country with coats, rain gear, etc.

CULTURAL OUTINGS

Art in a winery? A museum exhibit on winemaking? What else would you expect from Wine Country?

• *Drink in the art*
The Gallery at Cliff Lede Vineyards (www.cliffledevineyards.com, 800-428-2259 and 707-944-8642, 1473 Yountville Cross Rd., Yountville CA 94599; Open: 10 to 4; Admission: Free) The gallery, in the winery's original fermentation room, has a modern feel, with concrete floors and crisp walls. The collection includes Jim Dine's *Twin 6' Hearts* and contemporary works by San Diego artist Scott White. A bronze sculpture by Lynn Chadwick outside the gallery sets the stage for the work inside.

• *Immerse yourself in regional culture and history*
Napa Valley Museum (www.napavalleymuseum.org, 707-944-0500, 55 Presidents Circle, Yountville CA 94599: Open: Daily 10–5, closed Tues.; Admission: Adults over 17, $10, seniors $5, children free) Since its debut in 1997, this has been an impressive addition to the valley. Housed in a stylishly modern take on an old California barn, the $3.5 million museum is devoted to the history, culture, and art of Napa, with standing and touring exhibits. One of the standing exhibits is "California Wine: The Science of an Art," a highly interactive education in the making of wine.

• *Plan a night at the symphony*
Napa Valley Symphony (www.napavalleysymphony.org, 707-944-9910, Lincoln Theater, 100 California Drive, Yountville, CA 94599) This symphony dates to 1933, when Luigi Catalano first gathered a cadre of amateur and professional musicians. Today, the orchestra includes more than 75 musicians from Napa Valley and the Bay Area. Each of the season's five concerts features guest artists. Past soloists have included pianist Philippe Bianconi and violinist Robert McDuffie.

• *Enjoy music with Wine Country ambiance*
Music in the Vineyards (www.musicinthevineyards.org, 707-258-5559, various locations and sponsors) This festival of chamber music happens every August and draws musicians from around the country. Area wineries provide the backdrop, as well as the wine at intermission.

Robert Mondavi Summer Music Festival (www.robertmondavi.com/concerts/4, 888-766-6328, 7801 Hwy. 29, P.O. Box 106, Oakville, CA 94562) A tradition since 1969, these June-through-August concerts on the lush lawns of Mondavi's winery bring in top names in popular music, including Tony Bennett, David Benoit, and the Preservation Hall Jazz Band.

• *Take in a show*
Lincoln Theater (www.lincolntheater.org, 707-944-1300, 866-944-9199; Veterans Home of California, Yountville, CA 94599) LTNV is the performance home of the Napa Valley Symphony and Festival del Sole. Performance includes jazz, world music, rock, classical and ethnic dance, comedy, musical theater, opera, and touring theater companies.

• *Celebrate the seasons*
Napa Valley Mustard Festival (www.mustardfestival.org, 707-938-1133, various locations) Mustard, the beautiful yellow wildflower that blooms throughout Wine Country every winter, is the focus of this late-winter series of food and wine events.

Yountville Days Festival (707-944-2959, downtown Yountville, CA 94599) Commemorates Napa Valley's first settlement. This event, held the first Sunday in October, includes a parade, music, and food.

Festival of Lights (707-944-0904, downtown Yountville, CA 94599) Kick off the holiday season at the Festival of Lights, held annually the Friday after Thanksgiving. There's gourmet food and wine, holiday entertainment, late-night shopping, and even a visit with Santa. The street fair begins at 2 PM and culminates with the lighting of the town around 5:30 PM.

RECREATIONAL FUN

• *Get an altitude adjustment with a hot air balloon ride*
Napa Valley Aloft (www.nvaloft.com, 800-627-2759; 707-944-4400, 6525 Washington St., Yountville, CA 94599) Owners Carol Ann and Nielsen Rogers operate three Yountville balloon companies that offer pickup from San Francisco and Napa Valley hotels, champagne breakfast, and daily flights. Napa Valley's oldest balloon company even offers a minister who's available for in-flight weddings. Sunrise launches daily from the grounds of the V Marketplace in Yountville.

Napa Valley Balloons (www.napavalleyballoons.com, 707-944-0228, 800-253-2224, 6795 Washington St., Yountville, CA 94599) This highly regarded hot-air balloon company was founded in 1978. It offers a champagne brunch following flight. The meeting location is Yountville's Domaine Chandon.

• *Take the kids to the park*
If you're touring Wine Country with tykes, they need their share of fun too. Sometimes 30 minutes on a playground can go a long way. Grab a picnic or a snack and head to Yountville City Park, which features one of the best playgrounds in Napa Valley. Just off Madison Street on the north edge of town, it features a modern and well-maintained playground with recreational equipment for the kids, and the park offers plenty of shade for Mom and Dad. Best of all, it's free.

3

Oakville & Rutherford

THE VILLAGES OF OAKVILLE and Rutherford are a cross section of delectable cabernet country. The "Rutherford Bench" describes the middle of Napa Valley, where cabernet reigns. "Rutherford dust" is said to imbue wine with a dusty, berry, spicy quality.

While wine tasting, people often stop at the Oakville Grocery for high-brow picnic fixings—duck pâté, cold cuts, and caviar. Since when did picnics become so glamorous? When in Napa Valley . . .

The most prized resort in the area is Auberge du Soleil or "Inn of the Sun," which also has a restaurant and spa, a great place to relax after marathon tasting.

Roam these villages with an eye on cabernet and you'll find the top names—Robert Mondavi, Beaulieu, and Rubicon, to name a few.

> ### Insider Secret:
> Few know that a one-two punch was behind the breakup of brothers Robert and Peter Mondavi, originally vintners of Charles Krug Winery in St. Helena. The feud was reportedly instigated by Robert's extravagant purchase of a fur coat for his wife. Robert opened his namesake winery in 1966; Peter remained at Charles Krug. (www.robertmondavi.com)

Checking In

Best places to stay in and around Oakville and Rutherford.

Whether it's pampering you're after or a bed & breakfast with gourmet food, we have a couple of good options.

AUBERGE DU SOLEIL (www
.aubergedusoleil.com, 707-963-1211,
180 Rutherford Hill Rd., Rutherford,
CA 94573; Price: Very Expensive)
Auberge du Soleil is Napa Valley's most luxurious experience and it has a great perk: a world-class restaurant on the property (see listing under Restaurants). The style throughout the inn is

LEFT: Step back in time at Nickel & Nickel.   Tim Fish

Travel Like an Insider:

Our Top 10 Picks for Oakville & Rutherford

1. St. Supéry Vineyards and Winery (www.stsupery.com) The sauvignon blanc here is not to be missed, and the cabernet is tasty. The winery, with its science-museum approach, is a great place to tour. Sip and learn.

2. Oakville Grocery Co. (www.oakvillegrocery.com) What looks like an old country store, with its giant red Coca-Cola sign and wooden screen doors, is actually a gourmet grocery. Small and large picnic baskets and boxed lunches offer true Wine Country fare. Sandwiches include turkey with pesto mayo and a glorious lavash.

3. Opus One (www.opusonewinery.com) The wine—a blend of cabernet sauvignon, cabernet franc, and merlot—is a classic; one of Napa Valley's highest-profile wines since its first vintage in 1979. The winery—which blends classical European and contemporary American architectural elements—does not take a back seat.

4. Auberge du Soleil (www.aubergedusoleil.com) Auberge du Soleil is Napa Valley's most luxurious experience. Fifty-two rooms and suites are nestled in olive trees on a remote 33-acre hillside. A restaurant and spa are on premises, and both are destinations unto themselves.

5. Robert Mondavi Winery (www.robertmondaviwinery.com) Once too flamboyant for conservative Napa County, the Spanish mission-style winery now seems as natural as the Mayacamas Mountains. After setting out on his own from family-owned Charles Krug, Mondavi was the most outspoken advocate for California and its wines until his death in 2008.

6. Rubicon Estate (www.rubiconestate.com) Film director Francis Ford Coppola rescued the Inglenook chateau from potential oblivion in the mid-1990s and lovingly restored the chateau, the romantic ideal of what a Napa Valley winery should look like: a sturdy stone castle, shrouded in ivy and enveloped by vineyards.

7. Lake Berryessa (www.lakeberryessachamber.com) One of Northern California's most popular water-recreation areas, Lake Berryessa offers some of the best fishing in the state. There are full-service marinas, boat rentals (power and sail), waterskiing and Jet Ski equipment, and overnight accommodations from tent and RV camping to top-quality motels.

8. Mumm Napa (www.mummnapa.com) As its name suggests, Mumm Napa blends traditional French *méthode champenoise* with the distinctive fruit of Napa Valley, and the result is some of California's best sparkling wines.

9. PlumpJack Winery (www.plumpjack.com) At PlumpJack, cabernet is the flagship wine. The tasting room has Shakespearean whimsical touches, reflecting the winery's namesake: the roguish spirit of Sir John Falstaff.

10. Round Pond Winery (www.roundpond.com) The early results for this family-owned estate are promising: the cabernets are polished yet concentrated. The winery is a showplace, and there are a number of tastings and tours available, including one featuring Round Pond's olive oils.

Auberge Du Soleil is one of the most prestigious accommodations in Wine Country. Tim Fish

distinctly southern France, with deep-set windows and wood shutters and doors. Each room or suite has a terrace and private entrance, and most have spectacular views of the valley. All furnishings are chic yet casual, and terra-cotta tiling is used generously throughout on floors. After indulging yourself in the 7,000-square-foot Auberge Spa—one of the most luxurious in the valley—take in the sculpture garden set along a half-mile path.

RANCHO CAYMUS INN (www .ranchocaymus.com, 707-963-1777, 800-845-1777, 1140 Rutherford Rd., P.O. Box 78, Rutherford, CA 94573; Price: Moderate to Very Expensive) This romantic hacienda may recall the film *Like Water for Chocolate* (rose petals are optional). The stucco inn, with a red-tile roof, is built around a serene courtyard garden, and it's clear

an artist's hand was involved in the design. The original owner, sculptor Mary Tilden Morton, created an inn distinguished by stained-glass windows, hand-hewn beams, hand-thrown stoneware, and tooled wooden lamps. A generous continental breakfast is served either in the dining room by the fireplace or out in the courtyard. The staff is obliging.

> ### Insider Secret:
> Pampering takes on new meaning with the signature Head to Toe massages available at **Auberge Spa** at the Auberge du Soleil inn. And they mean head to toe—the service includes a scalp and foot treatment . . . complete spa heaven.

Local Flavors

Taste of the town—local restaurants, cafés, bars, bistros, etc.

RESTAURANTS

The villages of Oakville and Rutherford have a limited number of restaurants, but the two suggested here are top-shelf.

AUBERGE DU SOLEIL (www .aubergedusoleil.com, 800-348-5406, 180 Rutherford Hill Rd., Rutherford, CA 94573; Price: Very Expensive; Cuisine: California, French) If you want a picture-postcard view of Napa Valley, a tapestry woven of vineyards, make a reservation at Auberge du Soleil, located at the inn of the same name (see listing under Lodgings). Then, make sure you slip in early enough to grab a table on the outside deck. The check may cause a double take, but the experience is worth it. Auberge du Soleil, or "Inn of the Sun," is a page from *Metropolitan Home* magazine and suggests a villa in southern France. What arrives on the plate rivals the atmosphere, with rich dishes such as roasted Liberty Farms duck and seared ahi tuna. Although pricey, the wine list is one of the best in Northern California, with an extensive selection of wine by the glass, including champagne. Service, too, is impeccable but never overly attentive.

RUTHERFORD GRILL (www.hill stone.com/#/restaurants/rutherford Grill/, 707-963-1792, 1180 Rutherford Rd., Rutherford, CA 94523; Price: Moderate to Expensive; Cuisine: American) So you discovered a big burly cabernet sauvignon while wine tasting. What do you eat with it? California cuisine is not always cabernet-friendly, but this restaurant fills that niche: steak. The prime rib and filet mignon may not be the best you've ever had, but the beef is tasty and generally tender, and the portions are generous. Steaks and baby-back ribs are grilled over hardwood, and even the hamburgers are worth trying. The homemade Oreo ice cream sandwich with chocolate sauce is a worthy indulgence. The atmosphere is classy in a casual sort of way, with a decor that's steakhouse-meets-nightclub: dark wood and leather. The wine list is narrow but well focused on Napa, and the service is deft.

WINERIES

In Oakville and Rutherford, cabernet sauvignons are powerful, with a clear sense of place. There are many cult cabernet producers in this area, but we don't include those that aren't open to the public. However, the bigger players we include make killer cab and definitely are worthy of a stop.

BEAULIEU VINEYARD (www .bvwines.com, 707-967-5230, 800-264-6918, 1960 St. Helena Hwy., Rutherford, CA 94573; Tasting: Daily 10–5) If you could sum up the early history of Napa Valley winemaking with a single bottle of wine, it would be the Georges de Latour Private Reserve cabernet sauvignon by Beaulieu. Though no longer the best cabernet in the valley, it has been the yardstick against which all other cabernets have been measured. Pronounced "bowl-YOU" and called BV for short, Beaulieu is one of Napa's most distinguished wineries, dating back to 1900, when Frenchman Georges de Latour began making wine. In 1938 Latour hired a young Russian immigrant, André Tchelistcheff, who went on to revolutionize California cabernet. Today, though, Beaulieu

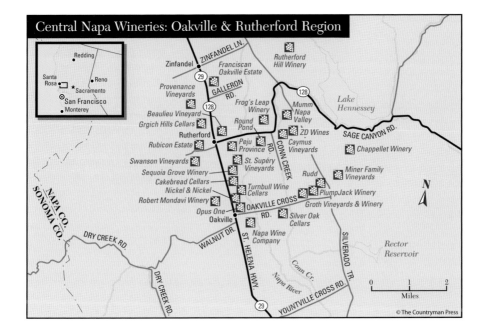

Central Napa Wineries: Oakville & Rutherford Region

struggles to maintain that rich tradition. Built of brick and covered with ivy, the winery isn't particularly impressive, but a tour can be an eye-opener, particularly when it passes the forest of towering redwood tanks. A video in the visitors' center briefs guests on Beaulieu's past and present. Three or four wines are offered; sip as you browse through the museum of old bottles and memorabilia.

CAKEBREAD CELLARS (www .cakebread.com, 707-963-5221, 800-588-0298, 8300 St. Helena Hwy., Rutherford, CA 94573; Tasting: By appointment) The Cakebread clan runs this winery set in prime cabernet sauvignon territory. Jack and Dolores Cakebread began making wine in 1973 and have won a loyal following. This striking winery looks like a modern rethinking of a historical California barn and is surrounded by gardens and vineyards. While you're in the tasting room, try the melony sauvignon blanc—one of the best. Cakebread's cabernet sauvignons and chardonnay, lean and crisp on release, bloom after a few years.

CAYMUS VINEYARDS (www.caymus .com, 707-967-3010, 707-963-4204, 8700 Conn Creek Rd., Rutherford, CA 94573; Tasting: Daily by appointment 10–4) In the past no American wine was more highly regarded than the Caymus Special Selection cabernet sauvignon. Upon its release, people would crowd the winery for the honor of paying $130 a bottle. While the Caymus SS remains a signature cabernet in Wine Country, it has lost its standing to other highbrow cult cabs. The winery is still a low-frills family outfit and tampers little with its wines. The main 40-acre vineyard lies east of the Napa River, in the heart of Napa Valley's cabernet country—a blessed location. The tasting room is in a modern winery made of sturdy fieldstone. Wines are poured at a seated tasting, and in addition to the cabernets, Caymus samples its zinfandel and sauvignon blanc, sold only at the winery.

FRANCISCAN OAKVILLE ESTATE
(www.franciscan.com, 707-963-7111, 800-529-9463, 707-967-3993, 1178 Galleron Rd., Rutherford, CA 94574; Tasting: Daily 10–5) Franciscan used to be one of our favorite stops along Highway 29, but the wines just haven't inspired us as they used to. Icon Estates, the wine giant that owns Franciscan, has expanded production of the cabernet sauvignon, merlot, and chardonnay—and it shows. The winery's latest addition is a sauvignon blanc, which is crisp, clean, and refreshing. Still, the visitors' center is big and roomy and sets a classy tone, and you can also taste the burly cabernets from sister winery, Mount Veeder.

FROG'S LEAP WINERY
(www.frogsleap.com, 707-963-4704, 800-959-4704, 8815 Conn Creek Rd., Rutherford, CA 94573; Tasting: By appointment) It's rare to find a winery with a sense of humor as well oiled as Frog's Leap. Printed on every cork is the word *ribbit*, and the weather vane atop the winery sports a leaping frog. The name, a takeoff on Stag's Leap Wine Cellars, was inspired by the winery's original site, an old St. Helena frog farm. Founders Larry Turley and John Williams parted ways in 1994, and Williams moved Frog's Leap south and restored a winery that dates to 1884. All five wines—Rutherford cabernet sauvignon, zinfandel, merlot, chardonnay, and sauvignon blanc—are reliable and often superb. Tasting takes place in the vineyard house behind the winery.

GRGICH HILLS ESTATE
(www.grgich.com, 707-963-2784, 800-532-3057, 1829 St. Helena Hwy., Rutherford, CA 94573; Tasting: Daily 9:30–4:30) French wine lovers worship

> **Insider Secret:**
> While the 2008 film *Bottle Shock* gives full credit to Jim Barrett for producing the winning chardonnay of the Paris Tasting of 1976, it was actually Mike Grgich who crafted the 1973 Chateau Montelena. Stop in at Grgich Hills Estate to taste his striking chardonnays.

the land, but in California, the winemaker is king. Cult followings have a way of developing—as with Mike Grgich, one of Napa Valley's best-known characters. The scrappy immigrant from the former Yugoslavia first gained renown as the winemaker at Chateau Montelena in Calistoga. Later, Grgich joined with Austin Hills and opened this winery. An ivy-covered stucco building with a red-tiled roof, Grgich's winery remains a house devoted to chardonnay. Grgich also makes a fumé blanc and has considerable luck with zinfandel and cabernet sauvignon and merlot. However, over the years all the wines have become inconsistent.

GROTH VINEYARDS AND WINERY
(www.grothwines.com, 707-754-4254, 750 Oakville Cross Rd., Oakville, CA 94562 Tasting: Mon.–Sat. by appointment 10–4) This California mission-style winery is a grand sight along the Oakville Cross Road. It's also home to a top-notch cabernet sauvignon, the Groth Reserve. Dennis Groth began making wine in 1982, and his graceful winery was completed a few years later. The tour is enlightening, beginning on a terrace that overlooks the vineyards, continuing past the bottling line and the cavernous barrel-aging room, and ending at the

Entrance to Grgich Hills Estate.

tasting bar. Groth cabernets typically have a lush elegance married to a firm backbone.

MINER FAMILY VINEYARDS (www.minerwines.com, 707-945-1270, 800-366-9463 ext. 17, 7850 Silverado Tr., Oakville, 94562; Tasting: Daily 11–5) Miner is making some impressive cabernet sauvignons and zinfandels. David Miner, a former software salesman, purchased a 60-acre vineyard high above the valley in 1989. A winery, situated above Silverado Trail, is a smart-looking edifice, done in rich golden hues and a modern, Mediterranean style. The tasting room, sleek in

its polished-wood tones, offers a grand view of the valley. Visitors can watch the winery in action through wide windows that overlook the barrel and fermentation rooms.

MUMM NAPA (www.mummnapa .com, 707-967-7770, 866-783-5826, 800-MUM-NAPA, 8445 Silverado Tr., Rutherford, CA 94573; Tasting: Daily 10–4:45) Mumm Napa may have a French pedigree, but it's a California child through and through. The winery is a long, low ranch barn with redwood siding and a green slate roof. Mumm blends traditional French *méthode champenoise* with the distinctive fruit of Napa Valley, and the result is some of California's best sparkling wines. The winery tour offers a detailed look at the French way of making sparkling wine. Brut Prestige is the main release, a snappy blend of pinot noir and chardonnay, and a zesty Brut Rose. The salon is quaint and country, with sliding glass doors that allow easy views of the Rutherford countryside.

NICKEL & NICKEL (www.nickel andnickel.com, 707-967-9600, 8164 St. Helena Highway, Oakville, CA 94562; Tasting: Mon.–Fri. 10–3, Sat.–Sun. 10–2) Nickel & Nickel was established by the partners of Far Niente, and the winery opened in July 2003. The idea was to produce 100 percent single-vineyard wines that best express the personality of each vineyard and varietal. Visiting the tasting room is like stepping back in time. It's housed in a building that dates back to 1882. Nickel & Nickel produces high-end chardonnay, merlot, Syrah, cabernet, and zinfandel, but it's best known for cab—and these pricy cabs are typically well worth the price.

OPUS ONE (www.opusonewinery .com, 707-944-9442, 7900 St. Helena Hwy., Oakville, CA 94562; Tasting: Daily by appointment 10–4:30) A joint venture between Robert Mondavi and France's Château Mouton-Rothschild, Opus One is an elegant temple, a

Insider Secret:

Few people know that the balcony off the tasting room at Opus One has one of the best views of the Napa Valley. Step out with your glass and take a peek.

cross between a Mayan palace and the *Battlestar Galactica.* Designed by the firm that created San Francisco's Transamerica Pyramid, the winery opened in 1991 but was largely inaccessible to the public until 1994. It's apropos that the winery makes a vivid architectural statement. Opus One has been one of Napa Valley's highest-profile wines since its first vintage in 1979. The wine—a blend of cabernet sauvignon, cabernet franc, petit verdot, malbec, and merlot—is a classic: rich, oaky, and elegant. The tasting room fee is extravagant (what do you expect for highbrow wine?), but the pour is generous.

PEJU PROVINCE (www.peju.com, 707-963-3600, 800-446-7358, 8466 St. Helena Hwy., Rutherford, CA 94573, Tasting: Daily 10–6) The grounds of this family-owned estate are lovely. There's good reason: Tony and Herta Peju ran a nursery in Los Angeles before coming north in the early 1980s. A row of beautiful sycamores leads to the French provincial winery, which is enveloped in white roses and other flowers. There is also a fine collection of marble sculptures. The tour doesn't take long; it's a small place. Cabernet sauvignon and cab franc are the specialties. Enjoy a bimonthly rotating art exhibit while tasting.

PLUMPJACK WINERY (www.plump jack.com, 707-945-1220, 620 Oakville Cross Rd., Oakville, CA 94562; Tasting: Daily 10–4) PlumpJack is named for the roguish spirit of Shakespeare's Sir John Falstaff. In the mid-1990s the company bought a century-old Napa Valley vineyard property renowned for producing cabernet of exceptional quality. Cabernet is still PlumpJack's flagship wine. The tasting room has Shakespearean whimsical touches, an uneven wavering fence outside, and iron decanters filled with flowers inside.

PROVENANCE VINEYARDS

(www.provenancevineyards.com, 707-968-3633, 866-946-3253, 695 St. Helena Hwy., Rutherford, CA 94573; Tasting: Daily 10:30–5:30) Provenance Vineyards makes appealing cabernet, sauvignon blanc, and merlot, and it gets particularly high marks for the latter. It's no wonder: winemaker Tom Rinaldi cut his teeth at Duckhorn Vineyards as founding winemaker, and he spent 22 vintages at the winery that exemplifies the best in merlot. Ironically, Rinaldi wanted to be a veterinarian, but because he worked with so many dissatisfied doctors who wanted to be winemakers, he opted for the latter. The modern-looking winery has a tasting room that's known for its French and American oak flooring constructed from strips of barrels—quite a conversation piece at the horseshoe-shaped tasting bar.

QUINTESSA

(www.quintessa.com, 707 967-1601, 1601 Silverado Tr., Rutherford, CA 94573; Tasting and Tours: Daily by appointment 10–4) This winery is somehow both inconspicuous and dramatically styled. Arching like a crescent moon from a wooded knoll in Rutherford, most of the winery is underground. The facade is rugged stone, and inside is a state-of-the-art, gravity-flow winery in which the grapes arrive on the roof and end up as wine in oak barrels in the underground cellar. On the rolling hills surrounding the winery are 170 acres of vineyards, mostly cabernet, and owners Valeria and Agustin Huneeus produce just one wine: Quintessa, the elegant red Bordeaux-style blend.

ROBERT MONDAVI WINERY

(www.robertmondaviwinery.com, 888-RMONDAVI option 2, 7801 St. Helena Hwy., Oakville, CA 94562; Tasting: Daily 10–5) We never thought we'd see it in our lifetime: the Robert Mondavi family without its namesake winery. Of course, Mondavi began to loosen his grip when the winery went public in 1993, but he and his family lost ownership interest after a $1.36 billion buyout by Constellation Brands of New York. The late Robert Mondavi was an innovator, such a symbol of the "new" Napa Valley that it's hard to believe he founded his winery in 1966. Once too flamboyant for conservative Napa County, the Spanish mission–style winery now seems as natural as the Mayacamas Mountains. After setting out on his own from family-owned Charles Krug, Mondavi became the most outspoken advocate for California and its wines. Few Napa wineries are busier on a summer day than Mondavi, which offers one of the most thorough tours in the valley. Mondavi bottles one of the most extensive lists of wines in the valley. Reds seem to be the winery's strong suit. The reserve cabernet sauvignons and pinot noirs become more magnificent every year—and so do the prices. Of course, the regular bottlings are hardly slackers.

ROUND POND WINERY (www
.roundpond.com, 707-302-2575,
888-302-2575, 875 Rutherford Rd.,
Rutherford, CA 94573; Tasting: Daily
11–4, some by appointment) The
MacDonnell family has been selling
cabernet sauvignon grapes to the likes
of Beaulieu and Franciscan for two
decades and today owns more than 400
acres in the Rutherford area. A few
years ago the family decided to build
their own winery and start making
wine. The early results are promising:
The cabernets are polished yet concentrated. The winery is a showplace, and
there are a number of tastings and
tours available, including an exploration of the olive oil press.

RUBICON ESTATE (www.rubicon
estate.com, 707-968-1161, 800-
RUBICON, 1991 St. Helena Hwy.,
Rutherford, CA 94573; Tasting: Daily
10–5) Film director Francis Ford Coppola rescued the Inglenook chateau
from potential oblivion in the mid-
1990s and lovingly restored the property, the romantic ideal of what a Napa
Valley winery should look like: a sturdy
stone castle, shrouded in ivy and
enveloped by vineyards. Visitors
approach the winery through a long,
tree-lined driveway. Coppola's affec-
tions for Inglenook date to the mid-
1970s, when he bought the former
home of Inglenook's founder, Gustave
Niebaum, which is next to the winery.
Coppola released his own wine, Rubicon, a stout yet elegant Bordeaux-style
blend, beginning with the 1978 vintage. Coppola's movie memorabilia,
formerly on display at Rubicon, is finding a new home at his latest winery
addition: Francis Ford Coppola Winery
in Sonoma County.

RUDD WINERY AND VINEYARDS
(www.ruddwines.com, 707-944-8577,
500 Oakville Cross Rd., Oakville, CA
94562; Tasting and Tours: Tues.–Sat. by
appointment) Leslie Rudd knows a
thing or two about luxury. He owns
upscale retailer Dean & DeLuca, several restaurants around the country,
and even a high-end gin distillery. In
the mid-1990s Rudd came to Napa and
transformed an underperforming winery into a showpiece. He replanted the
vines on the 55-acre estate and created
a stone winery with a 22,000-square-
foot cave. Cabernet is the star attraction, and the wines are powerful and
polished. The tour is an extensive
affair, offering a thorough overview of
Rudd and ending with a seated tasting.

RUTHERFORD HILL WINERY
(www.rutherfordhill.com, 707-963-
1871, 800-637-5681, 200 Rutherford
Hill Rd., Rutherford, CA 94573; Tasting: Daily 10–5) The winery here is a
mammoth barn, albeit a stylishly realized one, covered in cedar and perched
on the hills overlooking Rutherford.
Carved into the hillside behind are
among the largest man-made aging
caves in California, snaking a half mile
into the rock. The titanic cave doors
are framed by geometric latticework
that recalls the work of Frank Lloyd
Wright. A trek through the cool and
humid caves is the tour highlight. Merlot is the star here, and it's typically
fleshy, with a tannic backbone.

ST. SUPÉRY VINEYARDS AND
WINERY (www.stsupery.com, 707-
963-4507, 800-942-0809 x44, 8440 St.
Helena Hwy., Rutherford, CA 94573;
Tasting: Daily 10–5) Wineries, on the
whole, aren't the best places to take
kids. St. Supéry is an exception. It adds
a touch of science-museum adventure,
with colorful displays, hands-on activities, and modern winery gadgetry.
Windows reveal the bottling line, the
barrel-aging room, and the like. A
highlight is the "smellavision," where
noses are educated on the nuances of
cabernet sauvignon and sauvignon

blanc. Ever hear cabernet described as cedar or black cherry? Hold your nose to a plastic tube, and smell what these descriptions mean. Another display gives you a peek under the soil to see the roots of a grapevine. St. Supéry offers a solid cabernet sauvignon, Meritage, and an exceptional sauvignon blanc, among other wines.

SEQUOIA GROVE WINERY

(www.sequoiagrove.com, 707-944-2945, 800-851-7841, 8338 St. Helena Hwy., Napa, CA 94558; Tasting: Daily 10:30–5) Dwarfed by century-old sequoia trees, this winery is easy to overlook along Highway 29, but the cabernet sauvignons are worth the stop. Wine was made in the 150-year-old redwood barn before Prohibition, but the wine and the winery had been long forgotten when the Allen family began making wine here again in 1980. The chardonnay is solid, but the regular and reserve cabernets can achieve greatness.

SILVER OAK CELLARS (www.silver

oak.com, 707-942-7026, 800-273-8809, 915 Oakville Cross Rd., Oakville, CA 94562; Tasting: Mon.–Sat. 9–5) Not many wineries can live off one wine, but then Silver Oak isn't just any winery. Here, cabernet sauvignon has been raised to an art form. Low profile by Napa Valley standards, Silver Oak is known to cabernet lovers around the country, and that's all that matters. The Alexander Valley cabernet is typically more accessible than the Napa Valley bottling, but both are velvety and opulent and done in a distinct California style. Silver Oak was established in 1972 on the site of an old Oakville dairy. A fire destroyed much of the original cellar in 2006 and the winery rebuilt it from scratch, hoping to pay tribute to the past while looking toward the future.

SWANSON VINEYARDS (www.swan

sonvineyards.com, 707-754-4000, 1271 Manley Ln., Rutherford, CA 94573; Tasting: Thurs.–Sun. by appointment) The Swanson family moved to Napa Valley after Clarke Swanson realized that wine had more allure for him than banking and journalism. The winery produces a cabernet blend, merlot, and pinot grigio. The petite sirah is great, but it's not produced every year, and when it is, it's made in small batches. On the upside, there's a great supply of Alexis, the Bordeaux blend, so keep your eye out for that. The tasting room is extravagant, inspired by the sumptuous salons of 18th-century Paris. And don't forget to visit the Sip Shoppe, which is considered a candy store for adults, featuring fine wines, bonbons, caviar, and cheeses.

TURNBULL WINE CELLARS

(www.turnbullwines.com, 707-963-5839, 800-887-6285, 8210 St. Helena Hwy., Oakville, CA 94562; Tasting: Daily 10–4:30) This small redwood winery in the heart of cabernet sauvignon territory was designed by award-winning architect William Turnbull, a former partner in the winery, which originated in 1979. The cabernet is known for its distinct minty quality.

ZD WINES (www.zdwines.com, 707-

963-5188, 800-487-7757, 8383 Silverado Tr., Napa, CA 94558; Tasting: Daily 10–4:30) Chardonnay, pinot noir, cabernet sauvignon: ZD has a way with all three. The winery began life in 1969 in Sonoma Valley and transplanted to Napa 10 years later. Crowned with a roof of red tile, the winery was expanded a few years back by the de Leuze family. The star is chardonnay, an opulent beauty, while cabernets are dense and powerful. The pinots are light but intensely fruity.

Prep for a Wine Country picnic at Oakville Grocery Co.   Tim Fish

Palate Adventures

For a gourmet picnic . . .

Oakville Grocery Co. (www.oakville grocery.com, 707-944-8802, 7856 St. Helena Hwy., Oakville, CA. 94562) This iconic country store houses a gourmet grocery. The fare is well suited to a Wine Country picnic basket: everything from duck pâté and caviar to hearty sandwiches. There's also coffee by the cup, bakery treats, and local wines. It's open daily for coffee at 7 AM. This is a great stop before or after wine tasting. It's been purchased by Dean & DeLuca.

To Do

Check out these great attractions and activities . . .

CULTURAL OUTINGS

• *Develop a taste for art*
Mumm Napa (www.mummnapa.com, 707-967-7730, 8445 Silverado Tr., Rutherford, CA 94573) The long hallways of this winery are devoted to art, and it's a lovely space. Revolving shows are featured, and Ansel Adams's *Story of a Winery* is on permanent display.

Best Day in Napa Valley

Our tour of Napa Valley takes in the cities of Napa and Yountville as well as Oakville and Rutherford; see the individual city chapters for full listings. Here we set you up with a 24-hour itinerary, featuring wine tasting, an exotic Japanese dinner, and a show at the Uptown Theatre.

You can easily tailor this tour to the Napa Valley "home base" of your choice. We'll escort you to the most interesting places, offering plenty of options so you can create your own Best Day.

1. To begin, we sweep you off to Paris, or so it seems, but no passport is necessary at **Bouchon Bakery** (Yountville; www.bouchonbakery.com). You'll find exceptional treats, like melt-in-your-mouth croissants and coffee éclairs. (Overslept? No worries. Grab a sandwich. The bread is divine).

2. Time to trade up from a latte to a glass of wine. Morning sipping? You bet, and here are some great options.

Domaine Chandon (Yountville; www.chandon.com) As the house that Moët Hennessy built, Chandon knows sparkling wine. This ultramodern winery in the hills west of Yountville is the setting for informative tours as well as tastings. Outstanding exhibits by local artists rotate throughout the year.

Cliff Lede Vineyards (Yountville; www.cliffledevineyards.com) Canadian Cliff Lede bought the old S. Anderson Winery, where sparkling wine had been the focus, and transformed it into a producer of cabernet sauvignon and sauvignon blanc. Right out of the gate the wines were competing with the valley's best.

Stag's Leap Wine Cellars (Napa; www.cask23.com) This is the place that put California wine on the map in 1976, when its 1973 cabernet won the famous Paris Tasting. For wine lovers, a visit to Stag's Leap Wine Cellars is a pilgrimage.

3. After a morning of sipping, you'll need to refuel with a hearty lunch. **Oakville Grocery Co.** (Oakville; www.oakvillegrocery.com) fills the bill. Don't let the country-store facade fool you (the place has been in business since 1881): this is a gourmet grocery. Fare includes duck pâté, cold cuts, and caviar. Sandwiches include turkey with pesto and a glorious lavash.

4. Prepare for another round of sipping—Wine Tasting, Part II—with plenty of options. Go ahead, be choosy.

Opus One (Oakville; www.opusonewinery.com) Call it visually distinctive or just plain cool, the building housing this winery is a must-see. Opus One has been one of Napa Valley's highest-profile wines since its first vintage in 1979. The wine—a blend of cabernet sauvignon, cabernet franc, and merlot—is a classic: rich, oaky, and elegant.

Robert Mondavi Winery (Oakville; www.robertmondaviwinery.com) Once too flamboyant for conservative Napa County, the Spanish mission–style winery now seems as natural as the Mayacamas Mountains. After setting out on his own in 1966 from family-owned Charles Krug, Mondavi was the most outspoken advocate for California and its wines until his death in 2008.

Rubicon Estate (Rutherford; www.rubiconestate.com) Film director Francis Ford Coppola rescued the Inglenook chateau from potential oblivion in the

continued on next page

continued from previous page

mid-1990s. It is now lovingly restored, the romantic ideal of what a Napa Valley winery should look like: a sturdy stone castle, shrouded in ivy and enveloped by vineyards.

5. Now for an exotic dining experience at one of Napa Valley's newest and most exciting locales: **Morimoto Napa** (Napa; www.morimotonapa.com) This restaurant, under the direction of Iron Chef Masaharu Morimoto, serves contemporary Japanese cuisine (with a California twist, of course) in a sleek, dynamic space overlooking the River Walk.

6. Why not follow dinner with a show? **Uptown Theatre** (Napa; www.uptown theatrenapa.com) is the venue for live performance in Napa Valley. It's also been restored to its former art deco splendor. Check out current offerings on the website.

7. End the day with a nightcap at the swanky **Carpe Diem Wine Bar** (Napa; www.carpediemwinebar.com) Pair your libation with a light bite: yummy cheeses and charcuterie, grilled flatbreads, or perhaps you'd prefer something sweet. Another great addition to the Napa Valley scene.

8. A romantic getaway is in order. Prepare to be indulged at the **Milliken Creek Inn & Spa** (Napa; www.millikencreekinn .com) Guest rooms at the inn beckon you to relax and unwind. This place is set up to pamper: spa and massage services, yoga, breakfast in bed, Italian linens, and Napa River views. Sweet dreams.

Relaxation awaits at the Milliken Creek Inn.

Robert Mondavi Winery (www.robertmondavi.com, 888-766-6328, 7801 St. Helena Hwy., Oakville, CA 94562) This is one of the first wineries to show art. Rotating shows are on display in the Vineyard Room.

• *Enjoy music with a view*

Music in the Vineyards (www.musicinthevinyards.org, 707-258-5559, various locations and sponsors) This festival of chamber music happens every August and draws musicians from around the country.

Robert Mondavi Summer Music Festival (www.robertmondavi.com /concerts/4, 888-766-6328, 7801 Hwy. 29, P.O. Box 106, Oakville, CA 94562) A tradition since 1969, these June-through-August concerts on the lush lawns of Mondavi's winery bring in top names in popular music, including Tony Bennett, David Benoit, and the Preservation Hall Jazz Band.

• *Pamper yourself at a spa*

Auberge du Soleil (707-963-1211; 180 Rutherford Hill Rd., Rutherford, CA)
What would Napa Valley's most luxurious resort be without an excellent spa? The
facility is top-notch—but then, so is everything at this inn, hidden in the mountains above Napa Valley. Auberge du Soleil offers a variety of treatments, from
aromatherapy and facials to foot massages and Eastern-influenced massages. If
you're staying at the inn, consider an in-room massage.

• *Relax on the water, fish, sail, or ski*

Lake Berryessa (www.lakeberryessa.com) At about 26 miles long, Lake Berryessa
is one of the largest bodies of fresh water in California, Located about 15 miles
east of Rutherford along Highway 128, it's one of Northern California's most popular water-recreation areas. It offers full-service marinas, boat rentals for the avid
fisherman, sailboats, water-ski and Jet Ski equipment, and overnight accommodations from tent and RV camping to top-quality motels.

Lake Hennessey (4 miles east of Rutherford on Highway 128, closest town:
Rutherford, CA 94543) This is a water source for the city of Napa. Fishing and
boating are allowed, though the only facilities are a car-top launch ramp and
picnic grounds.

4

St. Helena

ST. HELENA IS A FOOD MECCA— the Culinary Institute of America at Greystone is housed here, in a castle that was once the Christian Brothers winery. It's a big draw for rookies and professionals who want to improve their craft. As for wine lovers, the Rudd Center on the premises, which was once a distillery, has two tasting theaters for serious sipping.

St. Helena is also home to the Meadowood Resort, perhaps the swankiest of all Wine Country resorts. Every year it hosts Auction Napa Valley, one of the most successful wine charity auctions in the country, second only to the Naples Winter Wine Festival in Florida.

Travelers here soon realize that food and wine dominate the itinerary, with perhaps the possibility of squeezing in some golf and tennis between palate adventures. Unique restaurants play to both California cuisine and comfort food, and top-name chefs include Hiroyoshi Sone and Cindy Pawlcyn, who have made food, quite simply, edible art.

Tasting rooms and wineries are plentiful, with vineyards not far from the center of town. Spotteswood is a favorite, but there are many wineries worth exploring.

Shoppers will enjoy downtown St. Helena's chic strip of stores. In fact, when you slip in to some of the shops, for a split second you think you're on Madison Avenue. Woodhouse Chocolate, for example, resembles a highbrow jewelry store, but instead of jewels under glass you'll find delectable confections.

The town, which seems quaint at first glance, is surprisingly sophisticated.

> **Insider Secret:**
> Oprah Winfrey, *Tonight Show* host Jay Leno, and *American Idol* host Ryan Seacrest have frequented the Auction Napa Valley, a charity event where $10 million is routinely raised in a single afternoon. When Oprah was here she said, "Napa Valley is my new favorite place. This is how people are supposed to live—sipping a glass of wine on a patio in the afternoon, looking out over a vineyard." (www.napavintners .com)

LEFT: The St. Helena street scene.   Tim Fish

Travel Like an Insider:

Our Top 10 Picks for St. Helena

1. Terra (www.terrarestaurant.com) Terra's Asian influence leaves an indelible mark on California cuisine. Chef Hiroyoshi Sone, a superb talent, adds a little daring to each dish. The black cod marinated in sake is a house specialty.

2. Culinary Institute of America at Greystone (www.ciachef.edu/california/) Housed in a castle, the California branch of the Culinary Institute of America, or CIA for short, is a haven for foodies. Greystone offers programs for culinary professionals, wine professionals, and food enthusiasts like the rest of us.

3. Meadowood Napa Valley (www.meadowood.com) This luxurious resort prides itself on reflecting the best of Napa Valley, from the guest rooms to the acclaimed restaurant and spa. The staff pampers with style, and a soothing sense of privacy prevails.

4. Go Fish (www.gofishrestaurant.net) The clever people behind Go Fish know that wine lovers can't subsist on red meat alone. The menu has a range of tasty offerings, including the option of "fish cooked your way," whether sautéed, wood grilled, or poached.

5. CADE Winery (www.cadewinery.com) California lieutenant governor Gavin Newsom and entrepreneur Gordon Getty are behind this winery atop Howell Mountain, at an altitude of 1,800 feet. The motto here is "Think Green. Drink Green." Smart politics?

6. Gott's Roadside Tray Gourmet (www.gotts.roadside.com) This is a classic old drive-in restaurant—though you have to walk to the window these days—but average joes and gourmands alike flock to Gott's for its updated, 1950s-style fast-food menu, which includes burgers, fries, beer, and wine. And if you're traveling with kids, it's a godsend, because Napa Valley is short on family restaurants.

7. Woodhouse Chocolate (www.woodhousechocolate.com) This shop is a bright and airy house of chocolates that resembles a highbrow jewelry store, with delectable chocolates instead of gems. It specializes in European-style fresh crème chocolate with no preservatives.

8. I Wolk Gallery (www.iwolkgallery.com) This is an excellent gallery, specializing in contemporary paintings, photography, and crafts by emerging American artists. Exhibitions feature single artists, but a wide range of artists is shown continuously.

9. Spottswoode Winery (www.spottswoode.com) The first Spottswoode wines were made in 1982 in the basement of this estate's 1882 Victorian. Intense and impeccably balanced, Spottswoode's cabernet sauvignon was quickly regarded as among the best in the 1980s, a stature it retains. Run by the Novak family, Spottswoode is a small enterprise that welcomes devotees of fine cabernet.

10. Napa Valley Olive Oil Manufacturing Co. This faded white barn is a glorious time warp. The shop dates to the 1920s, when Napa Valley was largely populated by Italian farmers. You're as likely to hear Italian inside as English, and the deli counter looks like your grandmother's kitchen—if your grandmother is from Naples. There are picnic tables outside.

Checking In

Best places to stay in and around St. Helena.

Accommodations in St. Helena serve a variety of interests and budgets: there are bargains here as well as luxe resorts for which you'll pay a premium.

ADAGIO INN (www.adagioinn.com, 707-963-2238, 888-823-2446,1417 Kearney St., St. Helena, CA 94574; Price: Very Expensive) The sun-soaked porch at this 1904 Victorian cottage offers relaxation after a day of shopping and wine tasting. The three guest rooms are spacious and done in romantically antique decor, and two of the rooms have large whirlpool tubs. The location is nearly ideal, in a quiet residential neighborhood a few steps from St. Helena's Main Street.

EL BONITA MOTEL (www.elbonita .com, 707-963-3216, 800-541-3284,195 Main St., St. Helena, CA 94574; Price: Moderate to Expensive) Don't let the "motel" in the name fool you. The 1950s meets the new millennium at El Bonita, a chic, art deco, pastel-hued classic. It's also Napa's best bargain. Built in 1953, the motel was renovated and newly landscaped in 1992. The garden and lawn span 2.5 acres, all sheltered from busy Highway 29. Trees and hedges also help cushion the steady hum of traffic. There's continental breakfast service in the lobby or—weather permitting—on the patio.

HARVEST INN (www.harvestinn.com, 707-963-9463, 800-950-8466, 1 Main St., St. Helena, CA 94574; Price: Expensive to Very Expensive) There's a bit of Old England in Napa Valley at the Harvest Inn, a stately English Tudor–style lodge built from the bricks

Croquet anyone? The immaculate grounds of Meadowood Resort.

Class is in session at the Culinary Institute of America at Greystone. Tim Fish

and cobblestones of old San Francisco homes. The lush landscaping also helps to create the aura of another time and place. The inn's Harvest Centre has a wine bar and dance floor, and a complimentary continental breakfast is served in the dining hall. The inn overlooks a 14-acre working vineyard and is within strolling distance of many wineries.

HOTEL ST. HELENA (www.hotel sthelena.com, 707-963-4388, 888-478-4355, 1309 Main St., St. Helena, CA 94574; Price: Inexpensive to Expensive) In the thick of St. Helena's shopping and dining, this hotel on the town's Main Street is richly furnished with antiques. Built in 1881, the hotel has 17 rooms and one suite. There's a wine bar, and a continental breakfast is served every morning. The hotel is air-conditioned.

INK HOUSE BED & BREAKFAST (www.inkhouse.com, 707-963-3890,

1575 St. Helena Hwy., St. Helena, CA 94574; Price: Moderate to Expensive) A glass-enclosed rooftop observatory with a 360-degree view of vineyards distinguishes this yellow, 1884 Italianate Victorian listed on the National Register of Historic Places. Just for fun, take a lesson on the antique pump organ in the parlor, or take in a sunset from the wraparound porch. A full gourmet breakfast is served, plus wine and hors d'oeuvres at night. This is an exceptional location and setting. Though it's right on Highway 29, the inn is remarkably quiet.

INN AT SOUTHBRIDGE (www.innat southbridge.com, 707-967-9400, 800-520-6800, 1020 Main St., St. Helena, CA 94574; Price: Very Expensive) A classy addition to St. Helena, this inn complex is a sleekly modern Italianate design. All 20 rooms are on the second floor and done in handsome ivory white and cream and hues with sophisticated wood accents. Just off the lobby is a family-style Italian restaurant called Pizzeria Tra Vigne; it's not bad for a quick pizza (see listing under Restaurants). Also part of the complex is the Health Spa Napa Valley. A continental breakfast is included.

MEADOWOOD NAPA VALLEY

(www.meadowood.com, 707-963-3646, 800-458-8080, 900 Meadowood Ln., St. Helena, CA 94574; Price: Very Expensive) Meadowood never falters in its interpretation of luxury. Its white-trimmed buildings, tiered with gabled windows and porches, are reminiscent of New England's turn-of-the-20th-century cottages. The staff pampers with style, and a soothing sense of privacy prevails. Most of the resort's 85 cottages, suites, and lodges—scattered around a gorgeous, wooded 250-acre property—have cathedral ceilings, skylights, ceiling fans, and air-conditioning. Breakfast is not included; however, a continental repast can be delivered to your door, or a full feast is available at the Grill. Better yet, try a light breakfast by the pool, surrounded by lush lawns and trees. Meadowood also has one of the finest health facilities in the valley, with aerobic and exercise rooms and a full spa.

SHADY OAKS COUNTRY INN

(www.shadyoakscountryinn.com, 707-963-1190, 399 Zinfandel Ln., St. Helena, CA 94574; Price: Expensive) Oak and walnut trees surround this friendly country inn consisting of five guest rooms with private baths, all furnished with antiques. A full gourmet champagne breakfast—eggs Benedict or Belgian waffles are the norm—is served in your room or in the dining room and garden patio, which is guarded by Roman columns. Wine and cheese are served in the evening. For those who are up for a little recreation,

there's a new boccie ball court in front of the inn.

VINEYARD COUNTRY INN

(www.vineyardcountryinn.com, 707-963-1000, 201 Main St., St. Helena, CA 94574; Price: Expensive to Very Expensive) This lovely inn takes its inspiration from a French country village. Surrounding a central court, the buildings are crowned with steeply pitched roofs and intricate brick chimneys. There are 21 elegant suites, with exposed-beam ceilings, redbrick fireplaces, king- or queen-sized beds, and wet bars with refrigerators. Many have balconies with vineyard views. For the breakfast buffet, small tables are grouped around the large dining room fireplace. The inn is on busy Highway 29, but the rooms are relatively quiet.

WINE COUNTRY INN

(www.winecountryinn.com, 707-963-7077, 888-465-4608, 1152 Lodi Ln., St. Helena, CA 94574; Price: Expensive to Very Expensive) This guest house is modern, but a tall stone tower gives it an old-world feel. There are 20 guest rooms, each decorated with country-style quilts and antiques; all have private baths, and many have fireplaces and decks or balconies with lush views. A buffet-style breakfast is served daily.

ZINFANDEL INN

(www.zinfandelinn.com, 707-963-3512, 800 Zinfandel Ln., St. Helena, CA 94574; Price: Expensive to Very Expensive) A striking example of a modern English Tudor, this luxury getaway is planted in the heart of Wine Country. A fountain and an arched doorway crowned with fieldstone greet you, while the dining room has a beautifully inlaid oak floor. All rooms have lavish, full hot breakfasts, whirlpool tubs, fireplaces, private balcony or deck, and air conditioning.

Local Flavors

Taste of the town—local restaurants, cafés, bars, bistros, etc.

RESTAURANTS

St. Helena is a great place for diners with an urge to explore. Terra's sea bass marinated in sake is one of many innovative dishes you'll find. At Go Fish, sometimes it's black cod and sometimes its sea bass, depending on the daily catch. Our advice? Go with the flow.

CINDY'S BACKSTREET KITCHEN (www.cindysbackstreetkitchen.com, 707-963-1200, 1327 Railroad Ave, St. Helena, CA 94574; Price: Expensive; Cuisine: California) Cindy's has quickly become one of our favorite restaurants in Wine Country. We always feel welcome, and we love the atmosphere: it's light and breezy, with exposed rafters, soothing hues, pine floors, and a distinct zinc bar. The restaurant is owned by Cindy Pawlcyn, the grande dame of Napa Valley and owner of Mustards Grill and Go Fish. The food is comforting but infused with flavor and is generally a welcome retreat from the traditional Wine Country cuisine. We're a sucker for the chicken fried steak and the Chinatown duck burger. Be sure to start with the backstreet fry, a crispy collection of calamari and fresh vegetables. The wine selection isn't large, but it has everything you need and is largely focused on Napa. The bar also has a fine list of ales and creative drinks such as a wild-apple martini.

GO FISH (www.gofishrestaurant.net, 707-963-0700, 641 Main St., St. Helena, CA 94574; Price: Very Expensive; Cuisine: California) This house of fish is a smart addition to Wine Country. The clever woman behind it, Cindy Pawlcyn, knows that wine lovers can't subsist on red meat alone. The menu has a range of tasty offerings, including the option of "fish cooked your way," whether sautéed, wood grilled, or poached. Every dish we tried exceeded our expectations. The wine list is fairly priced and appropriately weighted to whites. The service is knowledgeable, efficient, and friendly, while the decor is a feng shui haven. Go Fish is modern and clean yet cozy, as if it were a high-end home. The sushi bar dominates, running the length of the dining room.

MARTINI HOUSE (www.martini house.com, 707-963-2233, 1245 Spring St., St. Helena, CA 94574; Price: Very Expensive; Cuisine: California) If you've ever been to a Pat Kuleto–designed restaurant, you never forget it. The innovative restaurant designer and owner of such top San Francisco dining rooms as Boulevard, Farallon, and Jardinière is the man behind Martini House. Set in a 1923 Craftsman bungalow, the restaurant is dramatically stylish, with a design inspired by Napa history, including Indian-basket light fixtures, yet it remains as comfortable as an old leather coat. The patio is one of the valley's best outdoor dining

Insider Secret:

If the lobster roll is a special at **Go Fish,** order it in a whisper and don't let the people at the next table hear you. This appetizer is the Cadillac of sushi, and there's a limited supply. It's a great find; you'll marvel over it for months.

experiences. Chef and partner Todd Humphries, formerly of San Francisco's Campton Place, creates a menu of what Kuleto calls Napa Cuisine: hearty creations that focus on local, seasonal ingredients such as pan-roasted duck breast and butter-basted halibut, although the kitchen can be maddeningly inconsistent. The wine list is one of the best in the valley, however, with a wide range of varietals and regions.

PIZZERIA TRA VIGNE (www .travignerestaurant.com, 707-967-9999, 1016 Main St., St. Helena, CA 94574; Price: Moderate; Cuisine: Italian) This family-friendly house of pizza has a stylishly casual atmosphere and reasonable prices, which make it a good lunch stop while you're touring the valley. The dining room is big and airy, with a brick, wood-fired pizza oven in full view. There are cozy booths and large communal tables that seat 12 or more. Don't let the laid-back veneer fool you, though: the people behind this pizzeria are the same savvy folks behind the restaurant Tra Vigne. The menu is the same at lunch or dinner, and if you don't feel like eating the usual pizza, try something called *piadine,* a basic pizza topped with salad, which you fold and eat like a taco. The grilled chicken version is wonderful. The wine list is appealingly no-nonsense.

PRESS (www.pressthelena.com, 707-967-0550, 587 Hwy. 29, St. Helena, CA; Price: Very Expensive; Cuisine: Steakhouse) This is a first-class steakhouse. In fact, the 20-ounce, dry-aged "cowboy" bone-in rib eye is one of the best steaks we've ever tasted. It's pricy, but decadence this tasty is hard to resist, plus it's big enough for two. The menu is a carnivore's delight, but there are also a couple of tasty seafood options. The eclectic wine list is impressive but fairly expensive. The

service is first-class and the decor is inviting, uncluttered sophistication at its best—high ceilings, expansive glass, and black walnut accents. Good tip: If it's warm enough, sit outdoors by the fireplace.

TERRA (www.terrarestaurant.com, 707-963-8931, 1345 Railroad Ave., St. Helena, CA 94574; Price: Very Expensive; Cuisine: California Asian) At Terra, East meets West, and the restaurant's Asian influence leaves an indelible mark on California cuisine. Terra's chef, Hiroyoshi Sone, is a superb talent and adds a little daring to each dish. The setting is the historic Hatchery Building, and the decor is crisp and elegant: high ceilings; tall, arched windows; and fieldstone walls. The duo behind Terra has an impressive resume: Sone led the kitchen at Wolfgang Puck's Spago in Los Angeles, and his wife, Lissa Doumani, was a pastry chef. While the black cod marinated in sake is a menu staple and the best entrée in the house, any variation on squab or pork chop is worth a try. For dessert, the tiramisu is a knockout. The wine list is superb, and the by-the-glass selection has improved recently. The service at Terra is always attentive, gracious, and knowledgeable. Terra is a rare find, indeed.

TRA VIGNE (www.travignerestaurant .com, 707-963-4444, 1050 Charter Oak Ave., St. Helena, CA 94574; Price: Expensive; Cuisine: Italian, California) One of Napa Valley's most popular restaurants, Tra Vigne is a sensory delight, from the fragrance of roasted garlic wafting through the courtyard and the neo-Gothic atmosphere of the tall, stone building to the pool of herb-infused olive oil at your table. The food is generally cooked with a fiery passion. Most dishes linger on the palate (though a few muster only a mediocre rating). The odds are truly in your favor. Worthy dishes include the classic antipasto plate, Budino (a cheese custard with asparagus), and the restaurant's signature short ribs with three-cheese polenta. Everything is made at the restaurant, including prosciutto, breads, pastas, cheeses, and gelato. Tra Vigne, which means "among the vines," charms its guests with rows of grapevines just outside the courtyard. Inside, the decor is part Italian villa, part Hollywood, with gold stripes on the molding softened by earth tones. The restaurant swarms with beeper-clad waiters, and the service is impeccable. The wine list offers more than 400 wines from Napa and Italy and more than 25 by the glass.

WINE SPECTATOR GREYSTONE RESTAURANT (www.ciachef.edu /greystone/spectator/ index.html, 707-967-1010, 2555 Main St., St. Helena, CA 94574; Price: Expensive; Cuisine: Mediterranean) This restaurant is downright dramatic. It's in the north wing of the recently restored Greystone Cellars, a historic Wine Country castle once known as Christian Brothers and now home to the West Coast campus of the CIA. With stone walls and a towering ceiling, the room is cavernous and a bit noisy. The decor is accented with bright colors, and three open kitchen stations lend energy. The recent addition of a grand fireplace with a casual seating area has warmed the interior significantly. A

Catching a bite at Tra Vigne. Tim Fish

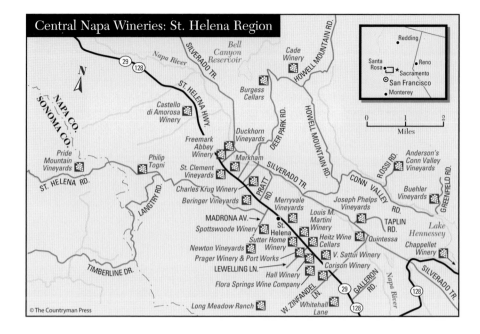

Central Napa Wineries: St. Helena Region

© The Countryman Press

particularly striking appetizer is the Temptation for Two, small bits put together by the chef, and it changes daily. The selection might include polenta, mixed tempura, or stuffed mushrooms. The wine list is solid, with an increasingly wide selection and an adequate offering by the glass. Service is professional but it could be more nimble.

WINERIES

St. Helena is a great destination for wine tasting because there's quite a range to explore, from big to boutique, from old to new. For example, we've listed Charles Krug Winery, a historic winery, along with Hall Winery, which has only been in the area since 2007.

ANDERSON'S CONN VALLEY VINEYARDS (www.connvalleyvine yards.com, 800-946-3497, 680 Rossi Rd., St. Helena, CA 94574; Tasting: By appointment) A small winery in the

foothills east of the valley, it's well off the beaten path, but its cabernet sauvignon is already one of Napa's rising stars. The 1987 vintage was the first for the Anderson family, and their cabernet is intense yet elegant. The Andersons are down-to-earth folks who welcome serious cab fans, although this isn't an extravagant venture, and refreshingly so.

Especially for Foodies in Napa Valley

French Laundry (p. 69) Note: At press time there was a two-month waiting list for reservations (if you can get them to answer the phone!)

Culinary Institute of America at Greystone (p. 110)

Woodhouse Chocolate (p. 107)

Terra (p. 99)

BERINGER VINEYARDS (www
.beringer.com, 707-963-8989, ext. 2222,
2000 Main St., St. Helena, CA 94574;
Tasting: Daily 10–5) There's something
almost regal about the Rhine House,
the circa 1874 mansion that forms the
centerpiece of Beringer Vineyards. Sitting amid manicured lawns and meticulously restored, the Rhine House
suggests that Beringer doesn't take
lightly its past or its reputation. This is
one of the few wineries that has it all. A
prime tourist attraction with a historical
tour, it's also one of Napa's most popular makers of cabernet sauvignon and
chardonnay. For a quick taste of wine,
visit the Old Winery for Beringer Classics Old Bottling, where you can take in
vino and history. The room is decorated
with artifacts such as a photo of Clark
Gable. To taste Beringer's top wines,
climb the staircase of the Rhine House
to the private reserve tasting room. The
reserve cabernet is stunning. Of course,
there's an additional fee.

BUEHLER VINEYARDS (www
.buehlervineyards.com, 707-963-2155,
820 Greenfield Rd., St. Helena, CA
94574; Tasting: By appointment)
"We're not at the end of the world,"
John Buehler Jr. likes to say, "but you
can see it from here." The winery, a
complex of handsome Mediterranean
buildings, is not that remote, although
it is secluded above the rocky hills that
overlook Lake Hennessey. The spot-
light here is on cabernet, but zinfandel
is also making noise. Don't miss a pour
of both.

BURGESS CELLARS (www.burgess
cellars.com, 707-963-4766, 800-752-
9463, 1108 Deer Park Rd., St. Helena,
CA 94574; Tasting: By appointment)
Built atop the vestiges of a stone winery that dates to the 1880s, Burgess has
a low profile and likes it that way. High
on the western slopes of Howell

Mountain, the two-story stone-and-
redwood winery is not one that tourists
happen upon. Tom Burgess began it in
1972 and built a reputation for cabernet, merlot, and Syrah.

CADE WINERY (www.cadewinery
.com, 707-965-2746, 360 Howell
Mountain Rd. S., Angwin, CA; Tasting:
By appointment) California lieutenant
governor Gavin Newsom and entrepreneur Gordon Getty are behind this
winery atop Howell Mountain at an
altitude of 1,800 feet. The motto here
is "Think Green. Drink Green." The
winery is eco-friendly, and the vineyards are in the process of earning
their organic certification. The focus
here is on cabernet sauvignon but the
sauvignon blanc will turn your head. So
will the view. On a clear day you can
spy Mount Diablo.

CHAPPELLET WINERY (www
.chappellet.com, 707-963-7136, 800-
4-WINERY ext. 4263, 1581 Sage
Canyon Rd., St. Helena, 94574; Tasting
and Tours: Mon.–Fri. by appointment)
Styled like a pyramid, this winery
would make a striking statement along
Highway 29. Instead, it's hidden among
the rustic hills east of the valley. Built
in the late 1960s by Donn and Molly
Chappellet, the winery was only the
second to open in the county after Prohibition. The vineyards are steeply terraced and produce a firm cabernet
sauvignon as well as something called
Mountain Cuvee and Bordeaux.

CHARLES KRUG WINERY (www
.charleskrug.com, 707-967-2229, 888-
682-KRUG, 2800 Main St., St. Helena,
CA 94574; Tasting: Daily 10:30–5)
After working under Agoston
Haraszthy in Sonoma, Charles Krug
built Napa Valley's first winery in 1861.
This massive stone winery was gutted
by fire the day after it was finished, but
Krug rebuilt. When the Mondavi fami-

ly bought Krug in 1943, another Napa dynasty began. Robert Mondavi began his own winery in 1966 after a falling-out with his brother Peter. In disrepair for many years, the historic winery building has recently regained much of its former glory. The winemaking now takes place in a facility just behind the first site. The winery bottles one of the valley's most exhaustive wine menus, and its cabernet sauvignons have recently regained their former stature.

CORISON WINERY (www.corison .com, 707-963-0826, 987 Hwy. 29, St. Helena, CA 94574; Tasting: By appointment) Winemaker Cathy Corison is a pioneer, among the first women winemakers in the valley. She's been making wine for close to 30 years, and her background includes a decade as winemaker for Chappellet Vineyards. At Corison the specialty is cabernet, and stylistically they're complex yet elegant. The winery resembles a 19th-century barn with gables, and the modest tasting room is in the middle of the cellar, with temperatures ranging from 55 degrees to a high of 70 degrees—quaint and chilly.

DUCKHORN VINEYARDS (www .duckhornvineyards.com, 888-354-8885, 1000 Lodi Ln., St. Helena, CA 94574; Tasting: Daily 10–4) Duckhorn has long reigned as the king of merlot in Napa, and the winery's cabernet sauvignon and sauvignon blanc are first-rate as well. The tasting room, set in the majestic estate house, is a chic den with a fireplace, done with polished wood and granite. Since its first release in 1978, Duckhorn has been a major presence on restaurant wine lists around the country.

FLORA SPRINGS WINE COMPANY (www.florasprings.com, 707-967-8032, 866-967-8032, Tasting Room: 677 St. Helena Hwy., St. Helena, CA 94574;

Tasting: Daily 10:30–5) This tasting room on the heavy tourist path of Highway 29 is a comfortable space, decorated with humorous murals, and there's a garden in the back where you can sip from a glass on a sunny day. The winery itself on Zinfandel Lane is a handsome stone edifice that dates to 1888, and current owners Jerome and Flora Komes arrived in 1977. After some shaky years, the wines are coming into their own, with a lineup that includes several solid chardonnays, an exotic sauvignon blanc named Soliloquy, and an intriguing red blend dubbed Trilogy.

FREEMARK ABBEY WINERY (www.freemarkabbey.com, 707-963-9694, 800-963-9698 ext. 3721, 3022 St. Helena Hwy., St. Helena, CA 94574; Tasting: Daily 10–5) Freemark Abbey was a leader in the 1960s and 1970s, with its Bosche vineyard cabernet sauvignon. But the wine floundered in the '80s and early '90s and only recently regained some of its stature. Winemaking on the site dates to 1886, when Josephine Tychson—likely the first woman to build a winery in California—constructed a wood winery. The present stone winery was built in 1895, and the tasting room is a lovely space with a wood-beamed ceiling.

HALL WINERY (www.hallwines.com, 707-967-2620, 866-667-4255, 401 St. Helena Hwy S., St. Helena, CA 94574; Tasting: Daily 10–5:30) This winery offers a glimpse into the lives of Kathryn Walt Hall, former US ambassador to Austria, and her husband, Craig Hall, a Texas businessman. They've made headlines in Wine Country with their $100 million Hall Winery project, largely because of their fiercely unconventional architect, Frank Gehry. Some have argued that Gehry—known for dramatic, ultramodern buildings in metal and glass such as Guggenheim Bilbao in Bilbao, Spain, and the Walt Disney Concert Hall in Los Angeles—isn't a good fit for rural Napa Valley and will congest the area with curious tourists. As for the wines, Hall has had good success with cabernet sauvignon, merlot, and sauvignon blanc.

HEITZ WINE CELLARS (www.heitz cellar.com, 707-963-3542, 436 St. Helena Hwy. S., St. Helena, CA 94574; Tasting: Daily 11–4:30) Driving along Highway 29, you might spot a line outside the tasting room, the wine faithful clamoring for a bottle of Heitz's Martha's Vineyard, the internationally acclaimed cabernet sauvignon. Curmudgeon and maverick Joe Heitz worked at Beaulieu before going his own way in 1961. Within a few years, he'd refurbished a stone winery in the hills of the valley's east side, keeping the old winery on Highway 29 as a tasting room. Joe died in 2000, but the winery is thriving with the second generation. The tasting room, in native stone and mahogany, showcases a library of old wines for sale, and typically two or three current wines are poured—though seldom the good stuff. Heitz also produces a chardonnay, and grignolino, a stout Italian varietal, has considerable charm.

JOSEPH PHELPS VINEYARDS (www.jpvwines.com, 707-963-2745, 200 Taplin Rd., St. Helena, CA 94574; Tasting: By appointment) This winery pioneered Bordeaux blends in California with its Insignia bottling, and it remains among the best of the breed. Bordeaux blends use the traditional grapes of that region: cabernet sauvignon, merlot, petit verdot, and the like. Phelps built his large and elegant redwood barn in 1973 and drew immediate attention. The current offerings include a toasty chardonnay and some

of the best cabernets in Napa Valley. We're also fans of the winery's Syrah and viognier, two lesser-known Rhone-style wines that merit a taste.

LONG MEADOW RANCH WINERY AND FARMSTEAD (www.longmeadowranch.com, 707-963-4555, 877-NAPA-OIL, 738 Main St. (entrance on Charter Oak Ave.) St. Helena, CA 94574; Tasting: Daily 11–6) Long Meadow Ranch is not just a winery, it's an agricultural experience. Nestled on 650 acres atop the Mayacamas Mountains, the ranch has a history that dates to the 1870s. Today, it's owned by the Hall family, and they're devoted to organic farming and produce a little of everything: eggs, olive oil, grass-fed beef, organic produce, and—of course—wine. Cabernet is the main selection, and it's a burly red that usually requires a few years in the cellar. The Halls offer a number of different tours, tastings, and excursions, some of them in Hummer-like all-terrain vehicles.

LOUIS M. MARTINI WINERY (www.louismartini.com, 707-968-3361, 800-321-WINE, 254 St. Helena Hwy., St. Helena, CA 94574; Tasting: Daily 10–6) Run by the third generation of Martinis, but owned since 2002 by the wine behemoth E&J Gallo, this large but unostentatious winery is one of Napa Valley's best known. That's one of the charms of visiting Wine Country: you know the label; why not visit the source? Martini is one of the valley's great overachievers, producing a voluminous roster that runs from cabernet sauvignon to port and other dessert wines. They're all capable and good values. Its top cabernet, Monte Rosso and Lot 1, has recently regained much of its glory. Originating in Kingsburg, California, in 1922, Martini moved to St. Helena in 1933. Napa's first post-

Prohibition success story, the winery flourished under founder Louis M. Martini, one the valley's great characters. Son Louis P. Martini brought the winery into the modern era.

MARKHAM WINERY (www.markhamvineyards.com, 707-963-5292, 2812 St. Helena Hwy. N., St. Helena, CA 94574; Tasting: Daily 11–5) Founded in 1978, Markham quietly went about its business until the Japanese firm Sanraku took over in 1988. Since then, the wines have been on a roller coaster ride of quality. Once known for its elegant merlot, the winery has had more recent success with whites such as chardonnay and sauvignon blanc. Following a multimillion-dollar facelift in the early 1990s, the winery became a popular tourist attraction. Beyond large fountains out front is an expansive and affluent tasting room.

MERRYVALE VINEYARDS (www.merryvale.com, 707-963-7777, 1000 Main St., St. Helena, CA 94574; Tasting: Daily 10–6:30) As Sunny St. Helena Winery, this historic stone cellar was the first winery built here after Prohibition, and in 1937 it was the Mondavi family's first venture in Napa Valley. It became home to Merryvale in 1985, when the building was renovated, updating its wine technology while retaining much of its historic charm. Done in rich wood, the tasting room feels like a large cabin, and behind the iron gates, you'll see the cask room with its massive 100-year-old cask. Profile, a cabernet blend that's the winery's flagship, is a wine to watch.

NEWTON VINEYARD (www.newtonvineyard.com, 707-963-9000, 2555 Madrona Ave., St. Helena, CA 94574; Tasting: By appointment) Perched high on Spring Mountain, this is one of the most spectacular wineries to visit in the valley, offering an eclectic mix of elaborate English gardens, Chinese red lanterns, and gates and vineyards carved into steeply terraced hillsides. Beneath all of this is an extensive cave system that extends several stories beneath the surface of the earth. As part of the tour, tastings are offered in a barrel-aging corridor deep inside one cave. The merlot and chardonnays are worth a taste.

PHILIP TOGNI VINEYARD (www.philiptognivineyard.com, 707-963-3731, 3780 Spring Mountain Rd., St. Helena, CA 94574; Tasting: By appointment) Creating a name for himself as winemaker for Mayacamas, Chappellet, Chalone, and Cuvaison, Togni began making his own wine in 1983. His cabernet sauvignon is an assertive beauty that has a legion of fans. Togni is a meticulous and hands-on winemaker, and the winery is a modest affair.

PRAGER WINERY AND PORT WORKS (www.pragerport.com, 707-963-7678, 800-969-7678, 1281 Lewelling Ln., St. Helena, CA 94574; Tasting: Daily 10:30–4:30) Bored with plain chocolate (cabernet sauvignon) and vanilla (chardonnay)? Try this small family winery that produces six styles of port, including two whites. (Port is a slightly sweet wine fortified with brandy.) Prager also makes small amounts of a petite sirah and a late-harvest Riesling. The winery is small, and the atmosphere is low key.

PRIDE MOUNTAIN VINEYARDS (www.pridewines.com, 707-963-4949, 4026 Spring Mountain Rd., St. Helena, CA 94574; Tasting: By appointment) Some 2,100 feet high on the crest of the Mayacamas Mountains, this estate straddles Napa and Sonoma counties. In fact, the county line is laid out on

Ribbed vineyards near St. Helena's Spottswoode Winery.

the crush pad so visitors can stand with one foot in each county. The current winery may just be a modest wood-beam affair, but the wines produced inside are exceptional. Bob Foley is a true talent when it comes to cabernet sauvignon, merlot, and chardonnay.

SPOTTSWOODE WINERY (www .spottswoode.com, 707-963-0134, 1902 Madrona Ave., St. Helena, CA 94574; Tasting: By appointment) The first Spottswoode wines were made in 1982 in the basement of this estate's 1882 Victorian. Intense and impeccably bal-anced, Spottswoode's cabernet sauvi-gnon was quickly regarded as among the best in the 1980s, a stature it retains. The cabernet's success is nearly matched by the sauvignon blanc, a

wine that's typically intense in citrus and mineral character. Run by the Novak family, Spottswoode is a small enterprise.

ST. CLEMENT VINEYARDS (www .stclement.com, 800-331-8266, 707-265-5000, 2867 St. Helena Hwy. N., St. Helena, CA 94574; Tasting: Daily 10–5) Built in 1878, St. Clement's exquisite Gothic Victorian was one of the earliest bonded wineries in the val-ley. Wine is no longer produced in the stone cellar; in 1979 a modern winery made of fieldstone was built in the hill behind the mansion, which now serves as a stately visitors' center. The wide wooden porch offers a soothing view of the valley below, and wines are poured in a small parlor. The winery has an excellent record with chardonnay and cabernet sauvignon.

SUTTER HOME WINERY (www .sutterhome.com, 707-963-3104, ext. 4208, 800-967-4663, 277 St. Helena Hwy., St. Helena, CA 94574; Tasting: Daily 10–5) Who'd have thought back in the 1970s that a simple, sweet rosé would become the Holy Grail—some would say Unholy Grail—of California wine? Since white zinfandel became one of Wine Country's hottest commodities, Sutter Home has grown from one of Napa Valley's smallest wineries to one of its biggest. In 1972 winemaker Bob Trinchero began tinkering with a rosé-style zinfandel. Sutter Home called it white zinfandel, and it became one of the best-selling varieties in America. There's no tour here—the wine is made elsewhere—but Sutter Home's tasting room is an expansive space that doubles as a folksy museum of wine and Americana. Visitors should try the red zinfandel as well as the white; it's sturdy and tasty.

V. SATTUI WINERY (www.vsattui .com, 707-963-7774, 800-799-2337, 1111 White Ln., St. Helena, CA 94574; Tasting: Daily 9–6) Just about every winery has a picnic table tucked somewhere, but V. Sattui is Lawn Lunch Central. The tasting room doubles as a deli shop. The front lawn is shaded by tall oaks and filled with frolicking kids. Picnickers won't find a heartier welcome in Napa Valley. While some wineries prefer simply to make wine and not deal with the public, V. Sattui is just the opposite. Its wines are available only at the winery. It's a busy place, yet the atmosphere is cordial, not frantic. The winery produces solid chardonnays and zinfandels, but for good picnic wines, try the light and fruity Johannisberg Riesling and Gamay Rouge.

WHITEHALL LANE WINERY (www.whitehalllane.com, 707-963-9454, 800-963-9454 ext. 19, 1563 St. Helena Hwy., St. Helena, CA 94574; Tasting: Daily 11–5:45) This handsomely modern winery is seemingly designed with geometric building blocks, and it's worth a visit, thanks to the Leonardini Family of San Francisco, who took control of the winery in 1993. The family updated the winemaking, instituted a new barrel-aging program, and was very particular when sourcing vineyards. The winery produces first-rate cabernet sauvignon and merlot.

Palate Adventures

From a retro fast-food joint to a highbrow chocolatier.

• *Go for 1950s-style fast food*
Gott's Roadside Tray Gourmet (www.gottsroadside.com, 707-963-3486, 933 Main St., St. Helena, CA) This is a classic old drive-in restaurant—though you have to walk to the window these days—but average joes and gourmands alike flock to Gott's for its updated, 1950s-style fast-food menu. Burgers, fries, milkshakes, and onion rings are top-notch. There's also beer on tap and wine by the glass or the bottle. Seating is strictly picnic table, but that's half the fun.

• *Be a chocoholic*
Woodhouse Chocolate (www.woodhousechocolate.com, 707-963-8413, 800-966-3468, 1367 Main St., St. Helena, CA) is a bright and airy house of chocolates that

resembles a highbrow jewelry store, but the prized gems here are, thankfully, edible. It specializes in European-style fresh crème chocolate with no preservatives. Don't miss this classy shop.

• *Treat yourself*
Model Bakery (707-963-8192, 1357 Main St., St. Helena, CA) Everything here is baked in a big brick oven. Sweet or sour baguettes are stacked like kindling in tall wicker baskets, and scones, muffins, and croissants compete for shelf space. Behind the counter are burly loaves of rye, powdered white on top. There's a full coffee bar, and seating for 30, with lunch items—sandwiches, pizzas, and salads—offered.

Insider Secret:
A burger joint like Gott's Road-side can only survive in a fancy-pants food haven like Napa Valley by acting like a fancy-pants restaurant. It's particular when it sources ingredients—egg buns from Sciambra Bakery in Napa, fresh halibut for the fish tacos, and sushi-grade tuna for ahi burgers.

• *Shop like a wine geek*
The specialty wine shops in Napa and Sonoma counties are, as you might imagine, among the finest in the nation, offering a huge variety as well as hard-to-find treas-

Woodhouse Chocolate showcases its candies like prized jewels.

ures. You'll be surprised to learn that wine is seldom less expensive at the wineries than it is at local retail shops, unless you catch a sale or buy by the case. You also run the risk, of course, of not being able to find a wine you love at the winery. It's your gamble.

Dean & DeLuca (707-967-9980, 607 S. St. Helena Hwy., St. Helena, CA 94574) This gourmet food store has a large and superb selection of all California wines. Prices are the going rate.

St. Helena Wine Center (707-963-1313, 1321 Main St., St. Helena, CA 94574) One of Napa's oldest, dating to 1953, this shop believes in the notion of "only the best," offering few bargains. It has a small but extremely select library of current Napa and Sonoma wines. There's also a tasting bar.

St. Helena Wine Merchants (707-963-7888, 699 St. Helena Hwy., St. Helena, CA 94574) There's a giant selection of new and older vintages but no bargains here. There's also a notable assortment of large bottles and a tasting bar.

• *Visit a wine collective and sample top-name brands*
Dozen Vintners (707-967-0666, 3000 N. Hwy. 29, St. Helena, CA 94574; www .adozenvint ners.com) Inside this cream-colored building is an art-deco-style tasting room with some top names in Napa Valley wine. The notables include Howell Mountain Vineyards and Fife.

• *Unleash your inner foodie*
St. Helena has its share of gourmet shops and markets.

Giugni's Sandwiches (707-963-3421, 1227 Main St., St. Helena, CA 94574) A fun Italian deli offering classic deli meats, including corned beef and pastrami, as well as a great chicken salad sandwich.

Napa Valley Olive Oil Manufacturing Co. (707-963-4173, 835 Charter Oak Ave., St. Helena, CA 94574) This faded white barn is a glorious time warp. The shop dates to the 1920s, when Napa Valley was largely populated by Italian farmers. You're as likely to hear Italian inside as English, and the deli counter looks like your grandmother's kitchen—if your grandmother is from Naples. There are picnic tables outside.

• *Do lunch*
You've got a number of options for daytime refueling.

Gillwood's Café (707-963-1788, 1313 Main St., St. Helena, CA 94574) This is a great stop for breakfast and lunch. There are delicious burgers, sandwiches, and salads, and if you're a breakfast person, Gillwood's serves it all day long.

Villa Corona (707-963-7812, 1138 Main St., St. Helena, CA 94574) Home-made flour tortillas and specialty sauces make for tasty burritos, particularly the super burrito. Some good breakfast dishes include the huevos con rancheros.

Pizzeria Tra Vigne (707-967-9999, 1016 Main St., St. Helena, CA 94574) Fine casual fare, and it's family-friendly (see full listing under Restaurants).

• *Make the brewpub scene*

Silverado Brewing Co. (www.silveradobrewingcompany.com, 707-967-9876, 3020 St. Helena Hwy., Suite A, St. Helena, CA 94574) We like the atmosphere of this spot. The hand-hewn stone building, built in 1895, was once a winery, but now it's a popular hangout for tourists and locals looking to wet their whistles.

• *Go to foodie school*

The Culinary Institute of America at Greystone (www.ciachef.edu/california, 800-888-7850 2555 Main St., St. Helena CA 94574) offers a variety of continuing-education programs for the food and wine enthusiast, in one of Napa Valley's most magnificent properties. Your classroom's in a castle!

• *Attend a wine event*

We're still waiting to see this sign along the road: "Garage Sale & Wine Tasting." Wine events are ubiquitous here. There's considerable appeal in sampling and comparing all sorts of wine at one location or in one sitting. Most of the events listed here are staged outside.

Napa Valley Wine Auction (707-963-3388, Meadowood Resort, St. Helena, CA 94574) *The* chic wine outing, this three-day June event is busy with extravagant parties, dances, and dinners. Auction tickets cost a fortune but are in high demand. All the big names of the Napa wine industry attend, and the auction raises millions for local charities.

Hometown Harvest Festival (707-963-5706, downtown St. Helena, CA 94574) A rich Napa tradition, celebrating the end of the growing season and the summer's bountiful harvest. One weekend in late October, there's scads of food, wine tasting, arts and crafts, music featuring local bands, a kids' carnival, and even a pet parade.

Napa Valley Mustard Festival (www.mustardfestival.org, 707-938-1133, various locations) Mustard, the beautiful yellow wildflower that blooms throughout Wine Country every winter, is the focus of this late-winter series of food and wine events.

To Do

Check out these great attractions and activities . . .

SHOPPING

You'll want to schedule a good 12-hour day of shopping in this quaint yet cosmopolitan Main Street USA. St. Helena has some of the best shopping in all of Wine Country. Our favorites: St. Helena St. Helena Antiques (707-963-5878, 1231 Main St., St. Helena, CA 94574)—yes, "St. Helena" *is* stated twice in the store name, a bit unusual, but then so is the shop. It has a large collection of corkscrews and 18th- and 19th-century antiques. Jan de Luz (707-963-1550, 1219 Main St., St. Helena, CA 94574) is a Frenchman, and his namesake store features his custom-designed linens, chandeliers, fountains, etc. Amelia Claire (707-963-8502, 1230 Main St., St. Helena, CA 94574), which carries upscale shoes from Aquatalia—100 percent waterproof shoes. Vanderbilt & Co. (707-963-1010, 1429 Main St., St. Helena, CA 94574) is brimming with accessories you might find while flipping through a glossy home

St. Helena has some of the best shopping in Wine Country. Tim Fish

and garden catalog. Pennaluna (707-963-3115, 1220 Adams St., St. Helena, CA 94574) is an eclectic home-accessories store that's a "must see" shop offering off-beat treasures such as an Eiffel Tower ornament and a colorful hammock. Calla Lily (707-963-8188, 1222 Main St., St. Helena, CA 94574) is the consummate bed-and-bath shop, offering furniture, jewelry and linens, lotions, etc. Fideaux (707-967-9935, 1312 Main St., St. Helena, CA 94574) is where PetSmart meets Fifth Avenue. Among the avant items you'll find here are a wine-barrel doghouse.

CULTURAL OUTINGS

Go ahead, get cultured. St. Helena also offers food for thought.

• *See a movie*
Cameo Cinema (www.cameocinema .com, 707-963-9779, 1340 Main St., St. Helena, CA 94574) This charming the-ater in downtown St. Helena was com-pletely refurbished in 1997. It shows first-run films—but as you might expect for a small town, a few weeks after release. The fare is mostly Ameri-can, though occasional art and foreign films come for a stay.

> *Insider Secret:*
> In Wine Country even dogs are connoisseurs with highbrow tastings. At **Fideaux** in St. Helena and Healdsburg, there's a lineup of biscuits in buckets so that dogs can pick out their favorite treat. The biscuits run the gamut—sweet potato, honey-glazed chicken with apple, and turkey with apple and cheese. (www.fideaux.net)

• *Visit a gallery*

I. Wolk Gallery (www.iwolkgallery.com, 707-963-8800, 1354 Main St., St. Helena, CA 94574; Open: Daily 10–5:30) This is an excellent gallery with serious intentions about art, specializing in contemporary paintings, photography, and crafts by emerging American artists. *Contemporary* does not necessarily read *abstract*; here the emphasis is on realist imagery. Exhibitions feature single artists, but a wide range of artists is continuously shown.

• *Hit the books*

One of Wine Country's two distinguished libraries is the Napa Valley Wine Library inside St. Helena Public Library (707-963-5244, 1492 Library Ln., St. Helena, CA 94574). It has a vast collection, including more than six thousand books, tapes, and so forth, detailing everything from the art of winemaking to the history of Napa wine to the current community of wineries throughout the valley.

• *Commune with a literary great*

Silverado Museum (www.silveradomuseum.org, 707-963-3757, 1490 Library Ln., P.O. Box 490, St. Helena, CA) Writer Robert Louis Stevenson was taken with Napa Valley. In 1880, the author of *Dr. Jekyll and Mr. Hyde* and *Treasure Island* honeymooned with his wife in a cabin near the old Silverado Mine. He wrote about the area in *The Silverado Squatters.* He called Napa's wine "bottled poetry," and Mount St. Helena was the inspiration for Spyglass Hill in *Treasure Island.* Although Stevenson spent only a few months in Napa Valley, he has been accepted as an adopted son. Part of the St. Helena Library Center, the museum has the feeling of a small chapel. Founded in 1969, on the 75th anniversary of Stevenson's death, Silverado is more a library than a museum. It contains more than eight thousand artifacts, including dozens of paintings and photographs, as well as original Stevenson letters and manuscripts. There are also hundreds of books and first printings.

RECREATIONAL FUN

Here are some good options for countering your caloric intake with a venture into scenic Wine Country.

• *Take a bike ride*

Want to slow the pace of your Wine Country tour? Try a bike. With terrain that varies from meandering valleys to steep mountains and a spectacular coastline, there are roads and trails to satisfy everyone, from the most leisurely sightseer to ambitious cycling fanatics. St. Helena Cyclery (www.sthelenacyclery.com, 707-963-7736, 1156 Main St., St. Helena, CA 94574) advertises its rental bike fleet as the best in Napa Valley.

• *Shoot for a hole in one*

Meadowood Resort (www.meadowood.com, 707-963-3646, 800-458-8080, 900 Meadowood Ln., St. Helena, CA 94574) This executive golf course is private to members and guests. It offers 9 holes, par 31, on a tree-lined, narrow course.

• *Get pampered*

Health Spa at Meadowood (www.meadowood.com, 707-963-3646, 800-458-8080, 900 Meadowood Ln., St. Helena, CA 94574) Want to be pampered? The Health Spa at Meadowood Resort is the place. One of Napa Valley's best spas, it comes at a price, yet a basic massage is priced competitively. Meadowood specializes in face and body treatments as well as wellness programs. The setting alone soothes the soul. The spa is set in the lush foothills of Howell Mountain, and the outside pool and Jacuzzi are surrounded by towering trees. Treatments include something called a citrus salt glow as well as facials, waxing, and various therapeutic combinations of all individual treatments. Massage rooms are dimly lit, and light music is piped in. Treatments are available to resort guests and members only. Sixty-minute massage with use of steam room, sauna, and pools: $135.

• *Play tennis*

Meadowood Resort (707-963-3646, 900 Meadowood Ln., St. Helena, CA 94574) The courts are open to members and guests, and a pro is on-site for private lessons. Court fees are $16 for singles and $24 for doubles.

St. Helena Public Courts (707-963-5706) are available at Robert Louis Stevenson School (1316 Hill View Pl., St. Helena, CA) and St. Helena High School (1401 Grayson Ave., St. Helena, CA). City-operated courts can be found at Crane Park (off Crane Avenue, St. Helena, CA). There's an active women's city league program for A and B players.

5

Calistoga

WHEN YOU COME TO CALISTOGA,
the goal is to relax at a spa and render
yourself a noodle al dente. "To spa" is,
of course, a verb, and in Wine Country
it's practically considered a form of
exercise.

The downtown strip is lined with
trees and there are local shops to
explore, volcanic mud baths to experience, and outdoor bistros that allow
you to take it all in. Calistoga has small-
town charm combined with the sophistication of a world-class wine region.
It's surrounded by vineyards and highbrow wineries, including the famous
Chateau Montelena, which is featured in the 2008 film *Bottle Shock*.

Another winery that history buffs won't want to miss is the architecturally
adventurous Castello di Amorosa. The postmodern Italianate castle took 14 years
to build, not to mention lots of *dinero*—$30 million to be exact.

Wineries aside, this resort town has always been popular for its natural hot
springs, drawing residents and visitors to the Napa Valley for over a hundred years.

> **Insider Secret:**
> Most people are surprised when
> they find out there's a Latin Mass
> held in the chapel at **Castello di
> Amorosa** every Sunday. It's for
> early-bird churchgoers, with
> mass at 8:30 AM. Women are
> asked to wear veils, and men, a
> tie. (www.castellodiamorosa.com)

Checking In

Best places to stay in and around
Calistoga.

There's plenty of lodging options in
Calistoga, from high end to low end
and everything in between.

LEFT: The streets of Calistoga. Tim Fish

BRANNAN COTTAGES INN
(www.brannancottageinn.com, 707-
942-4200, 109 Wapoo Ave., Calistoga,
CA 94515; Price: Moderate to Expensive) Built around 1860 by Calistoga
founder Sam Brannan, this inn is listed
on the National Register of Historic
Places and is the only guest house constructed for Brannan's Hot Springs

Travel Like an Insider: Our Top 10 Picks for Calistoga

1. Chateau Montelena (www.montelena.com) The whole world was watching when a 1973 Chateau Montelena chardonnay won the legendary Paris Tasting in 1976, beating out the best of Burgundy. Chateau Montelena's star has been shining brightly ever since.

2. Indian Springs Spa and Resort (www.indianspringscalistoga.com) Eighteen whitewashed bungalow-style cottages—one is a three-bedroom that sleeps six—overlook 16 acres of palm trees and views of Mount St. Helena. There's a gorgeous Olympic-sized mineral pool, and it's an easy walk to downtown shopping and dining.

The famed Chateau Montelena.

3. Clos Pegase (www.clospegase.com) Come to this winery for the architecture and the art, stay for the wine. The name derives from Pegasus, the mythical winged horse. And yes, you will be carried away.

4. The Wine Garage (www.winegarage.net) This value-oriented wine shop has more than two hundred wines under $25 and a current inventory of more than three hundred bottles. In keeping with the garage theme, shoppers can actually "pump" wine from stainless steel, gas-station-like nozzles.

5. Brannan's Grill (www.brannansgrill.com) Because this restaurant seats two hundred, you might expect the menu to be formulaic and the service to be anything but meticulous. Happily, you'd be wrong on both counts. The food is lively and the atmosphere is club-like cozy.

6. JoLe (www.jolerestaurant.com) This "farm to table" restaurant features small-plate cuisine, with dishes prepared in a tiled brick oven. The space includes a six-seat chef's counter and a wooden bar where microbrews and old-world wines are poured. A budget-conscious yet swanky choice for dinner.

7. Solbar at Solage Calistoga (http://solbarnv.com) This restaurant is driven by the seasons of Northern California, with an eye to fresh local produce. The menu combines light, healthful dishes with heartier fare (read: comfort food).

8. Chateau de Vie (www.cdvnapavalley.com) Surrounded by vineyards and with excellent views of Mount St. Helena, this B&B has an understated elegance appreciated by the discerning. Great gourmet breakfasts, and a perk for wine lovers: the inn produces its own Chateau de Vie label for guests.

9. Castello di Amorosa Winery (www. castellodiamorosa.com) This 121,000-square-foot, medieval-style fortress is complete with towers, turrets, a moat, a dungeon, and even a torture chamber. The tour is exhaustive but fascinating, rich with colorful frescos and a barrel cellar room underground with a dramatically arched ceiling.

10. Sterling Vineyards (www.sterlingvineyards.com) Sterling is an adventure. You board a tram and scale a tall knoll to reach a modern white villa. Sure, there's a touch of Disneyland to the experience, but the tram grants you access to an unsurpassed view at the top, not to mention a tasty glass of wine.

Resort, which still stands on its original site. Not surprisingly, it's also the oldest building in town. Restoration began in the 1980s: reconstruction of the gingerbread gable was based on enlarged vintage photographs. Today, an eclectic collection of furnishings, including plush and comfortable antiques, finishes the six guest rooms. The house is surrounded by gardens—weather permitting, the generous breakfast may be served in the courtyard under trees.

CALISTOGA RANCH (www.calistoga ranch.com, 707-254-2800, 800-942-4220, 580 Lommel Rd., Calistoga, CA 94515; Price: Very Expensive) Set on a 157-acre spread in the forested hills outside Calistoga, this luxury resort opened in the summer of 2004. It includes 47 individual guest lodges ranging in size from 600 to 2,400 square feet. The living areas open up onto mahogany decks that have retractable roofs, which lend an indoor-outdoor atmosphere. Activities center on the pool and health-spa bathhouse, but there are also 4 miles of hiking trails.

CARLIN COTTAGES (www.carlin cottages.com, 707-942-9102, 800-734-4624, 1623 Lake St., Calistoga, CA 94515; Price: Moderate to Expensive) Remember the old auto court motels of the 1950s? Well, Carlin Cottages is a souped-up version of those vanishing classics. There are 15 cottages—ranging from studios to two-room suites—and each is minimally but agreeably appointed with country Shaker-style furniture. There's a pool in the center of the courtyard, and mature trees shade the entire property. Located on a quiet residential street, Carlin Cottages is a good spot for families. A good value.

CHATEAU DE VIE (www.cdvnapa valley.com, 707-942-6446, 877-558-2513, 3250 Hwy. 128, Calistoga, CA 94515; Price: Expensive to Very

The colorful interior of the Castello di Amorosa.

Expensive) Surrounded by 2 acres of vineyards, this bed and breakfast has an understated elegance appreciated by the discerning. The inn has excellent views of Mount St. Helena and great gourmet breakfasts: fresh-baked scones, breads, and muffins; country sausage; and vegetable quiches. All three rooms have queen-sized beds and private baths. An eight-person whirlpool spa sits outside by the garden. A perk for wine-lovers: The inn produces its own Chateau de Vie label for guests.

CHELSEA GARDEN INN (www .chelseagardeninn.com, 707-942-0948, 800-942-1515, 1443 2nd St., Calistoga, CA 94515; Price: Expensive) Formerly known as Scott Courtyard, this stylish inn has a lushly landscaped courtyard that lends a wonderfully secluded feel. All five accommodations are one-bedroom suites, each with a private entrance and air-conditioning—a real comfort on those Calistoga summer days. Breakfast is served in the common room warmed by a stone fireplace or in the courtyard by the pool. This inn is near downtown but quiet, and the hospitality is first-rate.

CHRISTOPHER'S INN (www .christophersinn.com, 707-942-5755, 1010 Foothill Blvd., Calistoga, CA 94515; Price: Expensive to Very Expensive) This stylish inn has 22 rooms, all with private baths, and its rich antiques and Laura Ashley wallpaper and curtains evoke an English country inn. An architect by trade, Christopher Layton renovated three old summer cottages. A wing was added in 1997, and many of the new rooms feature fireplaces and whirlpool tubs. A modest continental breakfast is delivered to your room or served in the garden. Location is both an advantage and a bit of a disadvantage. Guests can

walk to town, but Highway 29 can be noisy during the day. It's practically a moot point, however, because all the rooms are soundproofed.

CHANRIC INN (www.thechanric .com, 707-942-4535, 877-281-3671, 1805 Foothill Blvd., Calistoga, CA 94515; Price: Expensive.) Set on a shady hillside, the Chanric Inn is an easy walk to Calistoga's main-street dining and shopping. All rooms have private baths and guests are pampered with fluffy down comforters, high-thread-count Egyptian cotton sheets, and plush bathrobes. The pool and spa boasts a view of the Palisades Mountains. A full breakfast emphasizes ingredients from local organic farms, and it can be served at an intimate table or at the big table where guests gather. The grounds are lovely, with beautiful roses and a trellised ancient grape vine.

COTTAGE GROVE INN (www .cottagegrove.com, 707-942-8400, 800-799-2284, 1711 Lincoln Ave., Calistoga, CA 94515; Price: Very Expensive) This classy inn is actually a group of 16 California Craftsman-style cottages, built on the site of Brannan's original Calistoga resort. The cottages, nestled in a grove of old elms, are a short walk to Calistoga's many spas. The inn offers wi-fi Internet access and flat-screen televisions. Some cottages are situated close to the street, but Lincoln Avenue is considerably quieter at night.

FOOTHILL HOUSE (www.foothill house.com, 707-942-6933, 800-942-6933, 3037 Foothill Blvd., Calistoga, CA 94515; Price: Expensive to Very Expensive) This cozy inn is a find. Shaded by tall trees and set amid lush gardens, the modest turn-of-the-20th-century farmhouse is a soothing getaway. Foothill House offers three elegant suites and a private cottage.

The cottage, called Quail's Roost, is accented in whitewashed pine and equipped with a kitchenette and a two-person whirlpool that looks out to a waterfall. Guests are pampered with a generous, gourmet breakfast delivered to their room or taken on the terrace. Afternoon wine and cheese in the sunroom is an extravagant spread.

GARNETT CREEK INN (www .garnettcreekinn.com, 707-942-9797, 1139 Lincoln Ave., Calistoga, CA 94515; Price: Expensive to Very Expensive) A 19th-century Victorian with a wraparound porch, this charming inn is located in the heart of Calistoga. There are five rooms in all, each with private bath and gas fireplace. The Lucinda Suite offers a deep soaking tub and sitting room with a bay window overlooking the garden. A continental breakfast is served in your room or on the porch, weather permitting.

HIDEAWAY COTTAGES (www.hide awaycottages.com, 707-942-4108, 1412 Fairway, Calistoga, CA 94515; Price: Moderate to Very Expensive) These 17 units are comfy but utilitarian, and all are set amid tall, mature trees on 2 acres on a quiet residential street close to Lincoln Avenue restaurants and shops. It's a good spot if you're planning an extended stay. Three deluxe cottages are available, and one of the cottages can accommodate groups of four or six. Air-conditioning and televisions are standard, and most units have kitchenettes.

MEADOWLARK (www.meadowlark inn.com, 707-942-5651, 800-942-5651, 601 Petrified Forest Rd., Calistoga, CA 94515; Price: Expensive to Very Expensive) This luxurious inn is just 2 miles outside Calistoga, and it has plenty of land to roam: 20 acres. There's a mineral pool on the property and a clothing-optional policy for the

hot tub and sauna. The bedrooms all have private baths and queen-sized beds, and all have private decks or terraces. Gourmet breakfasts are served, and guests are encouraged to enjoy the vistas from their terraces or decks. Well-behaved dogs are welcome.

MOUNT VIEW HOTEL (www .mountviewhotel.com, 707-942-6877, 800-816-6877, 1457 Lincoln Ave., Calistoga, CA 94515; Price: Expensive to Very Expensive) Restored mission revival and on the National Register of Historic Places, this elegant lodge was originally a European-style hotel built in 1917. There are 29 units and three cottages, including nine luxurious suites, one of which is furnished in art deco period pieces. It's in the heart of Calistoga shopping and dining. The hotel has its own superb spa and others are just a step away. The restaurant JoLe is on the premises (see entry under Restaurants).

PINK MANSION (www.pinkmansion .com, 707-942-0558, 800-238-7465, 1415 Foothill Blvd., Calistoga, CA 94515; Price: Expensive to Very Expensive) Postcard views of Napa Valley and lush forests await visitors who stay at this 1875 Victorian. The home's pink exterior will catch your attention, while the flowers, rare plants, and exotic palms will hold your interest. The inn features two rooms and four suites with fireplaces. There is also a 1,000-square-foot cottage with a loft and fireplace. The inn also has an indoor pool. Wine and cheese cap off the afternoon.

SOLAGE CALISTOGA (www.solage calistoga.com, 707-226-0800, 755 Silverado Trail, Calistoga, CA. 94515; Price: Very Expensive) A 22-acre complex includes 89 accommodations, from one-room studios to deluxe suites, as well as the Spa Solage and Solbar (see entry under Restaurants). The hip

Especially for those on a budget

If you're a budget-conscience traveler in Napa Valley, try these spots to make the most of your money:

Gott's Roadside Tray Gourmet (p. 107)

Golden Haven Hot Springs Spa and Resort (see below)

bistro offers healthful entrées as well as rich comfort food. Breakfasts are not part of the room rate, but include decadent dishes such as double-decker French toast and made-from-scratch blueberry buckwheat pancakes. This is a green resort, which means all the water is recycled and all the cleaning products are environmentally friendly. Solage Calistoga offers great views of the Palisades and the Mayacamas Mountains.

Spa Lodging
Some area establishments offer lodging/spa discount packages. ("Spa" in this context refers to Calistoga's natural hot springs and mineral pools; in some cases massage treatments are also offered.)

Calistoga Spa Hot Springs (www.calistogaspa.com, 707-942-6269, 1006 Washington St., Calistoga, CA 94515; Price: Moderate) Relaxed and unpretentious, this inn has the amenities of a resort but at more affordable prices. All 57 family-oriented units have kitchenettes, air-conditioning, TVs, and telephones. Features include a fitness room and four outdoor mineral pools. Children are welcome.

Calistoga Village Inn and Spa (www.greatspa.com, 707-942-0991, 1880 Lincoln Ave., Calistoga, CA 94515; Price: Moderate to Expensive) This inn has been everything from a motel to what some refer to as a Moonie indoctrination camp (it was once owned and run by the Rev. Sun Myung Moon's Unification Church). Rooms are pleasant but modestly appointed. Some suites have whirlpool tubs. Two outdoor mineral pools offer an expansive view of the mountains. There are an inside mineral whirlpool and sauna.

Dr. Wilkinson's Hot Springs (www.drwilkinson.com, 707-942-4102, 1507 Lincoln Ave., Calistoga, CA 94515; Price: Expensive) This spa has 42 spacious and functional rooms, many with kitchenettes. There are two outdoor mineral pools plus an indoor mineral whirlpool. Shopping and dining are within walking distance. Rooms, grounds, and pools have recently been upgraded and are very appealing.

Eurospa & Inn (www.eurospa.com, 707-942-6829, 1202 Pine St., Calistoga, CA 94515; Price: Moderate to Expensive) Each of the 13 rooms at this inn and spa is decorated in a different theme. Many rooms have private whirlpools and gas-burning stoves. There are an outdoor pool and whirlpool. It's close to downtown yet away from the main-street bustle.

Golden Haven Hot Springs Spa and Resort (www.goldenhaven.com, 707-942-8000, 1713 Lake St., Calistoga, CA 94515; Price: Inexpensive to Expensive) Amid towering oak trees and lush gardens, this inn and spa isn't fancy but offers 28 rooms, several of them two-room suites, five with kitchenettes, and all with refrigerators. Rooms with whirlpools and saunas are also available.

Indian Springs Spa and Resort (www.indianspringscalistoga.com, 707-

942-4913, 1712 Lincoln Ave., Calistoga, CA 94515; Price: Expensive to Very Expensive) Eighteen white-washed bungalow-style cottages—one is a three-bedroom that sleeps six—overlook 16 acres of palm trees and views of Mount St. Helena. There's a

gorgeous Olympic-sized mineral pool. It's an easy walk to downtown shopping and dining.

Lodge of Calistoga (707-942-9400, 1865 Lincoln Ave., Calistoga, CA 94515; Price: Moderate to Expensive) This motel offers 55 rooms; a hot mineral-water swimming pool, a hot mineral-water whirlpool, a sauna, a steam room, and a continental breakfast.

Roman Spa (www.romanspahot springs.com, 707-942-4441, 800-820-4461, 1300 Washington St.; Price: Inexpensive to Expensive) Lushly land-scaped grounds surround this older but well-tended 60-room motel-type resort. Half of the units have kitchenettes. There's an outdoor mineral pool and whirlpool plus a large indoor whirlpool and sauna.

Local Flavors

Taste of the town—local restaurants, cafés, bars, bistros, etc.

RESTAURANTS

Calistoga has some very appealing restaurants that play up California cuisine at its best. The town's longtime favorite on the downtown strip has been Brannan's Grill. But JoLe, at the Mount View Hotel, has become a popular contender. Its small-plate format is particularly appealing to the traveler who wants to get a taste of everything. Solbar at the resort Solage is also a hit. Revel in the possibilities.

ALL SEASONS BISTRO (www.all seasonsnapavalley.net, 707-942-9111, 1400 Lincoln Ave., Calistoga, CA 94515; Price: Expensive; Cuisine: California, Mediterranean) All Seasons has a soothing bistro menu matched with a

modest but urbane setting. Ceiling fans spin slowly over stained-glass lights; the floor is done in black, white, and green tile; and two walls of windows let you watch downtown Calistoga go by. The lunch menu focuses on salads, pizzas, pastas, and sandwiches, while dinner emphasizes upscale comforts of grilled fish, duck, beef, and chicken. The wine selection is fabulous, and service is professional and warm.

Brannan's Grill in downtown Calistoga. Tim Fish

BOSKOS TRATTORIA (www.boskos .com, 707-942-9088, 1364 Lincoln Ave., Calistoga, CA 94515; Price: Moderate; Cuisine: Italian) This Italian eatery serves basic and hearty food, and the price is right. The atmosphere is warm but casual and perfect for families. Lunch and dinner menus are the same, and portions are generous. Pastas range from the basic spaghetti and meatballs to fettuccine Alfredo to pizza from a wood-burning stove. The beer and wine list is adequate.

BRANNAN'S GRILL (www.brannans grill.com, 707-942-2233, 1374 Lincoln Ave., Calistoga, CA 94515; Price: Expensive; Cuisine: California, American) Brannan's Grill is more adventuresome than it seems at first glance. With seating for two hundred, we expected the menu to be less exciting. The food is lively and the atmosphere has a club-like coziness, with large windows that swing wide open when the weather is right. Seafood is something Brannan's does particularly well; consider starting your meal with a selection of local oysters on the half shell. For hearty eaters, there's a good selection of steaks. The

wine list showcases Napa Valley wines, but it's careful to include some less-traditional varietals. Rhone reds and whites, in particular, have a nice showing. The list is a bit pricey, but there's a good by-the-glass selection.

JOLE (www.jolerestaurant.com, 707-942-5938, 1457 Lincoln Ave., Calistoga, CA 94515; Price: Moderate to Expensive; Cuisine: American) JoLe features small-plate midsized cuisine, with dishes prepared in a tiled brick oven. Nearby is a six-seat chef's counter and a wooden bar where micro-brews and old world wines are poured. The wine list has good local flavor and the dishes showcase organic ingredients. This is a budget-conscious and yet swanky restaurant in the Mount View Hotel. On the main strip in downtown Calistoga, the restaurant is quaint and cozy. The lobby offers restaurant-goers a place to lounge before and after dinner.

SOLBAR (http://solbarnv.com, 707-226-0850, 755 Silverado Trail, Calistoga, CA 94515; Price: Expensive; Cuisine: California, America) This restaurant at Solage Calistoga (see entry under Lodging) is driven by the seasons of Northern California, with an eye to fresh local produce. And yet there is always room for comfort food á la buttermilk-fried quail with cheese grits. To get some insight into the range of the food served here, check out the chef's blog on the Solage website. The decor of the restaurant is contemporary and bright with an oversized fireplace to give the sleek design plenty of warmth. There's also outside dinning, which is a treat.

WINERIES

There are quite a few interesting wineries to explore in our Calistoga lineup. One of the most popular—and historic—is Chateau Montelena, which jolted the wine world by winning the legendary Paris Tasting in 1976. In fact, a bottle of the winery's 1973 chardonnay is in the Smithsonian, a testament to how the blind-tasting

upset led to the discovery of California wine, and in particular Napa Valley wine.

CASTELLO DI AMOROSA WINERY (www.castellodiamorosa .com, 707-967-6272, 4045 St. Helena Hwy. N., Calistoga, CA 94515; Tasting: Daily 9:30–6)

The wineries of Napa have often been called "castles," but in the case of Castello di Amorosa, it's true. Daryl Sattui, who owns the tourist-friendly V. Sattui Winery, spent 14 years and $30 million building this extravagant, 121,000-square-foot, medieval-style fortress. With 107 rooms on eight levels, it has towers, turrets, a moat, a dungeon, and even a torture chamber. The tour is exhaustive but fascinating, rich with colorful frescos and a barrel cellar room underground with a dramatically arched ceiling. Appropriately, the winery makes Italian-style wines, from pinot grigio to "Super Tuscan" blends, as well as mainstream wines like chardonnay and merlot and everything in between.

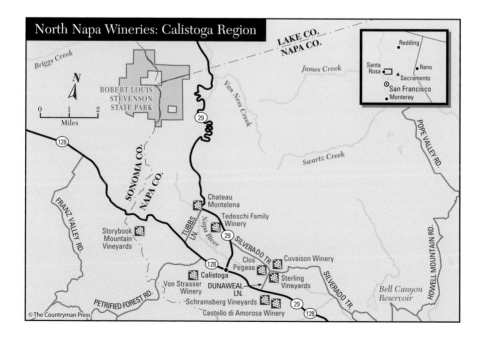

North Napa Wineries: Calistoga Region

The medieval-style Castello Di Amorosa in Calistoga.

CHATEAU MONTELENA (www
.montelena.com, 707-942-5105, 1429
Tubbs Ln., Calistoga, CA 94515; Tasting: Daily 9:30–4) "Not bad for a kid
from the sticks," was all Jim Barrett
said when Chateau Montelena stunned
the wine world by winning the legendary Paris Tasting in 1976. A Who's
Who of French wine cognoscenti
selected Chateau Montelena's 1973
chardonnay in a blind tasting over the
best of Burgundy. Chateau Montelena's
star has been shining brightly ever
since. No serious wine lover would
think of leaving Chateau Montelena
off the tour list. The wines are first-
rate, and the winery is an elegant and
secluded old estate at the foot of
Mount St. Helena. Alfred Tubbs
founded the original Chateau Montelena in 1882, and its French architect
used the great chateaux of Bordeaux
as inspiration. The approach isn't too
impressive, but walk around to the true
facade, and you'll discover a dramatic
stone castle. During Prohibition the
winery fell into neglect, but in 1958,
a Chinese immigrant, Yort Franks, created the Chinese-style Jade Lake and
the surrounding garden. It's shaded by
weeping willows, with swans and geese,
walkways, islands, and brightly painted
pavilions.

CLOS PEGASE (www.clospegase
.com, 707-942-4981, 1060 Dunaweal
Ln., Calistoga, CA 94515; Tasting:
Daily 10:30–5) Clos Pegase is architecturally flamboyant, a postmodern
throwback to the Babylonian temple—
a shrine to the gods of art, wine, and
commerce. This commanding structure
of tall pillars and archways, in hues of
yellow and tan, is the work of noted
Princeton architect Michael Graves.
The name Clos Pegase derives from
Pegasus, the winged horse that, according to the Greeks, gave birth to art and
wine. Owner Jan Shrem is an avid art
collector. The tour offers a glimpse of
the collection, including 17th- and

18th-century French statuary artfully displayed in the winery's massive underground cave. Pegase's wines include a ripe and complex cabernet sauvignon and a chardonnay that's typically refined but with plenty of forward fruit.

CUVAISON WINERY (www.cuvaison .com, 707-942-6266, 707-942-2468, 4550 Silverado Tr. N., Calistoga, CA 94515; Tasting: Daily 10–5) *Cuvaison* is a French term that describes the period in which the juice of grapes soaks with the skins and seeds to develop color and flavor. It's an appropriate name because Cuvaison's wines are often boldly flavored. Be sure to try the pinot noir. A white mission-style building with a red-tiled roof, Cuvaison is bordered by vineyards and a splendid landscaped picnic area. The tasting room is busy but retains a friendly tone.

Insider Secret:
If you like tasting exotic wines not available on the market, join Pegase Circle, the wine club of Clos Pegase. As a member you'll receive regular shipments of special reserve wines.

FRANK FAMILY VINEYARDS (www.frankfamilyvineyards.com, 707-942-0859, 1091 Larkmead Ln., Calistoga, CA; Tasting: Daily 10–5) Rich Frank, a longtime Disney executive, couldn't find the time to take long vacations, so he settled for short trips to Napa Valley and soon fell in love with Wine Country. Housed in the historic Larkmead Winery, the tasting room focuses on cabernet and zinfandel, but it also produced some tasty chardonnay and sangiovese. The

Clos Pegase looks like a Babylonian temple.

tasting room is located in the original yellow Craftsman house on the property.

SCHRAMSBERG VINEYARDS

(www.schramsberg.com, 707-942-4558, 800-877-3623, 1400 Schramsberg Rd., Calistoga, CA 94515; Tasting and Tours: Daily by appointment) No winery symbolizes the rebirth of Napa Valley better than Schramsberg. The late Jack and Jamie Davies were the quintessential post-Prohibition wine pioneers in their day. When they bought the old Schramsberg estate in 1965, it was rich in history but near ruin. Jacob Schram had established Napa's first hillside vineyard and winery in 1862 and, with the help of Chinese laborers, built a network of underground cellars. After a few years of sweat equity, Jack and Jamie became the country's premier producers of *méthode champenoise* sparkling wine. With their passing, son Hugh has taken over the business. As a tribute to Jack, the winery has been making a Diamond Mountain cabernet called J. Davies that's worth trying. The lovely grounds of Schramsberg are also worth exploring. The tour offers insight into the winery's history and the art of making bubbly. The highlight is the old cellar caves lined with walls of bottles.

STERLING VINEYARDS (www

.sterlingvineyards.com, 707-942-3344, 800-726-6136, 1111 Dunaweal Ln., Calistoga, CA 94515; Tasting: Mon.–Fri. 10:30–5, Sat.–Sun. 10–5) Sterling isn't just a winery, it's an experience. A modern white villa perched atop a tall knoll, it just may be Napa Valley's most dramatic visual statement. Sure, there's a touch of Disneyland—you ascend on an aerial tramway—but that's Sterling's appeal, and from the top the view is unsurpassed. Sterling retains such a contemporary look that

The barrel room at Castello di Amorosa in Calistoga.

it's hard to believe it was built in 1973. A well-marked, self-guided tour allows a leisurely glimpse of the winery's workings and leads you ultimately to one of Napa's most relaxing tasting rooms. A progressive-style tasting awaits you once you board the tram—usually a sample of sauvignon blanc. You're then greeted with another pour such as chardonnay after you step off the tram, and finish off with the remaining pours at the wine bar. Though its offerings have been inconsistent, Sterling occasionally achieves greatness, particularly with its Reserve Cabernet.

STORYBOOK MOUNTAIN

VINEYARDS (www.storybookwines .com, 707-942-5310, 3835 Hwy. 128, Calistoga, CA 94515; Tasting and Tours: By appointment) With a dramatic gate along Highway 128 and tucked amid rolling hills, Storybook Mountain earns its romantic name. The winery devotes itself to one wine: zinfandel. The regular and the reserve bottlings are typically powerful and long-lived. Jacob and Adam Grimm—the brothers Grimm, thus the Storybook name—made wine on the property back in the late 19th century. Jerry Seps restored it in 1976, and this small and unpretentious winery remains his baby. The wines reveal a hands-off attitude: the vineyards are organic, and Seps tinkers little with the wine in the cellar.

TEDESCHI FAMILY WINERY (www.tedeschifamilywinery.com, 707-337-5526, 2779 Grant St., Calistoga, CA 94515; Tasting and Tours: By appointment) The Tedeschi family has been in the Napa Valley for several generations. Eugene Tedeschi planted the first grapes on their Calistoga property in the 1960s. Today, Emil Tedeschi produces handcrafted wines in the tradition of his Italian heritage. The winery is bicycle-friendly, located in the north part of Napa Valley.

VON STRASSER WINERY (www.vonstrasser.com, 707-942-0930, 1510 Diamond Mountain Rd., Calistoga, CA 94515; Tasting and Tours: By appointment) Its first release arrived in 1993, and since then Von Strasser has caught the eye of cabernet sauvignon fans. Rudy and Rita von Strasser own prime vineyard space on Diamond Mountain, a stone's throw from the famous Diamond Creek Vineyards. The cab is intensely built and production is small, but the von Strassers are immersed, tending the vineyards and hand-sorting the grapes.

Palate Adventures

Seek out culinary adventures in Calistoga.

• *Shop for wine . . .*
in interesting places
Calistoga Wine Stop (www.calistoga winestop.net, 707-942-5556, 800-648-4521, 1458 Lincoln Ave., Calistoga, CA 94515) Housed in an 1866 Central Pacific railroad car in the oldest railroad depot in California, this shop has a solid lineup of current Napa and Sonoma wines. Prices are average.

Enoteca Wine Shop (www.enotecawineshop.com, 707-942-1117, 1348 B Lincoln Ave., Calistoga, CA 94515) Here you'll find great selection and a savvy staff to help you shop in a store that, surprisingly, resembles a cave. This shop specializes in local small-production wines as well as old-world wines.

Wine Garage (www.winegarage.net, 707-942-5332, 888-690-WINE, 1020 Foothill Blvd., Calistoga, CA 94515) This value-oriented wine shop, housed in a converted garage, has more than two hundred wines under $25 and a current inventory of more than three hundred bottles including their own label. The Wine Garage now has a half-gallon jug of either a Rhone or Bordeaux blend starting at $29.99.

• *Indulge your sweet tooth*
Candy Cellar (707-942-6990, 1367 Lincoln Ave., Calistoga, CA 94515) Relive your childhood as you browse this general store, with its wooden barrels stuffed with

goodies such as taffy, butterscotch, fireballs, candy necklaces, gum, A&W Root Beer barrels, and the like.

• Order a morning brew

Calistoga Roastery (www.calistoga roastery.com, 707-942-5757, 1426 Lincoln Ave., Calistoga, CA 94515) Here's a cozy and casual spot for the morning brew, with plenty of seating inside and out. A full array of freshly baked breakfast goods such as scones, bagels, and muffins is served. Salads, sandwiches, and smoothies are also available for lunch.

San Marco Espresso and Bake Shop (707-942-0714, 1408 Lincoln Ave., Calistoga, CA 94515) This recently expanded café still makes an uncompromising cup of coffee, and fruit, ice cream, and milk shakes are now also offered.

• Score a slice of pie

Checkers Pizza & Pasta (707-942-9300, 1414 Lincoln Ave., Calistoga, CA 94515; 523 4th St., Santa Rosa, CA 95401) If you like pizza with panache, check out Checkers. Both outlets are festive, with abstract art and polished pine and black tile. There are traditional pies of sausage and pepperoni, of course, but there's also Thai pizza, topped with marinated chicken, cilantro, and peanuts.

> **Insider Secret:**
> At the **Candy Cellar,** the high-brow homemade fudge is often overshadowed by the clamor for retro candy. Insiders know to ask for the Café Latte Fudge and the Calistoga Mud Fudge.

Be a kid again at the Candy Cellar. Tim Fish

To Do

Check out these great attractions and activities . . .

SHOPPING

The hot springs have brought visitors to Calistoga for more than 130 years. You'll be tempted to do nothing but soak in a mineral bath. But don't miss the shops. Our favorites: Casa Design (707-942-2228, 1419 Lincoln Ave., Calistoga, CA 94515), which offers custom furniture, linens, mirrors, and original artwork. Zenobia (707-942-1050, 1410 Lincoln Ave., Calistoga, CA 94515) is a whimsical space that sells candles, cards, clothing, and inspirational wall hangings. Copperfield's Books (707-942-1616, 1330 Lincoln Ave., Calistoga, 94515) is the only bookstore in town, and it carries candles and calendars and sponsors readings and book signings. Hurd Beeswax Candles & Hurd Gift & Gourmet (707-942-7410, 707-963-7211, 1255 Lincoln Ave., Calistoga, CA 94515) sells candles that are handcrafted from sheets of pure beeswax, and there are hundreds of designs. At Mudd Hens (707-942-0210, 1348-C Lincoln Ave., Calistoga, CA 94515) you can pick up plenty of personal care supplies, including lotions, massage oils, and all-natural body products. A Man's Store (707-942-2280, 1343 Lincoln Ave., Calistoga, CA 94515) features rugged and casual wear for men, as well as cigars. Attitudes (707-942-8420, 1333-B Lincoln Ave., Calistoga, CA 94515) focuses on women's lifestyle clothing, from business to yoga wear. Chateau Ste. Shirts (707-942-5039; 1355 Lincoln Ave., Calistoga, CA 94515) has stylish swimwear and sportswear and even sells the Ugg line of shoes. Bella Tootsie Shoes & More (707-942-8821, 1373 Lincoln Ave., Calistoga, CA 94515) sells shoes, purses, and hats.

CULTURAL OUTINGS

• *Drink in the art*
Clos Pegase (www.clospegase.com, info@clospegase.com, 707-942-4981, 1060 Dunaweal Ln., Calistoga, CA 94515) This winery is a work of art in itself. Designed by the award-winning architect Michael Graves, it looks like a postmodern Babylonian temple. A commanding edifice of tall pillars and archways done in bold hues of cream and terra cotta, Clos Pegase is an eye-catcher. The lawn and courtyard serve as a sculpture garden, which includes Richard Serra's provocative *Twins,* a minimalist masterpiece. The regular winery tour offers a glimpse of owner Jan Shrem's impressive art collection, including 17th- and 18th-century French statuary artfully displayed in the winery's massive underground cave. Also, a casual browse in the visitors' center reveals more treasures.

• *Revel in regional history and culture*
Sharpsteen Museum (www.sharpsteen-museum.org, 707-942-5911, 1311 Washington St., Calistoga, CA; Admission: Donation appreciated) If you want a quick lesson in early Napa life, this quaint museum is the place to go. Ben and Bernice Sharpsteen created the museum almost as a hobby after Ben retired as a producer for Walt Disney and the couple moved to Calistoga. Before long, it became a community project, and today it's run by volunteers. The first section of this museum is devoted to the Sharpsteens themselves and a miniature model of early Calistoga follows.

• *Check out the nightlife*

A great Calistoga hot spot is Barolo (www.barolocalistoga.com, 707-942-9900, 1457 Lincoln Ave., Calistoga, CA 94515). This popular eatery has great Italian food and a good wine list. Enjoy Barolo's happy hour daily from 4:30–6:30 PM, where $1 well drinks are a popular option. On a warm evening, try the patio bar at Calistoga Inn Restaurant & Brewery (www.calistogainn.com/brewery.html, 707-942-4101, 1250 Lincoln Ave., Calistoga, CA).

• *Take advantage of seasonal offerings*

Calistoga Downtown Jazz & Blues (707-942-6333, Napa County Fairgrounds, Calistoga, CA 94515) This event happens in early October, and tickets range from $40 to $165.

Napa County Fair (www.napacountyfair.org, 707-942-5111, fairgrounds, Calistoga, CA 94515) Every July, the fair offers down-home fun, but with a twist of chic Napa style that includes social gatherings and wine tastings. There are the usual rides, animals, produce, and music, plus wine, wine, wine.

RECREATIONAL FUN

• *Go two-wheeling*

Many inns allow guests the use of bicycles for casual day trips, and most bike shops offer daily rentals. Getaway Adventures (www.getawayadventures.com, 707-568-3040, 800-499-2453, 2228 Northpoint Pkwy, Santa Rosa Ca 95407) has a variety of organized tours and route suggestions. Another great place for rentals is the Calistoga Bike Shop (707-942-9687, 1318 Lincoln Ave., Calistoga, CA 94515).

• *Venture into the wild*

Bothe-Napa Valley State Park (707-942-4575, 3801 St. Helena Highway North, Calistoga, CA 94515; midway between St. Helena and Calistoga, off Hwy. 29) This 1,920-acre state park has 50 developed campsites. Campers up to 31 feet and trailers to 24 feet can be accommodated; no sanitation station is provided. Services include horseback-riding trails, hiking, swimming pool, picnic area, and exhibits. Handicapped accessible in all areas. Park admission: $8 for parking. There is an additional fee for horseback riding and use of swimming pool, to be paid at the park entrance.

Old Faithful Geyser (www.oldfaithfulgeyser.com, 707-942-6463, 1299 Tubbs Ln., Calistoga, CA 94515; 1 mile north of Calistoga) One of just three regularly erupting geysers in the world, it shoots steam and vapor 40 to 50 feet into the air for three minutes,

Best Bests for Kids in Napa Valley

Sterling Vineyards (www.sterlingvineyards.com) isn't just a winery, it's an experience, with a touch of Disneyland—you ascend an aerial tramway to enter.

Napa Firefighters Museum (www.napafirefightersmuseum.org) has antique and modern-day firefighting equipment on display. Every kid aspires to be a hero, right?

Candy Cellar (Calistoga) delights children, and grown-ups are transported to childhood.

Calistoga Sip 'n Cycle

Getaway Adventures (www .getawayadventures.com) offers a daylong bicycle wine tour led by professional local guides. The tour follows scenic country roads with stops at several wineries. Tour price includes hybrid bike and helmet rental and a gourmet picnic lunch. A great way to explore Wine Country.

and repeats this feat every 40 minutes. Because seismic activity influences the frequency of the eruptions, many believe Old Faithful predicts earthquakes. Open daily, the site includes picnic grounds. Admission: $7 per family with AAA, $10 adult, $7 seniors, $3 children 6–12, children under 6 free. Open daily seven days a week including holidays 9–5 (winter) and 9–6 (summer).

Petrified Forest (www.petrified forest.org, 707-942-6667, 4100 Petrified Forest Rd., Calistoga, CA 94515; 5 miles west of Calistoga) Here you'll find remains of a redwood forest turned to stone by molten lava from the eruption of Mount St. Helena three million years ago. The Petrified Forest was discovered in 1870 and immortalized by Robert Louis Stevenson in *The Silverado Squatters*. Included here are picnic grounds and a gift shop, and the site is open daily 9–6. Two trails are available, at different prices: Main Trail and Meadow Walk. Admission: $9/$15 seniors 62+ and juniors ages 12–17, $10/$16 adults, $5/free children 6–11, children under 6 are free.

• *Let the kids run free*
If you're touring Wine Country with tykes, you'll want to grab a picnic or snack and head to Pioneer Park, on Cedar Street just off Lincoln Avenue. It's free, and there's a pleasant little playground. The kids will thank you.

6

Healdsburg

"RUSTIC CHIC" is the phrase that comes to mind when we think of Healdsburg, a Sonoma County town where Range Rovers and BMWs cohabitate. It's the hub of three premier wine regions—the Dry Creek, Russian River, and Alexander valleys.

Steeped in wine culture, Healdsburg has attracted upscale hotels and restaurants like Les Mars and Hotel Healdsburg, with their respective restaurants Cyrus and Dry Creek Kitchen. Cyrus, by all accounts, rivals the French Laundry across the mountain in Napa Valley. But despite the flurry of five-star establishments, top-rate chefs, and celebrity sightings of such luminaries as Martha Stewart and Bob Dylan, Healdsburg continues to have a charming small-town feel. The fall harvest is a ritual that seems to ground everyone; it brings out the earthy farmer in vintners who endeavor to make peace with Mother Nature yet again. The prayer is always the same: *Please, oh please, let the grapes ripen before the rains come.*

> **Insider Secret:**
> **Powell's Sweet Shoppe** has been called the "Smithsonian of candy stores," a place where you can marvel over old relics, candies like Zagnut bars and Jujubes, which date back to the 1920s. Sweet nostalgia. (www .powellsss.com)

Checking In

Best places to stay in and around Healdsburg.

Healdsburg has a good range of lodging options, from the European-styled Les Mars to the contemporary Hotel Healdsburg, with plenty of bed & breakfasts also in the mix.

BELLE DE JOUR INN (www.belle dejourinn.com, 707-431-9777, 16276 Healdsburg Ave., Healdsburg, CA 95448; Price: Expensive to Very Expensive) A peaceful B&B inn on the northern outskirts of Healdsburg, Belle de Jour is set on a tranquil

LEFT: So many options. So little time. Tim Fish

Travel Like an Insider:

Our Top 10 Picks for Healdsburg

1. Cyrus (www.cyrusrestaurant.com) Cyrus is not only the top restaurant in Sonoma County, it's one of the best in Northern California, giving competition to the French Laundry across the mountain and the top kitchens of San Francisco.

2. Francis Ford Coppola Winery (www.franciscoppolawinery.com) North of Healdsburg, in Geyserville, is this self-styled "wine wonderland," a resort-style destination for the entire family, with a pool near the tasting room, boccie courts, a movie gallery, and more.

3. Seghesio (www.seghesio.com) This winery produces many Italian-style varieties such as sangiovese, barbera, pinot grigio, and arneis, but it's known for its supple yet intense zinfandel.

4. Jimtown Store (www.jimtown.com) An Alexander Valley landmark for a century, this former general store and gas depot, which had been abandoned for years, was resuscitated in 1991 with a touch of gourmet chic. Jimtown Store remains quaint yet sophisticated, drawing national attention along the way.

5. h2hotel (www.h2hotel.com) An eco-friendly establishment near the town square, h2hotel is a hot destination for the green traveler. Another draw is its ever-popular **Spoonbar** restaurant, which serves Mediterranean eats, inventive cocktails, and wines that are international in scope, yet accent the locals.

6. Bovolo (www.bovolorestaurant.com) This restaurant doesn't offer the usual soups and sandwiches. The rustic Italian food is prepared from scratch and with fervor.

7. Barn Diva (www.barndiva.com) Known as a hip restaurant with late-night appeal, you can order exotic drinks from the bar until 11 PM.

8. Honor Mansion (www.honormansion.com) Honor Mansion has won its share of honors, including being named one of the most romantic inns by American Historic Inns.

6-acre hilltop with lovely views of rolling hills and distant mountains. The Italianate main farmhouse, built around 1873, is where the innkeepers live and prepare scrumptious breakfasts. The five guest suites, all decorated with French-country-inspired furniture, are set behind the main house. The inn is centrally located for touring Napa and Sonoma, and the Hearns are superb hosts.

CAMELLIA INN (www.camelliainn .com, 707-433-8182, 800-727-8182, 211 North St., Healdsburg, CA 95448;

Price: Moderate to Expensive) This 1869 Italianate Victorian home entered the turn of the 20th century as Healdsburg's first hospital. It's now a magnificent inn with nine guest rooms and still has many of its original and unique architectural details, including the twin marble fireplaces in the double parlor. On a quiet residential street just two blocks from the plaza, the inn is named for the 50 or so varieties of camellias that grace its gardens. A full breakfast buffet is served in the dining room, dominated by a mahogany fireplace

The happening patio at Barn Diva. Tim Fish

9. At neighbors **Holdredge Wines** (www.holdredge.com) and **Davis Family Vineyards** (www.davisfamilyvineyards.com), vintners John Holdredge and Guy Davis make powerhouse wines. Their winemaking reveals they're inventors and artists, and yes, mad scientists.

10. Downtown Bakery and Creamery (www.downtownbakery.net) Tortes and cakes are ungodly delicious, as are the sticky buns, the monster Fig Newton–like cookies, and the blueberry scones.

mantel. The innkeepers are very friendly.

DRY CREEK INN BEST WESTERN (www.drycreekinn.com, 707-433-0300, 800-222-5784, 198 Dry Creek Rd., Healdsburg, CA 95448; Price: Inexpensive to Expensive) This motel is distinguished by its outstanding location for wine touring. There is fairly standard motel decor throughout, but a spectacular view of Dry Creek Valley is the payoff in many rooms. Rooms are equipped with refrigerators and coffeemakers, and a continental breakfast

is included—great for families. It's well situated for a day of wine tasting followed by dining downtown on the plaza. The downside: The inn fronts busy Highway 101, but the road quiets considerably at night.

GRAPE LEAF INN (www.grapeleaf inn.com, 707-433-8140, 539 Johnson St., Healdsburg, CA 95448, Price: Expensive to Very Expensive) The 12 elegant guest rooms in this 1900 Queen Anne Victorian are furnished with cast-iron beds, armoires, and warm oak accents, and all are named

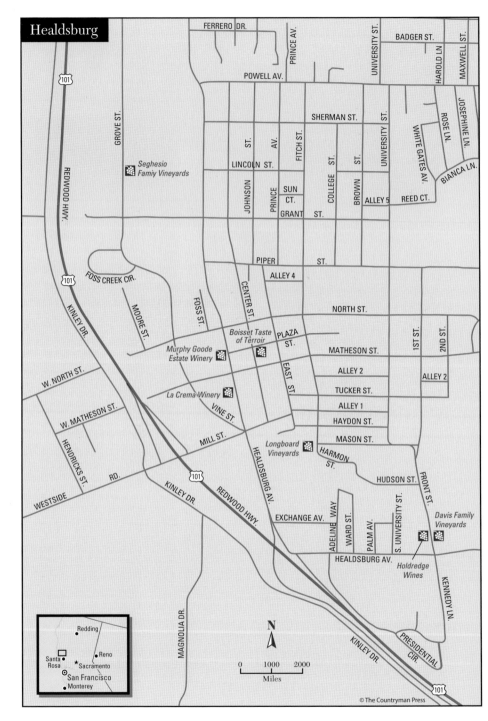

Healdsburg

FERRERO DR.

PRINCE AV.

UNIVERSITY ST.

BADGER ST.

HAROLD LN.

MAXWELL ST.

POWELL AV.

GROVE ST.

REDWOOD HWY.

SHERMAN ST.

UNIVERSITY ST.

ROSE LN.

JOSEPHINE LN.

WHITE GATES AV.

BIANCA LN.

Seghesio Famiy Vineyards

LINCOLN ST.

ST.

AV.

FITCH ST.

COLLEGE ST.

ST.

BROWN

UNIVERSITY ST.

JOHNSON

PRINCE

SUN CT.

ALLEY 5

REED CT.

GRANT ST.

PIPER ST.

FOSS CREEK CIR.

ALLEY 4

KINLEY DR.

MOORE ST.

FOSS ST.

CENTER ST.

NORTH ST.

1ST ST.

2ND ST.

Boisset Taste of Terroir

PLAZA ST.

Murphy Goode Estate Winery

MATHESON ST.

W. NORTH ST.

ALLEY 2

ALLEY 2

La Crema Winery

EAST ST.

TUCKER ST.

W. MATHESON ST.

VINE ST.

ALLEY 1

HAYDON ST.

HENDRICKS ST.

MILL ST.

MASON ST.

Longboard Vineyards

HARMON ST.

HEALDSBURG AV.

HUDSON ST.

FRONT ST.

WESTSIDE RD.

KINLEY DR.

REDWOOD HWY.

EXCHANGE AV.

ADELINE WAY

WARD ST.

PALM AV.

S. UNIVERSITY ST.

Davis Family Vineyards

KENNEDY LN.

HEALDSBURG AV.

Holdredge Wines

MAGNOLIA DR.

PRESIDENTIAL CIR.

KINLEY DR.

N

Redding

Reno

Santa Rosa

Sacramento

San Francisco

Monterey

0   1000   2000
Miles

© The Countryman Press

for grape varietals. The inn's quiet porch is perfect for unwinding after a day of wine touring. A full country breakfast is served in the dining room. Wine is served nightly, and the inn is within walking distance of Healdsburg's historic downtown plaza. For those who prefer a more exotic setting, the innkeepers have a unique offering: three guests cottages seven minutes from the inn, located amid a 10-acre, old vine zinfandel vineyard.

H2HOTEL (www.h2hotel.com, 707-922-5251, 219 Healdsburg Ave., Healdsburg, CA 95448; Price: Moderate to Expensive) Conveniently located near the town square, this "green" hotel describes its 36 guest rooms as "eco-chic." The furnishings are spare but aesthetically pleasing and intended to soothe: you'll find organic cotton linens and robes, bamboo floors, and ergonomic chairs. All rooms feature a private balcony or patio. Another draw is the hotel's ever-popular Spoonbar restaurant, which serves Mediterranean eats, inventive cocktails, and wines that are international in scope, yet accent the locals.

HAYDON STREET INN (www.haydon.com, 707-433-5228, 800-528-3703, 321 Haydon St., Healdsburg, CA 95448; Price: Moderate to Very Expensive) In a quiet residential area and surrounded by trees, this Queen Anne Victorian inn has nine charming guest rooms, all with hardwood floors, antiques, down comforters, and private baths. A generous breakfast buffet is crafted by owner John, a retired chef, and served in the dining room. The inn is a short walk to Healdsburg's plaza.

HEALDSBURG INN ON THE PLAZA (www.healdsburginn.com, 707-433-6991, 800-431-8663,110 Matheson St., Healdsburg, CA 95448; Price: Very

Insider Secret:
Who knew that choreography played a role in cocktail making? But mixologist Scott Beattie of h2hotel's **Spoonbar** says you can ruin a great drink with a shake instead of a stir. For the curious, he takes people behind the bar for cocktail classes.

Expensive) Right on Healdsburg's delightful downtown plaza, this 12-room inn welcomes guests through the main-floor gift shop.The solarium and roof garden is the common area where guests take breakfast and afternoon refreshments. In-room TVs and phones are available on request.

HONOR MANSION (www.honormansion.com, 707-433-4277, 800-554-4667, 14891 Grove St., Healdsburg, CA; Price: Expensive to Very Expensive) Honor Mansion has—appropriately—won its share of honors. It was named one of the most romantic inns by American Historic Inns. Built in 1883, this Victorian mansion attributes its name to Dr. Herbert Honor, whose family owned the property for more than one hundred years. The Fowlers bought the inn in 1994 and remodeled the entire building—and these innkeepers will spoil you outright, from mints on your pillow to scrumptious afternoon appetizers. There's a breakfast buffet, and you'll want to check out the inn's Honor Mansion Cookbook. Most of the guest rooms and suites feature queen and king-sized beds, fireplaces, comfy sitting areas, great views and many have spa tubs. A couple of rooms have claw-foot tubs. The inn is near the Healdsburg plaza and a short drive from many wineries in the area.

HOTEL HEALDSBURG (www.hotel healdsburg.com, 707-431-2800, 800-889-7188, 25 Matheson St., Healdsburg, CA 95448; Price: Expensive to Very Expensive) This contemporary, three-story hotel is right on the main square of Healdsburg, a small town that manages to be both quaint and cosmopolitan. The hotel is modern in decor but remains warm and inviting, with a stone fireplace in the lobby and—for those who like to people-

Especially for foodies in Sonoma County

Cyrus (p. 141)

Downtown Bakery and Creamery (p. 155)

Jimtown Store (p. 156)

Powell's Sweet Shoppe (p. 159)

Bovolo (p. 140)

Grapes ripening on the vine. Tim Fish

watch—a screened-in porch. Hotel Healdsburg has 55 rooms, all designed to pamper: oversized bathrooms done in Italian glass mosaic tile, 6-foot soaking tubs, private balconies, down comforters. In addition, a continental breakfast is delivered to your door. Right off the lobby is Dry Creek Kitchen, a restaurant owned by star chef Charlie Palmer—best known for his Aureole restaurants in New York and Las Vegas. Showcasing American cuisine and wine from Sonoma County, the restaurant serves lunch and dinner (see entry under Restaurants). The Healdsburg's location on the downtown square can be a drawback for guests sensitive to noise.

LES MARS (www.lesmarshotel.com, 877-431-1700 and 707-433-4211, 27 North St. Healdsburg, CA. 95448; Price: Expensive to Very Expensive) Les Mars feels like a European hotel on American turf. Its front lobby is elegant, with 17th- and 18th-century antiques, warm wood, and soft colors. It offers Old World luxury and 21st-century technology—such as entertainment amenities housed within a Louis XV armoire. Les Mars is one of the most decadent hotels in Wine Country, particularly for the palate. The restaurant with buzz—Cyrus—is on the hotel's premises and has quite a draw. Cyrus is as close to the French Laundry experience as you can get in Sonoma County. The hotel was wise to make it a power partner. If you want the ultimate in pampering, choose Les Mars and make a reservation—quick as you can—at Cyrus (see listing under Restaurants).

MADRONA MANOR (www.madrona manor.com, 707-433-4231, 800-258-4003, 1001 Westside Rd., Healdsburg, CA 95448; Price: Expensive to Very Expensive) This country inn and restaurant is the grande dame of Sonoma County. With its mansard roof, expansive porch, and surrounding lush gardens, this three-story Victorian built in 1881 is a majestic sight amid a glade of trees. Large and ornate antiques decorate most of the mansion's formal guest rooms. Well off the main road, Madrona Manor guarantees an unhurried stay and a return to the slower pace of the home's Victorian heyday. Buffet breakfast is included. The restaurant is also first-rate.

Local Flavors

Taste of the town—local restaurants, cafés, bars, bistros, etc.

RESTAURANTS

Picking the right eatery is crucial in Wine Country. There's the food to consider, and the service and the atmosphere as well. We have tested the waters to give you some great suggestions for Healdsburg restaurants in all price ranges.

BARN DIVA (www.barndiva.com, 707-431-0100, 231 Center St., Healdsburg, CA 95448; Price: Very Expensive, Cuisine: California) In Wine Country, Barn Diva is known as a hip restaurant with late-night appeal where you can order exotic drinks from the bar until 11 PM. It's also known for celebrating all things local, searching out the best local produce from local farmers, ranchers and vintners, etc. A safe bet is the "Rosemary Roasted Leg of Lamb" but a smart pick for the daring is the "Off the Hook," the chef's choice of wild fish. Whether you opt for lunch, an early dinner, or a nightcap, you won't be disappointed. The food is tasty, the drinks are festive, and though

At Bovolo, rustic Italian food is prepared from scratch. Tim Fish

the waitstaff may be young, they're dedicated. What's more, the decor charms. The restaurant is rustic-chic, a cedar barn with a 14-foot ceiling and a sleek mahogany bar. The wine list is sophisticated and fairly priced, with more than 150 bottles and about 10 specialty cocktails at the going rate. The menu follows suit. Good picks include fish and duck entrees. Tip: On a warm summer's night, the back patio is perfect.

BISTRO RALPH (www.bistroralph .com, 707-433-1380, 109 Plaza St., Healdsburg, CA 95448; Price: Expensive, Cuisine: California) Bistro Ralph recalls a Greenwich Village café: elegant in a spare, smartly industrial sort of way. Some might consider the atmosphere chilly, but it's never bothered us. Situated on the Healdsburg plaza, it's a handy spot for lunch or dinner. The food is typically excellent, particularly if chef-owner Ralph Tingle is in the kitchen, although there's an

occasional miss. At lunch the CK Lamb burger is a must and the Caesar salad is dependable. Bistro Ralph has an efficient and modestly priced wine list that plays up the area's best producers. Service is always relaxed and attentive.

BOVOLO (www.bovolorestaurant.com, 707-431-2962, Plaza Farms, 106 Matheson St., Healdsburg, CA 95448; Price: Moderate to Expensive; Cuisine: Northern Italian, California) Named for an Italian snail, Bovolo is not much to look at. It's little more than a glorified deli, but don't expect the usual soups and sandwiches. The rustic Italian food is prepared from scratch and with fervor. Chef John Stewart, who shares duties with chef/wife Duskie Estes, cures his own sopressata, coppa, bacon, and more. Pizza, pasta, and salads are also on the menu, and savory pork cheek and other hearty sandwiches are sold at lunch, while at night, there's a three-course dinner. The wine selection is quite small—a few dozen

are on the list—but it's loaded with
gems.

CAFÉ GRATITUDE (www.cafe
gratitude.com, 707-723-4461, 206
Healdsburg Ave., Healdsburg, CA;
Price: Inexpensive to Moderate; Cuisine: California, Organic, Vegan)
While Café Gratitude feels like a
throwback to the 1960s, it's actually a
cutting-edge alternative for the health-
conscious diner, offering organic and
vegan fare. The uninitiated might be
bemused by the menu, with its New
Age affirmations like "I am festive Taco
Salad," "I am dazzling Caesar Salad,"
and "I am thankful Coconut Curry

Soup." Despite it's out-of-the-box
designations—or perhaps because of
them—Café Gratitude is a popular
spot, and one of its most appealing
aspects seems to be its lineup of sugar-
free desserts.

CYRUS (www.cyrusrestaurant.com,
707-433-3311, 29 North St., Healdsburg, CA 95448, Price: Very expensive,
Cuisine: California, French, Asian)
This is not only the top restaurant in
Sonoma County, it's one of the best in
Northern California, giving competition to the French Laundry across the
mountain and the top kitchens in San
Francisco. Cyrus partners Nick Peyton
and Douglas Keane have created an
extravagant and formal food and wine
experience, but somehow the mood is
never stuffy. The dining room, with its
textured yellow walls and arched pillars
and vaulted ceiling, is at once dramatic
and warmly inviting. With Peyton
working the front of the house, service
is crisp and intuitive. Guests are greeted with Cyrus's trademark champagne
and caviar cart, a piece of showman-
ship that's quite tempting. The wine list

Cyrus in Sonoma County rivals The French Laundry in Napa Valley.

has more than seven hundred selections. It's worldly and expensive, but ripe with gems and classics. Chef Keane's dishes are rich and deeply flavored yet never over the top, even when he adds elements of Asia and American comfort foods. If you want to experience a taste of Cyrus without the full price tag, each course is available á la carte in the bar, although reservations are not accepted for bar dining, so arrive early.

DRY CREEK KITCHEN (www .charliepalmer.com, 707-431-0330, 317 Healdsburg Ave., Healdsburg, CA 95448; Price: Expensive; Cuisine: California) Given chef-owner Charlie Palmer's track record with his ever-expanding restaurant empire, it's not surprising that Dry Creek Kitchen has raised the culinary bar in Sonoma County. Palmer, who moved his family to Sonoma a few years back, divides his time between Wine Country and his restaurants in New York and Las Vegas. The decor is contemporary, with big columns that sweep dramatically toward the ceiling, and subtle colors: cream with pear-green trim. It's comfortable, clean, and simple. The menu follows the seasons and features local products almost exclusively: meat, seafood, produce, artisan cheeses, and, of course, wine. Palmer never gets in the way of these fine ingredients, yet somehow finds a way to give them an intriguing twist. The wine list is extensive and has a particularly good offering of pinot noirs and zinfandels, and though prices are generally high, there's no corkage fee for guests who bring in their own first two bottles of Sonoma County wine.

HEALDSBURG BAR & GRILL (www.healdsburgbarandgrill.com, 707-433-3333, 245 Healdsburg Ave., CA. 95448; Price: Moderate; Cuisine: California) The owners of Cyrus—Nick Peyton and Douglas Keane—opened this highbrow burger joint just a couple of blocks away from their upscale restaurant. The fact that Cyrus rivals the French Laundry across the mountain and the top kitchens in San Francisco should assure the casual diner they can expect good things at the Healdsburg Bar & Grill. It's no surprise that the burger—freshly ground All Natural Meyer Beef on a Toasted Costeaux Bakery Sourdough Bun—is a hit. Other appealing concoctions include the fries: get them with chipotle salt or truffle oil and Parmigiano-Reggiano.

MADRONA MANOR (www.madrona manor.com, 707-433-4231, 800-258-4003,1001 Westside Rd., Healdsburg, CA 95448; Price: Very Expensive; Cuisine: California, French) It's a shame to approach this 1881 Victorian in the dark. Rising three stories to a steep mansard roof, this inn is a majestic sight set in a quiet glade, amid lush gardens (see listing under Lodging). The dining rooms, which used to be as stark and formal as a starched white shirt, now have warmer yet elegant tones. Service is very attentive, and Madrona Manor has one of the best wine cellars around, particularly if you like newer "blue chip" wines. The location is the main reason for coming to the manor. The food is dependably good, if rather uninspired, and the evening overall is enjoyable. Perhaps the experience simply pales next to all the new competition in Healdsburg.

RAVENOUS (www.theravenous.com, 707-431-1302, 420 Center St., Healdsburg, CA 95448; Price: Expensive; Cuisine: California) There's no shortage of upscale restaurants in Healdsburg these days, but if you're looking for a casual lunch or dinner, this is a good choice. The setting is a 1930s bunga-low with a fireplace and wood floors and cheery colors on the walls. The menu changes daily—it's handwritten, in fact—and it's made up of lusty California cuisine, from one of the best hamburgers in the county to crab cakes and roasted poblano chili stuffed with potatoes, hominy, and cojita cheese. The wine list is extensive and eclectic and focused mainly on local wineries, with 40-50 wines by the glass are offered. The prices are fair. Service can be a little casual for our taste, but casual is what Ravenous is all about.

WILLI'S SEAFOOD AND RAW BAR (www.willisseafood.net, 707-433-9191, 403 Healdsburg Ave., Healds-burg, CA 95448; Price: Moderate to Very Expensive; Cuisine: Seafood, Eclectic) We love the energy of this place. You just want to pull up a chair or a bar stool and hang out. There's a hip, industrial feel to the joint, and the best seats are the private booths on the upper level. The menu is entirely small plates, with seafood and Latino spices playing a strong role. The flavors are bold and sometimes a dish goes over-board with too many ingredients, but we're generally won over. Plates range from fresh shellfish, ceviches, and tar-tars and New England–style sandwich rolls to skewers. The wine list is quite small, but the prices are fair and there's a decent selection by the glass.

ZIN RESTAURANT & WINE BAR (www.zinrestaurant.com, 707-473-0946, 344 Center St., Healdsburg, CA 95448; Price: Expensive; Cuisine: California Contemporary) Zin zealots con-verge at this restaurant, an expansive eatery that feels like an artist's loft: slabs of concrete walls beneath a high ceiling of wooden rafters. Contempo-rary and yet cozy, the walls are filled with colorful art. A long wine bar

Especially for the big spender in Sonoma County

When price is no object, **Cyrus** (www.cyrusrestaurant.com) should be your first choice for dinner, and **Les Mars** (www.lesmarshotel.com) is where you'll want to stay.

sweeps across one side of the restau-rant, and whether you're just in for a drink or in for a full meal, you'll love this custom-made menu focused on zinfandel. Even if zinfandel isn't your thing, you'll find plenty of other wines sharing second billing, and many are available by the glass. Regular menu items include applewood smoked and grilled Homestead Farms Natural pork chop with fresh apple sauce over andouille sausage and cornbread stuffing.

WINERIES

Let your palate roam through Wine Country. Whether you're a novice and an old pro, there's plenty to learn from bellying up to the bar. There are count-less wineries to choose from, in Healdsburg and just up the road in Geyserville.

Insider Secret:
You think of Wine Country as a place to drink, but this is also a place to gamble. **River Rock Casino** is right in the heart of Alexander Valley, but be sure not to gamble away your wine budg-et. (www.riverrockcasino.com)

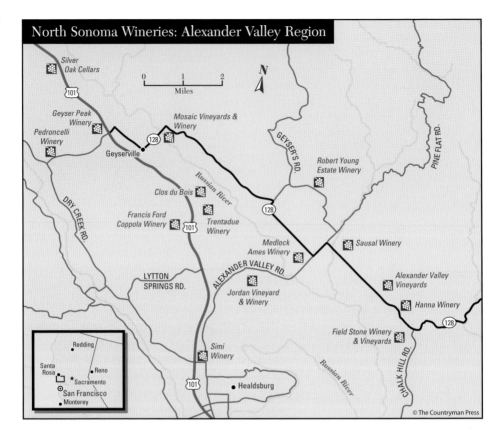

North Sonoma Wineries: Alexander Valley Region

Silver Oak Cellars

101

Geyser Peak Winery

Pedroncelli Winery

Geyserville

128

Mosaic Vineyards & Winery

GEYSER'S RD.

PINE FLAT RD.

Robert Young Estate Winery

Russian River

Clos du Bois

128

Francis Ford Coppola Winery

101

Trentadue Winery

Medlock Ames Winery

Sausal Winery

DRY CREEK RD.

LYTTON SPRINGS RD.

ALEXANDER VALLEY RD.

Alexander Valley Vineyards

Jordan Vineyard & Winery

Hanna Winery

128

Field Stone Winery & Vineyards

Russian River

CHALK HILL RD.

Simi Winery

101

Healdsburg

0   1   2
Miles

N

Redding

Santa Rosa   Reno

Sacramento

San Francisco

Monterey

© The Countryman Press

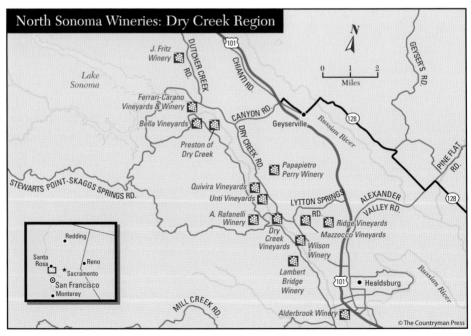

North Sonoma Wineries: Dry Creek Region

101

J. Fritz Winery

DUTCHER CREEK RD.

CHIANTI RD.

GEYSER'S RD.

Lake Sonoma

Ferrari-Carano Vineyards & Winery

Bella Vineyards

CANYON RD.

Geyserville

Russian River

128

Preston of Dry Creek

DRY CREEK RD.

PINE FLAT RD.

STEWARTS POINT-SKAGGS SPRINGS RD.

Papapietro Perry Winery

128

Quivira Vineyards

Unti Vineyards

LYTTON SPRINGS

ALEXANDER VALLEY RD.

A. Rafanelli Winery

RD.

Ridge Vineyards

Mazzocco Vineyards

Dry Creek Vineyards

Wilson Winery

101

Russian River

MILL CREEK RD.

Lambert Bridge Winery

Healdsburg

Alderbrook Winery

101

0   1   2
Miles

N

Redding

Santa Rosa   Reno

Sacramento

San Francisco

Monterey

© The Countryman Press

Healdsburg

ALDERBROOK WINERY (www.alderbrook.com, 707-433-9154, 800-405-5987, 2306 Magnolia Dr., Healdsburg, CA 95448; Tasting: Daily 10–5) With its wraparound porch, bleached-pine interior, and fireplace, Alderbrook's tasting room is a touch of New England in Wine Country—not that Alderbrook specializes in stout reds perfect for cool Vermont nights. White wine is the house forte, and the sauvignon blanc and chardonnay are consistently solid. Nevertheless, the zinfandel, syrah, and pinot noir are increasingly impressive.

ALEXANDER VALLEY VINEYARDS (www.avvwine.com, 707-433-7209, 800-888-7209, 8644 Hwy. 128, Healdsburg, CA 95448; Tasting: Daily 10–5) Cyrus Alexander, who lent his name to this beautiful valley, built his homestead here. His 1840s adobe remains. The Wetzel family planted vines in the early 1960s; in 1975 they built a winery with a cool cellar carved into a hill and a gravity-flow system that's less stressful to wine. The tasting room is a large homey, relaxed atmosphere with a beautiful fireplace. The cabernet sauvignons are elegant and easy to drink.

ARMIDA WINERY (www.armida.com, 707-433-2222, 2201 Westside Rd., Healdsburg, CA; Tasting: Daily 11–5) Three unique geodesic domes comprise this winery, which occupies the border of the Dry Creek and Russian River valleys. Wines include zinfandel, chardonnay, and pinot noir, all nicely done. Buy a bottle to share on the wooden deck, which offers an expansive view of Sonoma County.

A. RAFANELLI WINERY (www.arafanelliwinery.com, 707-433-1385, 4685 W. Dry Creek Rd., Healdsburg, CA 95448; Tasting and Tours: By appointment) If you want to try one of the best zinfandels in Wine Country, a trip to this small, folksy redwood barn is a requirement. The wines are nearly impossible to find otherwise. Rafanelli epitomizes old-school Sonoma County: good wine, no fuss. The Rafanellis have been growing grapes for generations and began making wine in 1974, believing their vineyards, not a winery with high-tech gadgets, did the talking. The winery makes great merlot and cabernet. The hospitality at the winery, once a bit snooty, has improved over the years.

BELLA VINEYARDS (www.bellawinery.com, 707-473-9171, 9711 West Dry Creek Rd., Healdsburg, CA 95448; Tasting: Daily 11–4:30) Situated at the far end of a country road, Bella isn't the sort of winery you stumble onto but it's well worth the trek. Scott and Lynn Adams are a passionate young couple who decided to live the dream and started Bella. The focus is zinfandel and Syrah, mostly from 80- or 100-year-old vines, and the wines are supple yet full of character. While you're tasting, be sure to check out the wine cave.

BOISSET TASTE OF TERROIR (tasteofterroir@boisset.com, 707-473-9707, 320 Center St., Healdsburg, CA 95448; Tasting: Daily 10:30–5:30) It's not news in Wine Country that Jean Charles Boisset and Gina Gallo are now married, so is this tasting room a wedding present from the bride to the groom? Boisset's Taste of Terroir is on the Healdsburg Square in the spot that Gallo of Sonoma had occupied for years. Boisset Family Estates has wine properties locally and abroad. Here it owns DeLoach Vineyards and Raymond Vineyards, and in France its brands include Domaine de la

Vougeraie and Jean-Claude Boisset, among others. Taste of Terroir will give people a chance to try wines from both Sonoma and Burgundy, which has occurred from time to time at DeLoach but will now be more formalized in one very fancy setting. For the celebrity-conscious, Boisset makes wine for Dan Aykroyd under the Dan Aykroyd Discovery Series name. Boisset has also been a leader in sustainable packaging with its line of French Rabbit wines.

DRY CREEK VINEYARDS (www.dry creekvineyard.com, 707-433-1000, 800-864-9463, 3770 Lambert Bridge Rd., Healdsburg, CA 95448; Tasting: Daily 10:30–4:30) Dry Creek Valley, we've always imagined, is what Napa Valley used to be: small, quiet, and unaffected by it all. It was a land of prunes and pears when Dave Stare, a former railroad engineer, arrived. The winery marked its 30th year in 2002. Designed after the small country wineries of France, Dry Creek has always reminded us of a simple country chapel. It only adds to the pleasure that Dry Creek's wines are consistently fine, often exceptional, as you'll discover in the tasting room. The atmosphere is laid-back, and the staff is chatty. Dry Creek has made its name with fumé blanc, a crisp wine that dominates the winery's production. The chenin blanc is so fruity and distinctive that we prefer it over many chardonnays. As for reds, the zinfandel is always one of the best, and the cabernet sauvignon has fine character and can be exceptional in a good vintage. The picnic area, shaded mostly by tall trees, is one of the best in Wine Country.

CHALK HILL WINERY (www.chalk hill.com, 707-657-4837, 10300 Chalk Hill Rd., Healdsburg, CA 95448; Tasting: Mon.–Fri. by appointment 10–3)

The white soil gives the Chalk Hill area its name—even though it's really volcanic ash, not chalk. Fred and his former wife Peggy Furth established this winery well off the beaten path in 1980 and hired a series of talented winemakers. In June of 2010 they sold winery to William Foley, the chairman of two Florida Financial companies, with the intent of keeping it family-owned. White wines thrive in the area, and chardonnay is the winery's specialty; it ranges from average to excellent. The sauvignon blanc is consistently a beauty. Be sure to try their new estate red— which is a California Bordeaux blend.

DAVIS FAMILY VINEYARDS (www.davisfamilyvineyards.com, 707-433-3858, Tasting Room: 52 Front St., Healdsburg CA 95448; Tasting: Thurs.–Sun. 11–5 pm) When you drink his wines, you can almost taste the passion Guy Davis has for winemaking. He produces a little of everything but seems particularly apt at pinot noir made from Russian River Valley grapes. The winery isn't fancy, but that's the charm. Best of all, you get to taste the wines right in the barrel room, and the staff is laid back and friendly.

FERRARI-CARANO VINEYARDS & WINERY (www.ferrari-carano.com, 707-433-6700, 8761 Dry Creek Rd.,

Insider Secret:

Vintner Guy Davis of **Davis Family Vineyards** makes an apple brandy called Apple-ation from the fruit of 100-year-old organic apple trees that's not to be missed. Davis is a clever inventor, and this brandy is a standout. (www.daviswines.com)

Villa Fiore at Ferrari-Carano is well known for its gardens.   Tim Fish

Healdsburg, CA 95448; Tasting: Daily 10–5) Ferrari-Carano seems to be on every restaurant wine list in America. The chardonnay is its flagship, a big, lush, complex wine. The fumé blanc is also impressive in its own right, while the cabernet sauvignon and merlot are both solid efforts. Don and Rhonda Carano own the Eldorado Hotel and Casino in Reno, so their arrival in Wine Country has been a dramatic one. Situated in northern Dry Creek Valley, Ferrari-Carano is a bold statement. Villa Fiore, the winery's visitors' center, was completed in late 1994, and it's an extravagant Mediterranean palace surrounded by brushy lawns, flowers (more than 18,000 tulips bloom every spring), and vineyards. The tasting room has a faux marble floor and a mahogany and black-granite tasting bar. Visitors descend the limestone staircase to what is possibly the most opulent underground cellar in Wine Country.

FIELD STONE WINERY AND VINEYARDS (www.fieldstonewinery .com, 707-433-7266, 800-54-GRAPE, 10075 Hwy. 128, Healdsburg, CA 95448; Tasting: Daily 10–5) Cozy inside an Alexander Valley knoll, this winery takes its name from the rugged stone that decorates the facade. Open the wide wooden door, and amble past the oak barrels to the tasting room—and you've pretty much taken the tour. A house specialty is petite sirah from circa-1894 vines. It's a ripe bruiser. The cabernet sauvignon is also recommended. The picnic grounds are superb.

FOPPIANO VINEYARDS (www .foppiano.com, 707-433-7272, 12707 Old Redwood Hwy., Healdsburg, CA 95448; Tasting: Daily 10–4:30) Five generations of Foppianos have tended vines here. John Foppiano arrived from Genoa in 1896 and planted a vineyard. Wine was sold in bulk and, later, in jugs. The family began moving into premium wine in the 1970s. The winery is unabashedly utilitarian, and the tasting room is in an unassuming wood cottage. The self-guided vineyard tour is worth a few minutes. Foppiano's star is its beefy petite sirah made from old vines.

GARY FARRELL WINES (www.gary farrellwines.com, 707-473-2900, 10701 Westside Rd., Healdsburg, CA 95448; Tasting: Daily 10:30–4) While Gary Farrell has moved on to boutique winemaking with his Aylsian brand in Forestville, this winery is still making great pinot noir. The Farrell's style, which you can still taste on the palate, is elegant, complex, and fruit-forward. The winery has a knack for pinot noir, chardonnay, and zinfandel. Situated like a mission-style chapel on a hill above Russian River, the tasting room offers wide and glorious views of the surrounding landscape.

HANNA WINERY (www.hanna winery.com, 707-431-4310 ext 116, Tasting Room: 9280 Hwy. 128, Healds-burg, CA 95448; Tasting: Daily 10–4) Noted cardiac surgeon Elias Hanna went into the wine business in 1985. Since the winery is well off the tourist path, Hanna opened a tasting room in the heart of its Alexander Valley vine-yard. The building–a Frank Lloyd Wright-style pagoda–makes for a strik-ing image among the rolling hills. Hanna owns prime vineyard space around Sonoma County, and the best wines to date are its bright sauvignon blanc, its sleek pinot noir plus a solid chardonnay.

HOLDREDGE WINES (www .holdredge.com, 707-431-1424, 51 Front St., Healdsburg, CA 95448; Tast-ing: Sat.–Sun. 11–4:30 or by appoint-ment) What started as a hobby for John Holdredge turned into a second job. A Santa Rosa attorney by day, he's a winemaker, grape grower, and wine salesman during what's left of his 24 hours. Wife Carri at first indulged him and then joined the winery when he launched in 2001. Tasting is a low-key affair amid the barrels in the winery, a historic old redwood barn on the out-skirts of Healdsburg. Pinot noir is the main focus, but Holdredge also makes a little zinfandel and Syrah, and stylisti-cally the wines are concentrated, lush and complex.

HOP KILN WINERY (www.hopkiln winery.com, 707-433-6491, 6050 West-side Rd., Healdsburg, CA 95448; Tast-ing: Daily 10–5) Hop Kiln began life as an ode to beer, not wine. Hops were a major crop along Sonoma County's Russian River at the turn of the 20th century. This is one of the few rem-nants from that era. Built in 1905, the unusual stone barn is topped with three pyramid towers. The tasting room inside is rustic but pleasant, warm with wood and history. Tasters can choose from any number of wines and the winery specializes HKG Estate Grown Russian River Valley wines including award winning HKG Pinot Noir. These wines are delightful, espe-cially for a picnic. Outside, a small lake is bordered by a sunny patch of picnic tables—be prepared to share your lunch with the ducks.

J. FRITZ WINERY (www.fritzwinery .com, 707-894-3389, 800-418-9463, 24691 Dutcher Creek Rd., Cloverdale, CA 95425; Tasting: Daily 10:30–4:30) This winery, in the farthest reaches of northern Sonoma wine country, is built like a bunker into the side of hill. Well off the road and hidden amid the scrub trees, J. Fritz blends into the country-side. J. Fritz takes zinfandel quite seriously, and it relies on gnarly old vines to make a burly yet graceful zin. Pinot noir, chardonnay and sauvignon blanc, too, are generally fine examples; try the melon, a white that's easy to quaff.

J VINEYARDS AND WINERY
(www.jwine.com, 707-431-3646, 11447 Old Redwood Hwy., Healdsburg, CA 95448; Tasting: Daily 11–5) The large tasting room is a stylish bar with angular concrete walls and bold modern art, and the winery produces a steely Brut as well as first-rate still wines such as pinot noir, chardonnay and pinot gris (sometimes known as pinot grigio). Wine and food pairing at most wineries is a cracker with a smear of something but J does it right. By appointment only and at an additional cost, the tour takes place in the reserve room, also called the "Bubble Room," where you begin with a glass of bubbly and onto a progressive food and wine pairing, ending with decadent chocolates and dessert wine. Visitors tour the winery along a concrete balcony that overlooks the entire plant, where the *méthode champenoise,* the French technique of making sparkling wine, is detailed.

JORDAN VINEYARD & WINERY
(www.jordanwinery.com, 707-431-5250, 800-654-1213, 1474 Alexander Valley Rd., Healdsburg, CA 95448; Tasting and Tours: By appointment) This spectacular French-style chateau rose from a former prune orchard in the mid-1970s to become one of Sonoma County's premier wineries. Covered in ivy, the chateau seems like a grand classic, but inside it's a state-of-the-art winery. The forest of towering wood tanks in its aging room is an impressive sight. Jordan's cabernet sauvignon is elegant and ready to drink on release—one reason it's such a popular wine in

restaurants. The tour explores the lush gardens, 18 acres of Olive trees and the winemaking facility.

LA CREMA WINERY (www.lacrema .com, 707-431-9400, Tasting Room: 235 Healdsburg Ave., Healdsburg, CA 95448; Tasting: Daily 10:30–5:30) La Crema has a long history in Sonoma County and has seen good times and bad, but the winery is now making some of its best wines to date. Pinot noir and chardonnay dominate the lineup. Both are typical plush and fruit-forward wines, and while prices have been creeping up in recent vintages, the cost-versus-quality ratio remains good. Part of the Jess Jackson family of wines, La Crema has a winery in West County but runs this smart-looking tasting room just off the Healdsburg plaza.

LAMBERT BRIDGE WINERY
(www.lambertbridge.com, 707-431-9600, 800-975-0555, 4085 W. Dry Creek Rd., Healdsburg, CA 95448; Tasting: Daily 10:30–4:30) Quaint is a woefully abused word, but we can't think of a better way to describe Lambert Bridge. Open since 1975, Lambert Bridge has maintained a low profile. This romantic little winery, with redwood siding and a porch shaded by wisteria, is a comfortable fit among the oaks and vines covering the hillsides overlooking Dry Creek. Inside, it's a comfortable space done in rich, dark wood. Merlot and chardonnay are specialties. There's a delightful picnic area out front, making this one of the best wineries around for a casual lunch.

LONGBOARD VINEYARDS (www .longboardvineyards.com, 707-433-3473, 5 Fitch St., Healdsburg, CA 95448; Tasting: Thurs.–Sat., 11–7; Sun. 11–5) A surfer tried and true, Oded Shakked named his winery after his surfboard of choice. In his mind, both surfing and winemaking require balance, harmony, and a respect for nature. A beach bum born near Tel Aviv, Shakked studied winemaking in California and for many years made bubbly at J Wine Co. before launching his own winery a few years back. The tasting room, inside a warehouse near downtown, is a hangout for surfer and wine drinkers alike. Merlot and cabernet are the specialties, but Shakked also makes a tasty Syrah and sauvignon blanc.

MAZZOCCO VINEYARDS (www .mazzocco.com, 707-431-8159, 800-501-8466, 1400 Lytton Springs Rd., Healdsburg, CA 95448; Tasting: Daily 11–5) This winery is hardly a visual treat, but it occupies prime zinfandel land. Founded by Tom Mazzocco in 1984, the winery has weathered ups and downs, but one constant has remained: great zinfandel—big and spicy, yet with considerable finesse. Cabernet sauvignon, sauvignon blanc, petite sirah, and chardonnay also have charm.

MEDLOCK AMES (www.medlock ames.com, tastingroom@medlock ames.com, 707-431-8845, 3487 Alexander Valley Rd., Healdsburg, CA; Tasting: Daily 10–5; Alexander Valley Bar: 707-431-1904; Open daily from 5 pm) What was once a century-old bar and store, is now a tasting room and bar extraordinaire. Medlock Ames's tasting room offers a full slate of wines and a glimpse of its earthy roots with homemade preserves, pickles and organic produce lining the walls. Certified organic, Medlock Ames has sustainable farming practices, using solar power, driving electric and biodiesel vehicles, deploying weed-eating sheep, and growing blocks of vegetables that they sell to local chefs. The vintners produce cabernet, pinot noir, merlot, red blends, rose, chardonnay and sauvignon blanc. There's not a bad wine in the lot, but the sauvignon blanc is particularly good. The Alexander Valley Bar offers another good place to sip on the property, and it's colorful, a cross between a saloon and a modern-day cocktail den.

MILL CREEK VINEYARDS (www .millcreekwinery.com, 707-431-2121, 1401 Westside Rd., Healdsburg, CA 95448; Tasting: Daily 10–5) It's hard to miss this tasting room, a redwood barn with a waterwheel. The Kreck family has been growing grapes since 1965 and bottled their first wine with the 1974 vintage. Mill Creek helped pioneer merlot but is not among the masters. Sauvignon blanc is the winery's best effort, and it's a delightful companion for a picnic on the winery's deck. Other wines include cabernet, zinfandel, and chardonnay.

MURPHY-GOODE TASTING ROOM (www.murphygoode.com, 1-800-499-7644, 20 Matheson St., Healdsburg, CA; Tasting: Daily 10:30–5:30) Murphy-Goode's tasting room is just off the historic Healdsburg Square and it's worth a stop. The winery has access to some of the best vineyards in Alexander Valley, and it shows in their wines. The house specialty is a crisp and complex fumé blanc, but Murphy-Goode—which is now owned by Kendall-Jackson—manages with finesse every wine, from an elegant cabernet sauvignon to a fruity zin.

MUTT LYNCH (www.muttlynch winery.com, 707-942-6180, 602 Limerick Ln., Healdsburg, CA; Tasting: By appointment) This winery claims to be the most dog-friendly in wine country with brands like Mutt Zinfandel and Unleashed Chardonnay. It also offers a

Yappy Hour with appetizers for humans and snacks for dogs. Check its website for the latest events. As *Dog Fancy* magazine puts it, "With the exception of Paris, you'd be hard pressed to find a more canine-inclusive place to sip wine in Sonoma County." The vintners use the money earned at dog-friendly events to benefit local animal-rescue organizations.

PAPAPIETRO PERRY WINERY (www.papapietro-perry.com, 707-433-0422, 4791 Dry Creek Rd., Healdsburg, CA 95448; Tasting: Daily 11–4:30) The winery name may be a little hard to pronounce, but you'll have no trouble drinking the wines. Ben Papapietro and Bruce Perry were bitten by the bug way back in the 1970s, when they used to help out at harvest at Williams Selyem Winery. After making their own homemade wine for years, they started the winery in 1998. Zinfandel and pinot noir are their passions, and these wines are ripe and richly structured. The winery and tasting room are located just off Dry Creek Road amid a rural complex of small producers.

PRESTON OF DRY CREEK (www.prestonvineyards.com, 707-433-3372, 800-305-9707, 9206 W. Dry Creek Rd., Healdsburg, CA 95448; Tasting: Daily 11–4:30) On the northern edge of Dry Creek Valley, this out-of-the-way winery has been quietly redefining itself in recent years. Lou and Susan Preston began as growers in 1973, specializing in grapes cherished by old Italian farmers: zinfandel and sauvignon blanc. A winery followed two years later, and Preston made its name with zinfandel and sauvignon blanc, but Rhone varietals have taken on importance in recent years. The tasting room of this grand California barn was expanded a few years back, and there's a plush lawn for picnicking just off the tasting room porch. An olive oil and bread fanatic, Lou Preston has his own bakery on the property and olive trees are scattered around the site.

QUIVIRA VINEYARDS (www.quivirawine.com, 707-431-8333, 800-292-8339, 4900 W. Dry Creek Rd., Healdsburg, CA 95448; Tasting: Daily 11–5) Quivira was a wealthy kingdom of legend that explorers believed was hidden in what is now Sonoma County. Though the name belongs to antiquity, this Quivira is a modern winery inside and out, and Quivira's zinfandel, sauvignon blanc and Rhone varietals are worth checking out.

RIDGE VINEYARDS (www.ridgewine.com, 707-433-7721, 650 Lytton Springs Rd., Healdsburg, CA; Tasting: Daily 11–4) This Sonoma County outpost of the popular Santa Cruz Mountain producer was once exclusively a destination for zinfandel lovers but now the winery has become part of the attraction. Environmentally friendly, it has a smooth, contemporary construction that was done with recycled lumber and straw bale-insulated walls. Solar panels produce up to 75 percent of the winery's energy. Ridge produces most of its zinfandels on the property, and there's a range offered for tasting. Be sure to sip the Lytton Springs bottling as you gaze out the window to the thick-fingered, century year-old vines that produced it.

ROCHIOLI VINEYARDS & WINERY (www.rochioliwinery.com, 707-433-2305, 6192 Westside Rd., Healdsburg, CA 95448; Tasting: Daily 11–4) The pinot noir vineyards of Rochioli are the envy of all winemakers. The top pinots in the business—Gary Farrell, Williams Selyem, and, of course, Rochioli (pronounced row-key-OH-lee)—begin here. Three generations of Rochiolis have been growing grapes along the Russian River. They stay close to the land, and because of that, they make great wine. In the modest tasting room, which looks out across vineyards toward the river, every wine is a winner. The chardonnay is ripe apple with crisp acidity and the sauvignon blanc, flowery and complex.

RODNEY STRONG VINEYARDS (www.rodneystrong.com, 707-431-1533, 800-678-4763, 11455 Old Redwood Hwy., Healdsburg, CA 95448; Tasting: Daily 10–5) A dramatic pyramid of concrete and wood, this winery has weathered many incarnations and owners over the years but it seems to be coming into its own again. The wines are reliable and frequently superb, with cabernet sauvignon, chardonnay, and pinot noir among the standouts. Balconies outside the tasting room overlook the tanks and oak barrels, so a tour may be academic.

SEGHESIO WINERY (www.seghesio .com, 707-433-3579, 14730 Grove St., Healdsburg, CA 95448; Tasting: Daily 10–5) Moving into its fourth generation, the great-grandsons of Italian immigrant Edoardo Seghesio are continuing the legacy that he began in 1895. The family owns more than 400 acres in Sonoma County, and the winery produces many Italian-style varieties such as sangiovese, barbera, pinot grigio, and arneis, but it's known for its supple yet intense zinfandel. The Tuscan-style tasting room is shaded by tall trees.

SAUSAL WINERY (www.sausalwinery .com, 707-433-2285, 800-500-2285, 7370 Hwy. 128, Healdsburg, CA, 95448; Tasting: Daily 10–4) Zinfandel is the top dog at this small winery. The Demostene family bought the ranch back in 1956 and inherited a plot of zinfandel that was planted before 1877. They began bottling in 1974, and specialize in the Old Vine Zinfandel which is full-bodied yet smooth. The tasting room sits snugly among the vineyards, and the vine-covered patio is a soothing spot to sip.

SIMI WINERY (www.simiwinery.com, 707-433-6981, 16275 Healdsburg Ave., Healdsburg, CA 95448; Tasting: Daily 10–5) If we had to choose only one winery to visit—akin to limiting yourself to one glass of champagne on New Year's Eve—that would be a tough call, but we vote for Simi, an alluring combination of history and high-tech. You

Brothers Pete and Ted Seghesio of Seghesio Winery and Seghesio Winery's old-vine zin.

never feel you're being herded through a factory, even though the winery is hardly small. The staff knows wine but doesn't lord it over you. And best of all: The wines are first-rate. Simi changed hands and is now owned by wine giant Icon Estates. Simi gives one of the best tours, offering peeks at everything from the oak-barrel aging room to the bottling line. The tasting room is a cordial spot. Try the sauvignon blanc, chardonnay, always delightful, and the impressive cabernet sauvignons. Summer brings a taste of authentic Italy to Simi's Pizza Café, now open May to October, Friday's 2 pm–6 pm. Enjoy good wine and New York style Pizza made to order from their hot brick oven. Life just doesn't get better than this.

UNTI VINEYARDS (www.unti vineyards.com, 707-433-5590, 4202 Dry Creek Rd., Healdsburg, CA 95448; Tasting: By appointment) One of the charms about driving through the back roads of Sonoma County is discovering a small winery such as Unti that sells most of its wine out the door. The Unti family began growing grapes in 1990 and started making wine in 1997. The winery is as basic as it gets— the "tasting room" is a plywood counter topped by polished stainless steel. Unti lets the wine do the talking, and the wines are intense and authentic. The zinfandel is elegant in the classic Dry Creek Valley style, and the grenache and barbera are full of personality. This place is a gem.

WILSON WINERY (www.wilson winery.com, 707-433-4355, 800-433-4602, 1960 Dry Creek Rd. Healdsburg, CA; Tasting: Daily 11–5) The Wilson family owns more than 220 acres of prime Dry Creek hillside vineyards, and that's part of the key to the winery's success. Wilson makes a wide range of wines but zinfandel is the strong suit, as you might expect, because that's Dry Creek's specialty. The zins here are powerful and peppery. The winery is in an old tin barn, a local landmark, and the tasting room in the backside of the barn offers a soothing view of the surrounding vineyards.

Geyserville

CLOS DU BOIS (www.closdubois.com, 707-857-3100, 800-222-3189, 19410 Geyserville Ave., Geyserville, CA 95441; Tasting: Daily 10–4:30) Clos du Bois, one of Sonoma's largest and most prominent wineries, seems to do everything well and a few things superbly. It may not produce big flashy wines, but its offerings are seldom disappointing—which is surprising, considering the larger roster of wines that range from values to collectibles. Vineyards are key to this success; the winery has access to some 1,000 prime acres in Alexander and Dry Creek valleys. The Calcaire chardonnay is a lush, Burgundian, fruit driven wine with minimal butter and oak, though we often prefer the straightforward character of the regular chardonnay. The cabernet sauvignons and merlots are generally impressive. The tasting room is a friendly spot, and the staff is knowledgeable, yet it never rolls an eye over novice questions.

DE LORIMIER WINERY (www.mosaicvineyards.com, www.delorimier winery.com, 800-546-7718, 2001 Hwy. 128, Geyserville, CA 95441; Tasting: Daily 10–4:30) Set amid a sea of vines in the north end of Alexander Valley, this winery—a modern barn with brown shingles—is well off the beaten path. It dates to 1986, when surgeon Alfred de Lorimier decided to make wine with the grapes he'd been growing for years. The biggest successes are sauvignon blanc. De Lorimier's latest focus is on Bordeaux blends and single vineyard cabernet sauvignon. The winery is owned by the Wilson Family (of Wilson Winery), which also owns Matrix, Mazzocco Vineyards, and Jackson Keys in Mendocino.

FRANCIS FORD COPPOLA WINERY (www.franciscoppolawinery .com, 707-857-1400, 1-877-590-3329, 300 Via Archimedes, Geyserville, CA; Tasting: Daily 11–6) This dramatic chalet, inspired by the old hop kilns that once spread across the Russian River Valley, was once Chateau Souverain but is now home to Francis Ford Coppola's new winery. Coppola is experimenting with a new family-oriented approach: "a wine wonderland." He's creating a resort-style wine experience for the entire family with a pool near the tasting room, boccie courts, a movie gallery, and more. Coppola, the Academy Award–winning director best known for the films *The Godfather* trilogy and *Apocalypse Now,* said: "When we began to develop the idea for this winery, we thought it should be like a resort, basically a wine wonderland, a park of pleasure where people of all ages can enjoy the best things in life." No age discrimination here. Check out the live music on Sundays and the zucchini fries at Rustic, the winery's full-service restaurant. The winery makes a full slate of wines, with the Diamond Series and the Director's Cut brands two of the best.

GEYSER PEAK WINERY (www .geyserpeakwinery.com, 707-857-2500, 800-255-WINE, 22281 Chianti Rd., Geyserville, CA 95441; Tasting: Daily 10–5) This winery went through a golden era in the 1990s, but production has expanded, and in recent vintages the wines have been good but not up to the old standards. Founded in 1880 by

Augustus Quitzow, the winery is a complex of buildings both old and new. The main, ivy-covered building has a commanding view of Alexander Valley. In the tasting room, the staff pours selections from Geyser Peak's large repertoire. Don't miss the Shiraz and cabernet sauvignon.

PEDRONCELLI WINERY (www .pedroncelli.com, 707-857-3531, 800-836-3894, 1220 Canyon Rd., Geyserville, CA 95441; Tasting: Daily 10–4:30) One of Sonoma County's oldest wineries—its origins date to 1904—Pedroncelli is also an old reliable. The winery and tasting room are agreeable but not elaborate. The wines are solid, though modestly scaled, and the prices are fair. Two generations of Pedroncellis tend the place. Try the cabernet sauvignon, sauvignon blanc, and zinfandel—all nicely done.

ROBERT YOUNG ESTATE WINERY (www.ryew.com, 707-431-4811, 4960 Red Winery Road, Geyserville, CA 95441; Tasting: Daily 10–4:30) Back in the early 1960s, many people thought Robert Young was crazy for planting a 14-acre cabernet vineyard in an old prune orchard, but he did it anyway and helped revive Alexander Valley as a wine region. These days, the Young family has 300 acres of vines, and after watching wineries such as Chateau St. Jean win medals with their grapes, they started making their own in 1997. The winery, appropriately, is in an old prune barn, and the tasting room is little more than a simple counter, but the chardonnay and cabernet are wonderful examples of how some places are uniquely suited for grape growing.

SILVER OAK CELLARS (www.silver oak.com, 707-857-3562, 800-273-8809, 24625 Chianti Rd., Geyserville, CA

95441; Tasting: Mon.–Sat. 9–5 and 11–5 Sun.) Cabernet sauvignon specialist Silver Oak considers Napa home, but it made its reputation on Alexander Valley cabernet. Consider this Silver Oak West. The winery, with its steeply pitched roof and flagstone courtyard, remains an elegant spot. While only the Alexander Valley bottling is produced here, all of Silver Oak's wines are poured when available.

TRENTADUE WINERY (www.trentadue.com, 707-433-3104, 888-332-3032, 19170 Geyserville Ave., Geyserville, CA 95441; Tasting: Daily 10–5) Trentadue makes Arnold Schwarzenegger wines: massive, muscular reds that won't be taken lightly. The Trentadue family has been making wine since 1969, favoring hearty classic Tuscan varietals such as carignane and sangiovese. After a spotty history, wine quality here took a leap in the 1990s. The tasting room is packed with gifts and picnic supplies, which you can put to fine use on the trellis-covered picnic patio. A fun feature is the tractor-powered gondola tour of the property. You can even taste wines along the way.

Especially for Sonoma County travelers with canine companions

The welcome mat is definitely out for you and your pup in Sonoma County. If dog is your copilot, you'll both enjoy these spots.

Mutt Lynch (p. 150) The dog-friendliest winery in Wine Country offers a Yappy Hour, with appetizers for humans and snacks for dogs. Check www.muttlynchwinery.com for the latest events.

Three Dog Bakery (p. 182) A professional chef bakes dog-friendly goodies without salt or refined sugar; treats are sweetened with applesauce or honey.

Palate Adventures

Great wine shops, coffee shops, and even a tasty taqueria.

• *Start the day off right*
Downtown Bakery and Creamery (www.downtownbakery.net, 707-431-2719, 308A Center St., Healdsburg, CA 95448) There are fabulous desserts here, but it doesn't look like much as you walk in. What's the secret? The Chez Panisse connection. Owner Kathleen Stewart is a veteran of that famed Berkeley kitchen. Tortes and cakes are ungodly delicious, as are the sticky buns, the monster Fig Newton–like cookies, galettes, and the blueberry scones. Don't miss the famous donut muffins, which were featured on the Food Network's *The Best Thing I Ever Ate* in February 2010. Breakfast is available Friday through Monday, and sandwiches, such as turkey on focaccia with homemade mayonnaise, are available for lunch. They also have great coffee and ice cream. Enjoy their new indoor seating or the downtown plaza across the street.

Flying Goat Coffee Roastery (707-433-9081, 324 Center St., Healdsburg, CA 95448; 419 Center St., Healdsburg, 95448) Here's a stylish spot for a cup of java. Have a muffin while you smell the roaster at work.

Café Newsstand (707-922-5233, 301 Healdsburg Ave., Healdsburg, CA 95448) Here, there's a modern, clean feel, and the sleepy-eyed reach for their

Treats galore at the Downtown Bakery and Creamery.

first cup of coffee and read the news of the day, although it's a worthy stop any time past morning. Coffee, panini sandwiches, and homemade ice cream are offered. The newsstand features more than two hundred different magazines and newspapers.

• Indulge your appetite for authentic Mexican
Ignore the atmosphere at Taqueria El Sombrero (707-433-3818, 245 Center St., Healdsburg, CA 95448) and relish the food just off the plaza. It uses whole beans, not canned refrieds, and grilled meat.

• Savor the ambience while you sample the fare
Dry Creek General Store (707-433-4171, 3495 Dry Creek Rd., Healdsburg, CA 95448) A few years back, Gina Gallo of Gallo of Sonoma Winery purchased this rural gathering spot, a landmark of Sonoma's rustic heritage. Keep your eye out for fancy trappings such as a wine rack and gourmet goodies amid the rustic charm. Drop into this charming country store for a delicious deli sandwich or simply enjoy a glass of local wine or a nice cold beer at the bar. In the summer on Thursday nights, don't miss the General's Store BBQ starting at 6:30 pm.

Jimtown Store (707-433-1212, 6706 Hwy. 128, Healdsburg, CA 95448) An Alexander Valley landmark for a century, this former general store and gas depot, which had been abandoned for years, was resuscitated in 1991 with a touch of gourmet chic. Today, Carrie Brown's Jimtown Store remains quaint yet sophisticated, drawing national attention along the way. Sandwiches are first-rate, and the aisles include old-fashioned candy, old-fashioned sodas, baked goods, antiques, toys, and memorabilia. Enjoy wine sold by the glass or bottle as you browse.

Insider Secret:
Breakfast at the **Downtown Bakery & Creamery** should include pancakes. Chef Kathleen Stewart tested countless recipes when she was writing an article for *Fine Cooking* magazine, and the rejects got tossed on Stewart's back patio, a feast for the pigeons, which, it turns out, weren't picky. The pancakes now served at the bakery made the final cut. (Breakfast served Friday through Monday.)

Oakville Grocery (707-433-3200, 124 Matheson St., Healdsburg, CA 95448) Napa Valley invaded Sonoma with this satellite of the successful upscale grocery. Goodies include duck pâté, cold cuts, cheese, olives, fresh produce, and artisan breads. Order a sandwich or pizza or a rotisserie chicken. There's even wine available by the glass. Take the food with you or eat on the patio. During the summer months of June to August, Oakville Grocery serves paella for Tuesday night's music on the plaza. Paella is a Spanish saffron-flavored dish containing rice, meat, seafood, and vegetables.

Plaza Farms (106 Matheson St., Healdsburg, CA 95448) A delightful spot on the Healdsburg square with a range of tasty purveyors such as DaVero Olive Oil, Bellwether Farm Cheese, and Tandem Winery. Not to be missed is Bovolo, the café in the back, which makes everything from scratch from pizzas and gelato to its signature pork dishes (see entry under Restaurants).

• Head to the town square for one-stop sipping
Who needs a designated driver when you can sip on the square? There are tasting rooms aplenty, some old and some new. Here are the latest: Boisset Taste of Terroir, 320 Center St., www.boissettasteofterroir.com, 707-473-9707; Edmeades Tasting Room, 20 Matheson St., www.edmeades.com, 707-857-1528; Healdsburg Tasting Room, 337 Healdsburg Ave., www.kj.com/visit/healdsburg-tastingroom/, 707-433-7102; Murphy Goode, 20 Matheson St., www.murphygoodewinery.com, 707-431-7644; La Crema, 235 Healdsburg Ave., www.lacrema.com, 707-431-9400; Thumbprint Cellars, 102 Matheson St., www.thumbprintcellar.com, 707-433-2397; Vintage Wine Estates, 308 B Center St., www.vintagewineestates.com, 707-921-2893.

Affronti (235 Healdsburg Ave., www.affrontihealdsburg.com, 707-431-1113) is a savvy wine bar with bar bites and small plates that won't break the bank. Appetizers include mushroom, bacon, and thyme tartine and sundried tomato, gorgonzola, and walnuts bruschetta. The wine bar offers handcrafted Sonoma selections, Southern European imports, and a splash of Lake and Mendocino County wines; 20-plus wines are poured by the glass, and the bar also offers locally made microbrews on tap. *Affronti* means "the place," and this is a worthy one.

Bear Republic Brewing Co. (345 Healdsburg Ave., www.bearrepublic.com, 707-433-Beer) This brewery may be Healdsburg's hottest nightspot, featuring food, live music, and some excellent handcrafted beers. The Scottish-style Red Rocket Ale is a specialty, and they also make a yummy Hefeweizen (pronounced HEF-ay-vite-zen), a light German brew perfect for a warm summer day. The atmosphere is lively, and from your table or the bar, you can watch brewing at work. As for the food, stick with the basic pub fare—burgers etc.—and you won't go wrong.

• Take part in a Wine Country ritual

Barrel Tasting along the Wine Road (www.wineroad.com, 707-433-4335, Russian River Wine Rd., countryside surrounding Healdsburg, CA) Typically the first spring event of the wine season, barrel tasting helps lift wine lovers out of the winter doldrums. Besides, everyone loves a sneak preview of wine that hasn't been bottled yet. There are 100-plus wineries pour samples.

To Do

Check out these great attractions and activities . . .

SHOPPING

Once you take a close look at Healdsburg, you realize that it's an interesting mix: countrified chic, cosmopolitan, yet down to earth—more Land Rover than BMW. Here's a look at Healdsburg's quaint town-square primo shopping. Our favorites: Copperfield's Books (707-433-9270, 104 Matheson St., Healdsburg, CA 95448) provides locals and tourists alike with thousands of titles to choose from. Levin & Co. (707-433-1118, 306 Center St., Healdsburg, CA 95448) is a lively shop that caters to the book and music lover, specializing in the classics and quality fiction. Clutch (707-433-8189, www.clutch healdsburg.com, 307 Healdsburg Ave., Healdsburg, CA 95448) features men's and women's accessories. M Clothing (707-431-8738, 381 Healdsburg Ave., Healdsburg, CA 95448) has hip, smart clothing for women, with lines that include

Sweet treats at Powell's Sweet Shoppe.

Nanette Lepore and Diane Von Furstenberg. Circe (707-433-8482, 311 Healdsburg Ave., Healdsburg, CA 95448) is an upscale women's clothing store with lines including Luna Luz and Ivan Grundahl. Susan Graf Limited (707-433-6495, 100 Matheson St., Healdsburg, CA 95448) carries upscale women's clothing, with lines such as Kate Spade and Delman. Saint Dizier Home (707-473-0980, 259 Center St., Healdsburg, CA 95448) features Ralph Lauren Collection furnishings, with some Henredon furniture in stock. Francophiles will want to step into Myra Hoefer Design (707-433-2166, 309 Healdsburg Ave., Healdsburg, CA 95448). Hoefer is the designer-owner and this shop carries mostly French or French-inspired antiques and accessories. Fideaux (707-433-9935, 43 North St., Healdsburg, CA 95448) caters to cats and dogs with whimsical items that include wine-barrel doghouses and breed-specific clocks. Powell's Sweet Shoppe (707-431-2784, 322 Center St., Healdsburg, CA 95448) has the feel of an old-time candy store, but it also carries toys and gelato. Options (707-431-8861, 126 Matheson St., Healdsburg, CA 95448) has a clear sense of style, and it's stocked with one-of-a-kind items and sophisticated collectibles. Look for jewelry, furniture, baskets, pottery, and ceramics. Galeria Two-O-Six (707-431-1234, 111 Mill St., Healdsburg, CA 95448) carries the work of more than 80 local artists and offers custom-designed furniture, with a focus on the kitchen and bathroom. Plaza Gourmet (707-433-7116, 108 Matheson St., Healdsburg, CA 95448) could outfit Martha Stewart's kitchen. It has a wide range of kitchenware, tableware, books, and candles.

CULTURAL OUTINGS

• *See it*

Raven Film Center (707-433-6335, 415 Center St., Healdsburg, CA 95448) The main Raven Theater is easily the finest movie house in Wine Country, but sadly, the downtown Healdsburg theater seldom shows films these days. Four smaller theaters were added behind the original theater, and they show first-run movies and the occasional art film.

Erickson Fine Art Gallery (707-431-7073, 324 Healdsburg Ave., Healdsburg, CA 95448) This attractive gallery is just off the square in downtown Healdsburg. It has a fine collection of serious art with only a smattering of frivolous landscapes.

Healdsburg Museum (707-431-3325, 221 Matheson St., Healdsburg, CA 95448; Tues.–Sun., 11–4) This museum is devoted to early Healdsburg and Northern Sonoma County history, including Indian artifacts and fifteen thousand photographs.

• *Hear it*

Healdsburg Plaza Tuesday Concert Series (707-433-6935, downtown Healdsburg, CA 95448) Held June through August, this series offers an eclectic array of music and livens Tuesday afternoons from 6 to 8 PM on this lovely plaza.

Rodney Strong Music Series (707-433-0919, 11455 Old Redwood Hwy., Healdsburg, CA 95448) There's a summer-long series of concerts on this winery's lawn.

Bear Republic Brewing Co. (707-433-BEER, 345 Healdsburg Ave., Healdsburg, CA) makes excellent handcrafted beers, and has music occasionally during the summer. Karaoke on Thursdays is popular during the winter.

Best Day in Sonoma County

Our tour of Sonoma County finds its base in Healdsburg. Here we set you up with a 24-hour itinerary, featuring wine tasting, a massage and swim, dinner at the most reputable place in Sonoma County, and a nightcap fit for a diva.

1. Naturally, we begin with a scrumptious breakfast to get ourselves percolating with caffeine: **Downtown Bakery and Creamery** (Healdsburg; www.downtownbakery.net) Tortes and cakes are ungodly delicious, as are the sticky buns, the monster Fig Newton–like cookies, and the blueberry scones.

The Prohibition Speakeasy Wine Bar is a great way to cap off the day.

2. Next up, wine tasting, of course. Here are two great options:

Seghesio (Healdsburg; www.seghesio.com) The winery produces many Italian-style varieties such as sangiovese, barbera, pinot grigio, and arneis, but it's known for its supple yet intense zinfandel.

Francis Ford Coppola Winery (Geyserville; www.franciscoppolawinery.com) A resort-style wine experience for the entire family, with a pool near the tasting room, boccie courts, a movie gallery, and more.

3. Lunch at a place that stocks both gourmet food and memorabilia: **Jimtown Store** (Healdsburg; www.jimtown.com). An Alexander Valley landmark for a century, this former general store and gas depot was resuscitated in 1991 with a touch of gourmet chic. Today, Carrie Brown's Jimtown Store remains quaint yet sophisticated, drawing national attention along the way. Sandwiches are first-rate, and the aisles are full of old-fashioned candy, toys, and memorabilia.

4. Unwind. Have a massage and swim at the **Spa Hotel Healdsburg** (Healdsburg; www.hotelhealdsburg.com). There's an understated sophistication to this spa, which is secluded deep inside this downtown hotel. Treatments range from pedicures to facials to hot stone massages and detoxifying seaweed wraps. Guests have access to a whirlpool tub and pool.

5. Go first class at the most highly regarded restaurant in Sonoma County, **Cyrus** (Healdsburg; www.cyrusrestaurant.com). It's not only the top restaurant in Sonoma County, it's one of the best in Northern California, giving competition to the French Laundry across the mountain.

6. Go for a nightcap at **Barn Diva** (Healdsburg; www.barndiva.com), where you can order exotic cocktails until 11 PM. in a rustic-chic cedar barn. The drinks and the decor charm.

7. End the day at **Honor Mansion** (Healdsburg; www.honormansion.com), named one of the most romantic inns by American Historic Inns. Tomorrow you'll enjoy a full gourmet breakfast, with complimentary mimosas.

Raven Performing Arts Theater (www.raventheater.org, 707-433-5448, 115 North St., Healdsburg, CA 95448) This venue stages musical acts—everything from rap to Bo Diddley and Taj Mahal—as well as dance and theatrical performance. Check website for current offerings.

RECREATIONAL FUN

• *Go down to the river*
Because the Pacific Ocean is chilly and the surf is a bit rugged, the Russian River is a good alternative for a leisure day on the water. During the hot summer, riverside beaches are popular with families who enjoy swimming in the refreshing water while canoes glide past. Canoes and kayaks can be rented near Healdsburg or Guerneville for a leisurely trip, with stops to relax or swim along the way. Don't be surprised if you spot a few nude sunbathers. The county doesn't condone it, but the freewheeling '60s still live in West County. River's Edge (800-345-0869, www.riversedgekayakandcanoe.com, 13840 Healdsburg Ave., CA 95488) offers two-day, full-day, and half-day trips down the river. Its Web site details each trip.

• *Commune with nature*
Lake Sonoma (707-433-9483, 3333 Skaggs Spring Rd., Healdsburg CA; near Dry Creek Road) Forty miles of trails wind through the 3,600 acres of redwood groves and oak woodlands surrounding Sonoma's newest man-made lake. A visitors' center is located at the base of the dam. There are also camping, boating, swimming, and a fish hatchery.

• *Court Lady Luck*
River Rock Casino (www.riverrockcasino.com, 3250 Highway 128, Geyserville, CA. 05441) is a quirky place in Wine Country. The tribal-owned casino has slot machines featuring classics like video poker, and offers everything from penny slots to $100 pulls.

• *Luxuriate*
A Simple Touch (www.asimpletouchspa.com, 707-433-6856, 239C Center St., Healdsburg, CA.) An intimate spot just off the Healdsburg square, this spa is a welcome addition to northern Sonoma County. With a large tub room, one couple's room and two treatment rooms, Simple Touch offers individual care. The lobby welcomes you with warm tones, a bit of Tuscany. Mud baths are fango style—a light and warm chocolate—milklike blend of mineral water and powdered mud. There are champagne baths as well as herbal facials, Swedish deep tissue massage, sports massage, and hot rocks massage.

Spa at Hotel Healdsburg (www.hotelhealdsburg.com, 707-433-4747, 327 Healdsburg Ave., Healdsburg, CA) There's an understated sophistication to this spa, which is secluded deep inside this downtown hotel. There are six treatment rooms, and the décor blends soothing colors with plantation shutters and pecan word floors. Guests have access to a whirlpool tub and pool. Treatments range from pedicures and facials to hot stone massages and detoxifying seaweed wraps.

7

City of Sonoma

THE OLD WORLD-STYLE Sonoma Plaza is the heart of a family-friendly downtown, and buildings like the Sebastiani Theatre, circa 1933, speak of a less complicated time. The central plaza is arguably the most charming of all town squares in Wine Country. It's an 8-acre park with two ponds, populated with ducks and geese, a play structure, and a rose garden. Shops, galleries, coffeehouses, and tasting rooms line the streets adjacent to the square.

On a historical note, the Bear Flag Monument is the place where the Bear Flag was raised in 1846, proclaiming the end of Mexican rule. The monument has a backdrop of lush greenery, and there are plenty of kids roaming the grounds, with mothers nursing lattes not far behind. There is a laid-back, lazy-Sunday-afternoon feel to the square at all times, which is particularly appealing to tourists who come to Wine Country to revive themselves, to take a hiatus from their cell phones, to be unreachable, off the grid.

> **Insider Secret:**
> The vintners of **Benziger Family Winery** in Glen Ellen are brothers, known in these parts as the "Bad, Bad Benziger Boys." They take the stage at the Sonoma Valley Harvest Wine Auction every year with a sexy skit to introduce their lot, which features a summer bash at their winery. (www.benziger.com)

Checking In

Best places to stay in and around Sonoma.

Now for choosing that special spot to stay. In Sonoma, there are plenty of options. Do you want a resort-like setting or a bed & breakfast? Is it crucial to have a spa on the premises? We're here to help.

LEFT: Mission San Francisco Solano is one of the most popular historic attractions in Wine Country. Tim Fish

BELTANE RANCH (www.beltane ranch.com, 707-996-6501, 11775 Sonoma Hwy., Glen Ellen, CA 95442; Price: Expensive) This former bunkhouse was built in 1890 and has been everything from a turkey farm to a historic farmhouse with ties to the Underground Railroad. The ranch was even rumored to be a brothel, but now it's a quiet and unpretentious B&B. It sits on 1,600 acres of land, amid vineyards and olive trees. (The inn even raises its own grass-feed beef, makes its own Beltane Ranch Olive Oil, and released for the first time this year a sauvignon blanc that was well received by *Wine Spectator*). A full breakfast featuring the inn's own produce and farm-raised eggs is served in the wood-paneled dining room or on the wraparound veranda. An added bonus is the remarkable hiking trail on the property, which takes you past vineyards.

BUNGALOWS 313 (www.bungalows 313.com, 707-996-8091, 313 1st St. E., Sonoma, CA 95476; Price: Expensive to Very Expensive) Located just a half block from the Sonoma Plaza, this inn is near the best restaurants, shops, and historical sites but is hidden in a secluded compound. There's a lovely little garden with a stone fountain, perfect for relaxing in a chair with a good book. There are five bungalows in all, each with a kitchenette and a distinct personality and modern furnishings. Dolce bungalow and Vita bungalow both have two-story lofts, and each overlooks a private garden.

THE COTTAGE INN AND SPA/THE MISSION BED-AND-BREAKFAST (www.cottageinnand spa.com, 707-996-0719, 800-944-1490, 310 1st St. E., Sonoma, CA 95476; Price: Expensive to Very Expensive) These two inns are side by side on 1st Street East, not far from the downtown plaza, but still a quiet oasis. A Mediterranean-style courtyard is enclosed by a high stucco wall and features a fountain and whirlpool. Many have private entries or patios; some have fireplaces and whirlpool baths. Fresh-baked goodies are delivered each morning, allowing guests a private continental breakfast.

EL DORADO HOTEL (www.hotel eldoradosonoma.com, 707-996-3220, 800-289-3031, 405 1st St. W., Sonoma, CA 95476; Price: Expensive) The El Dorado is a special hotel. Restored to its original elegance, it has 27 rooms, all with private baths. The hotel offers four street-level bungalows for easy entry and are handicapped-accessible. The lobby restaurant, El Dorado Kitchen, serves California cuisine.

FAIRMONT SONOMA MISSION INN AND SPA (www.fairmont /sonoma.com, 707-938-9000, 800-441-1414, 100 Boyes Blvd., Sonoma, CA 95476; Price: Very Expensive) Sonoma County's premier hotel, and now part of the prestigious Fairmont chain, the Sonoma Mission completed an impressive $60 million facelift in 2005. The inn was built on a site once considered a sacred healing ground by Native Americans. By the turn of the 20th century, the area had become a getaway for well-heeled San Franciscans, who came to the Sonoma hotel to "take the waters." The spa has also received

---

Insider Secret:

In Wine Country, celebrity sightings abound, especially at the **Fairmont Sonoma Mission Inn & Spa.** Tom Cruise, Billy Crystal, and Sylvester Stallone have all stayed here.

Travel Like an Insider:

Our Top 10 Picks for Sonoma

1. Lisa Kristine (www.lisakristine.com) Kristine is a gifted photographer who has been honored by the United Nations for her ingenuity in capturing images of indigenous peoples and the lives they lead.

2. Macarthur Place (www.macarthurplace.com) This resort is Wine Country at its most luxurious. Special features include Saddles Steakhouse, a pool, health spa, and glorious gardens.

3. The Inn at Ramekins (www.ramekins.com) This inn has to rate as one of the most food-savvy B&Bs of all. The six guest rooms are on the second floor of Ramekins Sonoma Valley Culinary School, well within reach of delectable aromas.

4. Mission San Francisco Solano (www.missiontour.org/sonoma) This is where European settlement in the area truly began. Though technically the Russians established the first outpost at Fort Ross, the true origins of Napa and Sonoma lie at Sonoma's Mission San Francisco Solano. The white adobe mission with its red-tile roof is probably the most popular historic attraction in Wine Country.

5. Café La Haye (www.cafelahay.com) This restaurant is classy yet simple in its sophistication. More important, the food stands up to the best in Wine County. If you're looking for a great meal on Sonoma Square, this is the spot.

6. Sonoma Enoteca Wine Shop (www.sonomaenoteca.com) This wine collective offers pours from about 10 boutique wineries including Brutacao, Manzanita Creek, and Madrone Ridge. What sets it apart from other collectives is its daily olive oil tastings, and its nifty gifts, including tea light holders made from barrel staves.

7. Maya (www.mayarestaurant.com) This Mexican restaurant is fun, plain and simple. The atmosphere is festive, with warm wood accents, colorful Mexican decor, and artifacts, and a bar stacked as high as a Mayan Temple with upscale tequilas.

8. Sebastiani Sonoma Cask Cellars (www.sebastiani.com) This winery is another way to spell "Sonoma" for many. It's the epitome of the county's wine tradition: an unpretentious family winery—big, old, and Italian.

9. Gloria Ferrer Champagne Caves (www.gloriaferrer.com) This house of sparkling wine is away from the high-traffic areas. Sitting dramatically on the gentle slope of a hill, the winery, done in warm tones of brown and red, is a bit of Barcelona.

10. Roessler Cellars (www.roesslercellars.com) Roessler is a great place to explore boutique winemaking at its best. The focus is almost entirely on pinot noir, with a few bottlings of chardonnay.

a complete makeover and is among the most luxurious in Wine Country. Guests of the resort have privileges to Sonoma Golf Course. The 13-acre grounds also include two restaurants.

Santé is the inn's upscale fine dining restaurant; it has received a Michelin Star, but sadly the food is not quite up to the price tag; the Big 3 is an adequate spot for breakfast, lunch, and

Find serenity in a Zen suite at Gaige House Inn.

dinner. If there's a drawback to the Sonoma Mission Inn, it's location. Though convenient to wineries and historic sites of Sonoma Valley, it's located along a hectic and well-developed thoroughfare. The grounds, however, remain peaceful.

GAIGE HOUSE INN (www.gaige .com, 707-935-0237, 800-935-0237, 13540 Arnold Dr., Glen Ellen, CA 95442; Price: Expensive to Very Expensive) This exceptional inn is a sanctuary off the beaten path. A Queen Anne Italianate built in the 1890s, it has 23 guest rooms, all elegantly done in modern tones. A new addition contains eight Zen suites done in sleek Asian design, some overlooking the nearby creek. A European continental breakfast is served daily which is included in the rate. The pool is in a lovely setting, and there's a whirlpool tub in the garden. It's in an ideal location for wine touring and Sonoma dining.

INN AT RAMEKINS (www.ramekins .com, 707-933-0452, 450 W. Spain St., Sonoma, CA 95476; Price: Expensive to Very Expensive) This has to rate as one of the most food-savvy B&Bs of all. The six guest rooms are on the second floor of Ramekins Sonoma Valley Culinary School, well within reach of delec-table aromas. A continental breakfast is served daily. It also offers in-house wine tasting as well as at several local wineries. Ramekins is also just a few blocks from the historic Sonoma Plaza.

KENWOOD INN AND SPA (www .kenwoodinn.com, 707-833-1293, 800-353-6966, 10400 Sonoma Hwy., Kenwood, CA 95452; Price: Very Expensive) This intimate resort looks like a small Tuscan village in a grove of oak trees. The inn includes 29 rooms situated around three courtyards on the 2.5-acre property. At the heart of the compound are the pool, gardens, and spa facility. A full country breakfast is included, and a lunch menu is also offered poolside. Dinner—Mediterranean-inspired cuisine—is offered to guests nightly. Traffic along Highway 12 quiets dramatically at night.

LEDSON HOTEL AND HARMONY LOUNGE (www.ledsonhotel.com, 707-996-9779, 480 1st St. E., Sonoma, CA 95476; Price: Very Expensive) This luxury two-story hotel is situated on the charming Sonoma Plaza. Six individually decorated rooms are on the upper floor, while the Harmony Lounge and Wine Tasting Bar covers the entire ground floor. The heart of Wine Country appears to be shifting from Sonoma Valley to Healdsburg and St. Helena, making retail shops on Sonoma Plaza less vibrant than in years past, but this hotel is still a lovely place to stay.

LODGE AT SONOMA RENAISSANCE RESORT AND SPA (www.thelodgeatsonoma.com, 707-935-6600, 888-710-8008, 1325 Broadway, Sonoma, CA 95476; Price: Very Expensive) One of the newest and largest hotels in Sonoma Valley, this 182-room lodge is part of the Renaissance /Marriott family of hotels. The 9-acre complex features a main lodge and 18 cottages. The lodge is elegantly designed in classic California mission style. The courtyard is impressive, with its towering Canary Island date palms. The spa features private cabanas and a mineral water pool. There are two fire pits located on the upper pool decks where you can sit and sip cocktails at night with blankets provided for guests. Be sure to check out Carneros Bistro and Bar, the lodge's restaurant, a handsome space that features fresh pastas, wood-fired pizzas, and steaks, seafood, and other treats from the rotisserie.

MACARTHUR PLACE (www .macarthurplace.com, 707-938-2929, 800-722-1866, 29 E. MacArthur St., Sonoma, CA 95476; Price: Very Expensive) MacArthur Place is Wine Country living at its most luxurious. Sixty-four rooms and suites are set in a private 7-acre compound lush with gardens and

sculptures. The property was once a working vineyard and ranch, and the original house—a grand Victorian built in the 1850s—includes 10 rooms. Twenty-nine deluxe suites were added, and each includes a wood-burning fireplace, king-sized bed, whirlpool tub, and TV with DVD player with six-speaker sound. Guests of the resort can enjoy a complimentary wine and cheese reception nightly and continental breakfast every morning. The property's historic barn is now home to a conference center as well as a cocktail bar and the valley's premier steak house, Saddles.

SONOMA VALLEY INN, BEST WESTERN (www.sonomavalleyinn .com, 707-938-9200, 800-334-5784, 550 2nd St. W., Sonoma, CA 95476; Price: Moderate to Expensive) "An

Once a working vineyard and ranch, MacArthur Place is now a luxurious inn and spa.   Tim Fish

Listen up, Romeo wannabes!

Try these romantic spots in Sonoma County with your sweetheart.
Gloria Ferrer Champagne Caves (www.gloriaferrer.com) A romantic place to sit and sip some bubbly.
Sonoma Valley Bike Tours (www.lifecycleadventures.com) Riding a bicycle built for two is a romantic way to see the sights.

Local Flavors

Taste of the town—local restaurants, cafés, bars, bistros, etc.

RESTAURANTS

There are more Sonoma restaurants than ever that are worth a visit, running the gamut from palatial chateaux to storefront bistros, along with ethnic eateries offering Mexican, Chinese, and Thai fare. There is more to dining out than just the food, of course. We also consider atmosphere and service.

CAFÉ CITTI (www.cafecitti.com, 707-833-2690, 9049 Sonoma Hwy., Kenwood, CA 95452; Price: Moderate; Cuisine: Italian) A trattoria in the strictest Italian sense—casual atmosphere with hearty wine and yummy, inexpensive pasta—Café Citti is a pleasure. There's a menu, but most people rely on the chalkboard on the wall. Customers order from the counter, cafeteria style. Lunch includes sandwiches: sweet Italian sausage and the usual cold deli fare. Pasta is mix and match; choose penne, linguine, and the like, and pair it with your sauce (marinara or Bolognese, to name a couple) of choice. Other offerings include a zesty Caesar salad and homemade focaccia, plus a luxurious risotto with mushrooms and garlic and a traditional Italian herb-roasted chicken that is to die for. For dessert, don't miss the crème brûlée or the tiramisu. For those traveling with kids, this is a perfect place to stop.

CAFE LA HAYE (www.cafelahaye .com, 707-935-5994, 140 E. Napa St., Sonoma, CA 95476; Price: Expensive; Cuisine: California) Café la Haye is classy yet simple in its sophistication.

intimate hotel" may be the best way to describe this exceptional lodge just a block from Sonoma Plaza. Rooms and furnishings are well above average, and many are equipped with kitchenettes, wet bars, whirlpools, and fireplaces. Most of the rooms open onto a lovely courtyard. It's ideal for families visiting the valley. Complimentary continental breakfast is included and delivered to the rooms.

INN 2 REMEMBER (www.aninn2 remember.com, 707-938-2909, 800-382-7895, 171 W. Spain St., Sonoma, CA 95476; Price: Expensive to Very Expensive) This inn is decorated throughout with Victorian furniture and decor. Each of the six guest rooms (two in the main house and four in the adjacent cottage) has a private bath, air-conditioning, and a ceiling fan. Five rooms have private decks and entrances. Three rooms have gas fireplaces, and three are equipped with large whirlpool tubs. Another whirlpool tub is in the garden. A full gourmet breakfast is served in the dining room or on the deck. This is a charming inn, reasonably priced and in an excellent location for strolling to all of Sonoma's finest. A selection of bicycles is available to guests.

More important, the food stands up to the best in Wine Country. If you're looking for a great meal on the Sonoma town square, this is the spot. Entrées include porcini-dusted dayboat scallops with champagne beurre blanc, truffled whipped potatoes, and green beans. The wine list complements the menu, and it's well focused, with a good selection of wines from Sonoma County and Napa Valley. As for the decor, the restaurant is tiny but seems spacious, with high wooden rafters and an upper level of seating—yet it still manages to feel cozy.

CARNEROS BISTRO AND BAR (www.carnerosbistro.com, 707-931-2042, 1325 Broadway, Sonoma, CA 95476; Price: Expensive; Cuisine: Wine Country Bistro) Carneros aspires to be a serious dining destination, and it nearly pulls it off. The food is good and the service shows promise. The restaurant is part of the Lodge at Sonoma, a 182-room complex owned by Renaissance Hotels. Carneros is the wine-growing region at the southern base of Napa Valley and Sonoma County, and the restaurant emphasizes wines produced from Sonoma County's 11 appellations. The portions are big and so are the flavors. Just consider one of the menu trademarks: Sonoma duck patty melt, a decadently rich sandwich made with foie gras and onion rings. Bring your cholesterol medicine! Prices on the wine list are the going rate, and it's a good selection that emphasizes wines of the region. The room itself has a large and airy atmosphere, with an open kitchen and cathedral ceiling, but there's something rather generic about the place.

DELLA SANTINA'S (www.della santinas.com, 707-935-0576, 133 E. Napa St., Sonoma, CA 95476; Price: Moderate; Cuisine: Italian) Ah, the mighty aromas that escape from this

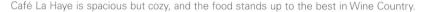

Café La Haye is spacious but cozy, and the food stands up to the best in Wine Country.

café! Don't overlook this Italian trattoria just off bustling Sonoma Plaza. The food is as authentic and unfussy as the best from Mama's kitchen. In summer, the intimate dining room gives way to a glorious garden patio, shady and green. The warm din of the kitchen mingles with Puccini and Verdi. Appetizers include a Caesar salad that's a vibrant cut above the usual, and the antipasto plate is everything it should be: fat with prosciutto and olives. Pastas are first-rate, and roasted meats—particularly chicken and rabbit and duck—are a specialty, yet quality varies. At one meal the chicken is dry and flavorless, but at the next, it's tender and heavenly. The wine list is modest but well suited to the food.

ESTATE (www.estate-sonoma.com, 707-933-3663, 400 W. Spain St., Sonoma, CA 95476; Price: Inexpensive to Expensive; Cuisine: Italian influenced) This 20th-century Victorian house is a true showplace. Former owner Suzanne Brangham revitalized this once-dilapidated pink house, which belonged to General Mariano Vallejo's daughter Natalia, and opened the General's Daughter in 1994. Today it's owned by Sondra Bernstein, who's best known in the area for her restaurant Girl & the Fig. Estate is a buttercup-colored Victorian but it has a less formal interior, with chandeliers swapped for basket lamps. The Italian menu plays to small plates, but entrées also include braised rabbit pappardelle, wood-fired baby squid, and all incarnations of pizza. For the sweet tooth in the famly, sometimes the menu includes this dessert: sugar doughnuts with Nutella dipping sauce.

GIRL & THE FIG (www.thegirlandthefig.com, 707-938-3634, 110 W. Spain St., Sonoma, CA 95476; Price: Expensive; Cuisine: French Country) The Girl & the Fig has its fans, even though the food and service are maddeningly inconsistent. Certainly, the restaurant is both appealing and convenient on Sonoma Plaza, adjacent to the lobby of the Sonoma Hotel, and with its tall, broad, wood-framed windows and light, mustard-colored walls, it's a pretty stop to spend a couple of hours here. The whole place feels breezy. The menu offers plenty of comfort, ranging from a salami and Brie sandwich and sirloin burger to duck confit and grilled polenta. Be sure to sample something from the cheese cart. The wine list is refreshing, even daring, and fairly priced. It focuses on California-produced, Rhone-style wines, with an emphasis on California Syrahs. Few will complain that it's limited in scope, because there's plenty to choose from, and Rhone-style wines are food friendly.

GLEN ELLEN INN (www.glenelleninn.com, 707-996-6409, 13670 Arnold Dr., Glen Ellen, CA 95442; Price: Expensive; Cuisine: California Fusion) The Glen Ellen Inn is not the quaint little dining room we once loved, but owners Chris and Karen Bertrand have added some sophistication to its small-town charm—and in this quiet corner of the world, Chris holds his own with Wine Country's finest chefs. The Bertrands have continually expanded their restaurant over the years, adding an oyster grill, martini bar, and collection of cottages in recent years. The food certainly hasn't suffered from the expansion. As for service, it's still first-rate, and the wine list specializes in the best Sonoma Valley wines. It includes a smart list by the glass. Bertrand, schooled at the Fifth Avenue Grill in Manhattan, cooks with a French accent, relying on fresh, local ingredients. Salads are exceptional. Specialties include luscious seafood and just about anything Bertrand does with filet mignon and salmon. For dessert, give in to the ever-popular Glen Ellen Inn sundae or the warm bread pudding.

HARVEST MOON CAFÉ (www .harvestmoonsonoma.com, 707-933-8160, 487 1st St. W., Sonoma CA 95476; Price: Expensive; Cuisine: California) This café on the Sonoma Plaza is a cozy retreat with sidewalk seating as well as a patio out back. Inside, rich warm colors and great aromas make you feel like you're dining at a friend's house. Harvest Moon offers comfort food at its best, with dishes such as the rib eye steak and specialty pastas. Tasty lighter fare includes the grilled California white bass. Entrées change daily. The wine list has a good showing of local wines with a strong sampling of imports.

KENWOOD RESTAURANT AND BAR (www.kenwoodrestaurant.com, 707-833-6326, 9900 Sonoma Hwy., Kenwood, CA 95452; Price: Moderate to Expensive; Cuisine: California) This bistro, a California roadhouse turned upscale, is in the heart of the Valley of the Moon, one of the most beautiful spots in Wine Country. The patio offers marvelous views of Sugar Loaf Ridge, where vineyards rib the lower slopes. The charm of sipping wine made nearby should not be underestimated, and Kenwood's wine list is a Who's Who of Sonoma Valley vintners. The decor and chef-owner Max Schacher's food are well matched: both paint a refined picture with subtle strokes. The dining rooms have steep wood ceilings and are done in muted tones brightened by colorful paintings. Likewise, Schacher believes in artistic presentation paired with a sense of understatement, with dishes that emphasize the quality of local duck or fish rather than exotic

creations. Frankly, we'd like more adventure. Also, the same menu is served lunch and dinner, which makes for a pricey lunch.

MAYA (www.mayarestaurant.com, 707-935-3500, 101 East Napa St., Sonoma, CA 95476; Price: Moderate to Expensive; Cuisine: Mexican, Yucatan Style) This place is fun, plain and simple. The atmosphere is festive, with warm wood accents, colorful Mexican decor and artifacts, and a bar stacked as high as a Mayan temple with upscale tequilas. The food is not your typical Mexican cuisine, and it's generally quite appealing. It takes its inspiration from the Mayan region in southern Mexico, but the kitchen also offers its own take on dishes such as hanger steak and a mixed grill of steak, prawns, and chicken served with tortillas. Signature dishes include a luscious grilled chicken breast stuffed with habanero jack cheese and *mole rojo.* The wine list is limited, but there's a creative offering of drinks such as margaritas, sangria, and specialty tequilas.

SADDLES (www.macarthurplace.com, 707-933-3191, 29 E. MacArthur St., Sonoma, CA 95476; Price: Moderate to Expensive; Cuisine: Steak and Seafood) If you want to order up a 10-ounce martini and a steak on the side, this is the place to go. Saddles is located in the MacArthur Place resort (see entry under Lodging). In Wine Country, a good steak house is a rare find, and the prime-cut meats here are outstanding—but don't expect to be wowed by the service. The western theme, a bit overdone, carries throughout the restaurant: cowboy boots, hats, and branding irons. The steaks are good, but oh, that price tag! The wine list has a solid selection of newer, mostly California wines. Prices are reasonable. A plus: those great martini offerings!

SANTE-FAIRMONT SONOMA MISSION INN (www.fairmont.com /sonoma, 707- 939-2415, 100 Boyes Blvd., Sonoma, CA 95416; Price: Very Expensive, Prix Fixe: $95 and $105; Cuisine: California with French Influences) Santé is a handsome, mission-style dining room, with dark wood beams, iron chandeliers, and wooden floors—but it's never a good sign when the best thing you can say about a restaurant involves its decor. The food doesn't live up to the price, though that isn't unusual at many hotel restaurants. The menu promises rich and deeply flavored dishes but the result is too often ill-conceived and boring. The wine list is one of the best in Sonoma County, although it comes at premium. If you're a hotel guest and prefer to eat in rather than out, this is a comfortable spot, but if you have the energy, there are far better places to dine nearby.

YETI RESTAURANT (www.yeti restaurant.com, 707-996-9930, 14301 Arnold Drive, Suite 19, Glen Ellen, CA; Price: Inexpensive to Moderate; Cuisine: Indian) Arguably the best Indian restaurant in all of Wine Country, Yeti is a rare find. The food is as authentic and tasty as you'd find in New York City and the service is just as smart. The naan is particularly good, and the curries are rich and complex. There are simply no misses on the menu. The decor takes you to India, and dining here is a relaxed affair.

WINERIES

We have a great lineup of wineries, including the historic Buena Vista Winery, which is said to be the oldest in all of Wine Country. We also give you at peek at the Benziger Family Winery, which is a respected leader in organics. Roessler Cellars is another great pick, it being a great example of boutique winemaking.

ARROWOOD VINEYARDS & WINERY (www.arrowoodvineyards .com, 707-935-2600, 800-938-5170, 14347 Sonoma Hwy., Glen Ellen, CA 95442; Tasting: Daily 10–4:30) Richard Arrowood was one of the first high-profile winemakers in Sonoma County. After toiling at a number of wineries over the years, Arrowood and his wife, Alis, opened this winery in 1986, and the wines are among the best in California. The visitors' center features a dramatic two-story limestone fireplace and views of the vineyard. The king here is chardonnay, rich and complex. Cabernet sauvignon and merlot are also first-rate. Beginning in 2000, Arrowood changed hands a number of times and is now owned by Jess Jackson of Kendall-Jackson. Richard Arrowood is no longer with the winery.

BENZIGER FAMILY WINERY (www.benziger.com, 707-935-4076, 888-490-2739, 1883 London Ranch Rd., Glen Ellen, CA 95442; Tasting: Daily 10–5) If this winery seems familiar, there's a reason. Millions know this spot along the gentle slope of Sonoma Mountain as Glen Ellen Winery, the king of the $5 bottle of vino. From a run-down grape ranch purchased from a naked hippie doctor in 1981, the Benziger clan built a multimillion-dollar Goliath. Weary, they sold the Glen Ellen brand in 1994 but kept the ranch, which dates to 1860, and now concentrate on their premium Benziger label. The Benzigers may have downsized, but the winery grounds are more beautiful than ever and are now entirely biodynamic; Benziger is at the forefront of California's "true wine" movement. Past an old farmhouse and down the hill is the wooden ranch barn that serves as aging cellar and tasting

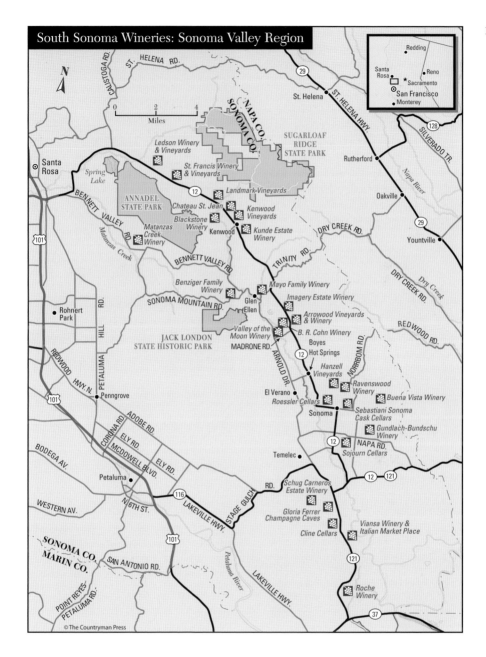

South Sonoma Wineries: Sonoma Valley Region

© The Countryman Press

room. The Benziger Tribute is a Bordeaux-style wine and was selected by *Wine and Spirits Magazine* in 2009 as the best cab blend in America. Cabernet sauvignons can be a knockout in a good vintage, and the citrusy sauvignon blanc is usually a winner.

BLACKSTONE WINERY (www.black stonewinery.com, 707-833-1999, 800-955-9585, 8450 Sonoma Hwy., Kenwood, CA 95452; Tasting: Daily 10–4:30) With the cost of wine rising so quickly, it's good to see that some winemakers still have value on their mind. Blackstone is part of the giant beverage company Constellation, and it offers a wide range of wines at decent prices. The house style is ripe and fruit forward, and the merlot is particularly reliable. Real winemaking is limited in Kenwood, but the tasting room is in a small cottage, and it's as easy going and laidback as the wines. The winery is one of the best kept secret in Sonoma County. Bordeaux and cabs are fast-growing favorites. It has big reds and its whites are tasty as well.

B. R. COHN WINERY (www.brcohn.com, 707-938-4064, 800-330-4064, 15000 Sonoma Hwy., Glen Ellen, CA 95442; Tasting: Daily 10–5) Manager for the Doobie Brothers and other rock bands, Bruce Cohn began a second career in wine when he bought Olive Hill Ranch in 1974. Cohn sold his grapes until 1984, when he bottled his first cabernet sauvignon. Ripe and concentrated, it was an immediate hit. Subsequent vintages have fared similarly, but his chardonnay and merlot are more routine. The tasting room has a handsome mahogany bar and marble fireplace and sits on a knoll covered with olive trees. Olive oil is Cohn's latest passion.

BUENA VISTA WINERY (www.buenavistacarneros.com, 707-256-1472, 18000 Old Winery Rd., Sonoma, CA 95476; Tasting: Daily 10–5) This is where it all began: California's oldest premium winery. Buena Vista is where Agoston Haraszthy, known as the Father of California Wine, started his experiments in 1857. Though others had made wine in Sonoma before this, they had used only the coarse mission variety grapes brought north by Spanish missionaries for Mass wine. Haraszthy was the first to believe that the noble grapes of Bordeaux and Burgundy could thrive in California. Visi-

Buena Vista is California's oldest premium winery.   Tim Fish

tors to Buena Vista stroll down a gentle, quarter-mile path, past thick blackberry bushes and tall eucalyptus trees, to the tasting room set inside the thick stone Press House, built in 1863. The wine is made a few miles away. Buena Vista's reputation has varied widely over time, but the wines have improved significantly in recent years.

CHATEAU ST. JEAN (www.chateaustjean.com, 707-833-4134, 800-543-7572, 8555 Sonoma Hwy., Kenwood, CA 95452; Tasting: Visitors' Center Daily 10–5; Reserve in Old Chateau Daily 10-4:30) Surrounded by luxuriant lawns and tall trees, with Sugarloaf Ridge in the distance, Chateau St. Jean—a modern version of a medieval French castle—is a visual treat. Opening in 1973, Chateau St. Jean drew immediate acclaim for its white wines, particularly the Robert Young Vineyard chardonnay, a luscious and oaky beauty that helped set the standard for chardonnay. Today, Chateau St. Jean is owned by wine and beer giant Foster's of Australia. Ironically, its red wines are now drawing attention. Its cabernet sauvignons and merlots are lush and well structured. There's a spacious visitors' center behind the chateau. Buy a bottle of the Riesling, chardonnay, or sauvignon blanc to pour with a picnic; the winery has one of Sonoma's best picnic grounds.

CLINE CELLARS (www.clinecellars.com, 707-940-4000, 800-546-2070, 24737 Arnold Dr., Sonoma, CA 95476; Tasting: Daily 10–6) Cline was Rhone before Rhone was popular. Fred Cline got started in the East Bay in 1982, preferring unsung Rhone-style grapes such as carignan and mourvèdre. Cline then took up shop in Sonoma's Carneros District in 1991. The tasting room is housed in an 1850s farmhouse with a wraparound porch; the pleasant grounds have duck ponds and rose gardens. Nearby, viognier and Syrah, Cline's latest Rhone passions, are newly planted. The winery has also had great success with zinfandel.

GLORIA FERRER CHAMPAGNE CAVES (www.gloriaferrer.com, 707-933-1917, 23555 Carneros Hwy., Sonoma, CA 95476; Tasting: Daily 10–5) If you've had the pleasure of paying a mere $10 for Cordon Negro, the simple but tasty little sparkling wine in the ink-black bottle, then you already know the people behind Gloria Ferrer. Freixenet of Spain is the world's largest producer of sparkling wine, and it was drawn to the great promise of California. Gloria Ferrer, named for the wife of Freixenet's president, makes consistently good bubbly at fair prices. It also makes admirable still wines: merlot,

Syrah, pinot, and chardonnay. The Carneros location places Gloria Ferrer away from the high-traffic areas. Sitting dramatically on the gentle slope of a hill, the winery, done in warm tones of brown and red, is a bit of Barcelona. Gloria Ferrer's tour has great appeal, particularly tours of the caves carved from the hillside where the sparkling wine ages.

GUNDLACH-BUNDSCHU WINERY (www.gunbun.com, 707-939-3015, 2000 Denmark St., Sonoma, CA 95476; Tasting: Daily 11–4:30) Passionate about wine and the Sonoma Valley, Jim Bundschu doesn't take himself too seriously. At a wine auction a few years back, he dressed as Batman, and his winery's humorous posters are classic. He even hijacked the Napa Valley Wine Train and—gasp!—handed out samples of Sonoma Valley wine. Behind all this frivolity is great wine and rich history. Since 1858, six generations have tended the winery's home vineyard, Rhinefarm—but wine wasn't bottled from Prohibition until Jim restored the original stone winery in the early 1970s. Located down a winding road, it's worth the trek. Take time to tour the winery's 10,000-square-foot cave.

HANZELL VINEYARDS (www.hanzell.com, 707-996-3860, 18596 Lomita Ave., Sonoma, CA 95476; Tasting and Tours: By appointment) The original boutique winery, Hanzell has greatly influenced California winemaking. The late ambassador James Zellerbach, who founded the winery in 1956, patterned it after the chateaux of Burgundy. The winery, with its dark wood and pitched roof, was modeled after Clos de Vougeot, and Hanzell was first in California to barrel-ferment chardonnay and use French oak barrels for aging. The winery went through a few rough years, but the pinot noir and chardonnay are now up to the old standards.

IMAGERY ESTATE WINERY (www.imagerywinery.com, 707- 935-4500, 877-550-4278, 14335 Hwy. 12, Glen Ellen, CA 95442; Tasting: Mon–Fri 10–4:30, Sat. and Sun. 10–5:30). Art and single-vineyard wines are the focus of this energetic winery run by the Benziger family. The artist collection series features boldly designed labels and offbeat varietals such as tempranillo and sangiovese, while the vineyard collection features distinctive cabernets, merlots, and other grapes from one unique place. The wines are sold almost exclusively at the winery, so you know you'll be able to taste a wine you'll never be able to buy back home.

KENWOOD VINEYARDS (www .kenwoodvineyards.com, 707-833-5891, 9592 Sonoma Hwy., Kenwood, CA 95452; Tasting: Daily 10–4:30) Don't let Kenwood Vineyards fool you. The tasting room might be in a rustic little barn, but behind the simple charm is a savvy winery, one of Sonoma County's largest. Here's a homey and relaxed tasting room with wines that will please everyone in your group. Built by the Pagani brothers in 1906, the winery is now owned by Gary Heck, who also runs Korbel Champagne Cellars. Kenwood doesn't really have a specialty. Whites or reds, they have luck with both. There's no better wine with fresh oysters than Kenwood's lemony sauvignon blanc. Try Kenwood's cabernet sauvignons, particularly the expensive but outstanding Artist Series—big wines with great aging potential.

KUNDE ESTATE WINERY (www .kunde.com, 707-833-5501, 9825 Sonoma Hwy., Kenwood, CA 95452; Tasting: Daily 10:30–4:30) Since 1904, five generations of Kundes have grown grapes. Stopping production during World War II, the clan began making wine again in the late 1980s. The Kundes have 2,000 acres of vineyards, and they know the personality of each varietal grape and put that to use. They also brought in a fine winemaker, David Noyes, who worked at Ridge for 10 years. The strengths so far are chardonnay, typically elegant and creamy, and a muscular zinfandel made from one-hundred-year-old vines. The winery is housed in a stylish white barn. In the hillside beyond, the Kundes have carved out a $5 million cave to age their wine. Visitors to the tasting room can watch the winery in action through picture windows.

LANDMARK VINEYARDS (www .landmarkwine.com, 707-833-0218, 101 Adobe Canyon Rd., Kenwood, CA 95452; Tasting: Daily 10–4:30) This attractive mission-style winery, in the shadow of Sugar Loaf Ridge, is a house of chardonnay. Landmark began in Windsor in 1974, but suburban squeeze forced a move south in 1989, when Damaris Deere Ethridge assumed control. The menu includes two impressive chardonnays and a pinot noir. The tasting room is an appealing space, with a cathedral ceiling, fireplace, and granite bar. The cloistered courtyard looks onto the eastern slopes.

LEDSON WINERY AND VINEYARD (www.ledson.com, 707-537-3810, 7335 Sonoma Hwy., Kenwood, CA 95409; Tasting: Daily 10–5) From the road, this winery looks a bit like Wayne Manor in the old *Batman* TV show. Originally designed as the Ledson family home, the 16,000-square-foot gothic "castle" turns heads on Sonoma Highway. Make your way up the long drive and through the vines, enter through the portico, and you'll see that the interior is just as extravagant as the outside. The wines are good but not great, with sauvignon blanc and chardonnay generally leading the pack.

MAYO FAMILY WINERY (www .mayofamilywinery.com, 707-938-9401, 13101 Arnold Dr., Glen Ellen, CA 95442; Tasting: Daily 10:30–6:30) Owner Henry Mayo had a career in real estate, but in 1990 he decided to forsake his business for grapes. It all began with a property in Kenwood he transformed into Laurel Hill Vineyards. By 1993 the Mayo family was bottling wine. The tasting room opened in July 2003, a more accessible location than the main winery nearby in the hills. Mayo produces more than a dozen varietals, but zinfandel and pinot steal the limelight. Mayo also maintains several other tasting rooms around the county.

RAVENSWOOD WINERY (www .ravenswood-wine.com, 707-933-2332, 888-669-4679, 18701 Gehricke Rd., Sonoma, CA 95476; Tasting: Daily 10–4:30) Zin lovers have long been wise to Ravenswood, an unassuming stone winery built into the side of a hill—and the location fits the label: a classic image of a circle of ravens. The old tasting room is a busy spot but made soothing by a crackling fire. If you're lucky, Ravenswood will pour one of its top zinfandels: Cooke, Old Hill, Dickerson. A sure way to sample the good stuff is to visit in the late winter and spring, when the zins are still in the barrel. Ravenswood's tour typically includes a walk through the vineyard and a barrel tasting. Because the

Landmark Vineyards, in the shadow of Sugar Loaf Ridge, is a house of chardonnay. Tim Fish

winery is small, the tour is brief, but guides are detailed in their discussion of Ravenswood's natural approach to winemaking.

ROCHE WINERY TASTING ROOM (www.roachwinery.com, 707-935-7115, 800-825-9475, 122 West Spain Street, Sonoma CA 95476; Tasting: Daily 11–5:30) This quaint tasting room is in a 1940s Craftsman-style building right off the historic Sonoma Plaza. Here they have an indoor tasting bar and an outdoor one. House specialties include chardonnay and pinot noir, but Syrah and merlot also deserve a taste. Joe and Genevieve Roche, both physicians, decided to live the dream and they brought their family to Sonoma Valley, where they reared both vines and children.

ROESSLER CELLARS (www .roesslercellars.com, 707-933-4440, 380 1st St. W., Sonoma, CA, 95476; Tasting: Daily 11–6) This is a great place to explore boutique winemaking at its best. Roessler features single vineyard designated wines, focusing almost entirely on pinot noir, with a few bottlings of chardonnay. Roger Roessler found his way into the wine world by way of the restaurant wine list. He spent 40 years in the business, with his restaurants placing more and more emphasizes on wine. Is writing a great wine list a prerequisite to being a winemaker? In Roessler's case, yes.

SCHUG CARNEROS ESTATE WINERY (www.schugwinery.com, 707-939-9363, 800-966-9365, 602 Bonneau Rd., Sonoma, CA 95476; Tasting: Daily 10–5) Nestled against a windswept hill on the western edge of Carneros is a little bit of Germany. Architecturally, Schug's winery would be more at home along the Rhine, where the winemaker was raised. His wines, too, reflect his European heritage. Schug established his impressive credentials at Joseph Phelps, where he was winemaker from 1973 to 1983. His current wines, poured in a cozy tasting room, are distinctive and more European in style than those produced by most California wineries.

SEBASTIANI SONOMA CASK CELLARS (www.sebastiani.com, 707-933-3230, 800-888-5532, 389 4th St. E., Sonoma, CA 95476; Tasting: Daily 10–5) For many people, Sebastiani is another way to spell "Sonoma." It's the epitome of the county's wine tradition: an unpretentious family winery—big, old, and Italian. Once among Sonoma County's largest wineries, Sebastiani trimmed production considerably a few years back to focus on quality. It remains one of Sonoma's most popular tourist attractions. The winery dates to 1896, when Samuele Sebastiani crushed his first grapes—zinfandel, to be precise—and the press he used is still on display in the tasting room. Samuele's son August, a man with an affinity for bib overalls and stout, simple wines, built the winery's reputation on inexpensive jug wines. Since his death in 1980, the family has concentrated on premium wines. Visitors can taste Sebastiani's wide range of wines. Try the Sonoma County cabernet sauvignon and merlot, delightful wines and excellent bargains.

SOJOURN (www.sojourncellars.com, 707-938-7212, 141 E. Napa St., Sonoma, CA 95476; Tasting: Daily by appointment 10–5) The partners behind this venture—Craig Haserot and Erich Bradley—met on a tennis court. Isn't that were most business ventures begin? When they realized they both wanted to make handcrafted wine, they figured they both won the match. They say their winemaking style is decidedly New World with old-world sensibilities. The focus here is on pinot noir, with about a half a dozen bottlings released each year, while the cabernet is limited to a few. They are making noise with both varietals, so check them out.

ST. FRANCIS WINERY AND VINEYARD (www.stfranciswinery .com, 707-833-4666, 888-675-9463, 100 Pythian Rd., Kenwood, CA 95409; Tasting: Daily 10–5) Merlot is the current popular flavor, and St. Francis makes two of the best, a regular and a reserve. Both are gorgeous and full-bodied, with enough muscle to age a few years. Another success story for St. Francis is its chardonnay, done in a lean and fruity style. Its old-vine zinfandel packs a punch of brilliant fruit. They can all be sampled at the lovely mission-style visitors' center located near the winery.

VALLEY OF THE MOON WINERY (www.valleyofthemoonwinery.com, 707-939-4500, 777 Madrone Rd., Glen Ellen, CA 95442; Tasting: Daily 10–4:30) When Gary Heck—who owns Korbel and Kenwood Vineyards—bought this winery a few years back, it was rundown, and the wines had a nasty reputation. Just about the only thing left from the old days is the winery's original 110-year-old foundation. The new tasting room is sleek and modern, and so is the winery's bottle design, a stark yet dramatic etched bottle. But what about the wines? They're good and getting better, particularly the zinfandel and Syrah.

VIANSA WINERY AND ITALIAN MARKET PLACE (www.viansa.com, 707-935-4700, 800-995-4740, 25200 Arnold Dr., Sonoma, CA 95476; Tasting: Daily 10–5) This tribute to Tus-cany is situated high atop a knoll in the Carneros District. Done in warm shades with a terra-cotta tile roof and Italian opera music in the background, Viansa is one of Wine Country's most festive spots. Even the stainless-steel wine tanks are adorned with colorful faux marble frescoes. The marketplace offers sumptuous picnic fare, plus a picnic area with a dramatic view. Viansa is concentrating increasingly— and with considerable success—on Italian-style wines such as barbera and nebbiolo and blends that recall a hearty Chianti.

WINE COLLECTIVES

These tasting rooms offer a broad range of boutique wines—labels made in such small quantities that they typically aren't found in retail shops. Enjoy these rare offerings.

Cornerstone Place (707-933-3010, www.cornerstone place.com, 23570 Arnold Dr./Hwy.121, Sonoma, CA 95476) A one-stop shop for tasting some of Sonoma County's best wines. The lineup includes Artesa, Roshambo, Larson Family Winery, and Ridgeline. The collective is a rare find because it's also an eye-catching hub of interesting shops such as Artefact Design & Salvage and 20 plots of gardens.

The Cellar Door (707-938-4466, www.sonomacellardoor.com, 1395 Broadway, Sonoma, CA 95476) A group of Sonoma Valley vintners banded together in this co-op to show off their latest releases. Wineries include Mayo Family, Sunset Cellars, and Richardson Vineyards.

Sonoma Enoteca Wine Shop (707-935-1200, www.sonomaenoteca .com, 35 E. Napa, Sonoma, CA 95476) This wine collective offers pours from about 10 boutique wineries including Brutacao, Manzanita Creek and

Madrone Ridge. What sets it apart from other collectives is its daily olive oil tastings, and its nifty gifts, including tea light holders made from barrel staves. Roots (707-934-4090, www .rootsinsonoma.com, 23574 Arnold Dr./Hwy. 121 Sonoma, CA. 95476) Grape grower Tom Larson and the wines of viticulturalist Tom Meadowcroft are pouring their individual brands, along with two brands they created together: Roots in Sonoma and Friendship Road. There's a lovely vineyard behind the tasting room, a great viewing when you get your pour.

Family Wineries Kenwood (888-433-6555, www.familywines.com, 9380 Sonoma Hwy (Hwy 12), Kenwood, CA 95492) Originally built as a schoolhouse in the 1890s, this locale now serves as a cozy farmhouse tasting room. More than 32 wines, including 3 unique sparkling wines and 17 varietals. Local wineries include: Collier Fall Vineyards, David Noyes Wines, Macrae Family Winery, SL Cellars and many more.

The Wine Room at the Adler Fels Tasting Room (707-833-6131; www.the-wine-room.com; 9575 Sonoma Hwy., Kenwood, CA 95452) When his career slowed in the 1970s, comedian Tommy Smothers bought a Kenwood ranch and planted grapes. Smothers Brothers wines soon followed, depending on how distracted Tom was by comedy. Dick Arrowood makes the bulk of the wine—now called Remick Ridge—and recent vintages have been impressive. These days, Smothers shares the tasting room with a number of other Sonoma Valley wineries, including Moondance, Sonoma Valley Portworks, and Family Dog Winery.

Palate Adventures

In Sonoma Valley, epicurean delights abound . . .

• *Step out for a bite to eat, an artisanal creation, or maybe a brew*
Artisan Bakers (707-936-7320, 720 W. Napa St., Sonoma, CA 95476) Some of the finest bread in Wine Country is made right here. Look for loaves in markets around Sonoma County and Napa Valley, or stop in at the bakery itself. In 1996, during the baking equivalent of the Olympics, owner Craig Ponsford achieved the impossible: he baked a better baguette than the French.

Basque Boulangerie Café (707-935-7687, 460 1st St. E., Sonoma, CA 95476) More than a bakery, this stylish storefront has a deli, a coffee bar, and even some wine selections. Popular sandwiches include chicken salad and prosciutto and Brie. For some reason, however, it has yet to master the classic croissant.

Sunflower Café (707-996-6645, 421 1st St. W., Sonoma, CA 95476) This rustic-style café is housed in an adobe built in the 1830s. It has a lovely garden patio with a wine bar, Mediterranean-influenced food, and an art gallery.

Olive Press (707-939-8900, www.theolivepress.com, 24724 Hwy. 121 at Jacuzzi Family Winery, Sonoma, CA 95476) Had your fill of wine tasting? Perhaps

**Especially for those on
a shoestring budget**

If you're a budget-conscience
traveler in Sonoma County, these
places will help you stretch your
vacation dollar:

Café Citti (p. 168)

Kenwood Vineyards (p. 176)

it's time to branch out. This smart den makes and sells olive oils that rival Italy's best. Enjoy a complimentary taste.

Olive & Vine Marketplace and Café (707-996-9150, 14301 Arnold Dr., Glen Ellen, CA 95442) This marketplace is home base for its catering company, and it has scrumptious panini sandwiches, pizzas, and soups. The grilled pork loin sandwich is also a hit.

Sonoma Cheese Factory (707-996-1931, 2 W. Spain St., Sonoma, CA 95476) The Viviani family began making cheese in Sonoma in 1931. Although it's a "factory" in name only (the cheese is now made in Crescent City), this supermarket-sized gourmet deli has much appeal, with made-to-order gourmet sandwiches, gift items, and Sonoma Valley wines. There's a coffee and gelato bar, and tasty samples abound. Shady Sonoma Plaza is nearby.

Vella Cheese Company (707-938-3232, 800-848-0505, 315 2nd St. E., Sonoma, CA 95476) The dry jack is to die for. This is a Sonoma classic that dates to 1931 and is worth a visit.

Ledson Hotel and Harmony Club Wine Bar (707-996-9779, 480 1st St. E., Sonoma, CA 95476) The wine list offers more than 30 selections, with a natural emphasis on Sonoma County, including Ledson's new Harmony Collection. The live piano music is a plus.

Chocolate Cow (707-935-3564, 452 1st St. E., Sonoma, CA 95476) These folks are "udderly" cow crazy—the black-and-white heifer image is everywhere, from T-shirts to stuffed animals. The place also stocks candy, chocolates, fudge, and ice cream.

Murphy's Irish Pub (707-935-0660, 464 First St. E., Sonoma, CA 95476). This pub in Sonoma Valley is small but cozy and offers a great selection of imported ales.

• *End the summer with a bash*
Sonoma Wine Country Weekend (www.sonomawinecountryweekend.com, 800-939-7666, 783 Broadway, Sonoma, CA 95476) A bit less chichi than its Napa counterpart (Auction Napa Valley), this remains quite an elegant affair. The gala over Labor Day weekend includes tastings and parties, highlights being the Taste of Sonoma and, best of all, the irreverent Sonoma Valley Harvest Wine Auction.

To Do

Check out these great attractions and activities . . .

SHOPPING

Today the plaza has high-style clothing stores, gourmet food shops, and ethnic stores, and it can get plenty crowded on weekends. Expect to jockey for a parking spot. Our favorites: Artifax International Gallery & Gifts (707-996-9494, 450-C 1st St. E., Sonoma, CA 95476) is a true sensory experience. Here you'll find Asian imports, Chinese baskets, soaps, exotic textiles, beads, and jewelry, etc. Baksheesh (707-939-2847, www.vom.com/baksheesh, 423 1st. St. W., Sonoma, CA 95476) is a great find. Persian for "gift," Baksheesh, which vows fair-trading practices, is replete with pieces made by artists who live in developing countries. It has an interesting mix of clothing, jewelry, toys, games, and even musical instruments. Tiddle E. Winks (707-939-6933 or 707-93-WOWEE, 115 E. Napa St., Sonoma, CA 95476) is a shop full of fun retro items. Owner Heidi Geffen says she rounds up her old toys, tins, and pendants by traveling back in time—boarding a Pan Am flight back to the 1950s. The Candlestick (707-933-0700, 38 W. Spain St., Sonoma, CA 95476) offers clever specialty candles, oil lamps, and even whimsical nightlights. Harvest Home Stores (707-933-9044, 107 W. Napa St., Sonoma, CA 95476), has lovely custom furniture, sofas, and leather chairs. Sonoma Home (707-939-6900, 497 1st St. W., Sonoma CA 95476) has great ideas for home decor and garden, from furniture and books to pillows. Readers' Books (707-939-1779, 127 E. Napa St., Sonoma, CA 95476), though perhaps not the City Lights of Sonoma County, has the reputation of being urbane and literary. Expect great classics and fiction, an expansive cookbook section, and myriad books for children. Sonoma Bookends Bookstore (707-938-5926, 201 W. Napa St., Suite 15, Sonoma, CA 95476) is a general bookstore catering to the tourist, with expanded travel and wine sections. Chico's (707-933-0100, 29 E. Napa St., Sonoma, CA 95476) offers chic women's clothing and accessories. Three Dog Bakery (707-933-9780, 526 Broadway, Sonoma, CA. 95476) is a real bakery (for dogs) that offers goodies made without salt and refined sugar; treats are sweetened with applesauce or honey.

> **Insider Secret:**
> At **Three Dog Bakery,** 90 percent of the customers are, surprisingly, tourists who stop in because they're homesick for their pooches. FYI: The hands-down favorite dog treat is the carrot cake. (www.threedog.com)

CULTURAL OUTINGS

• *Experience the world through an artist's eyes*

Lisa Kristine Gallery (www.lisakristine.com, 707-938-3860, 452 First Street East, Sonoma, CA., 95476) The photographer Lisa Kristine has been recognized by the United Nations for capturing striking images of indigenous peoples. This gallery on the Sonoma Plaza takes you a world away, revealing a glimpse into other cultures. "Each image is made with reverence for the subject," Kristine says. "In order for me to photograph a person in the unaffected environment of self there must be a trust between us. Without this, a stirring image cannot be created."

• *Marvel at architecture*

The oldest city in the area, Sonoma also has many of the oldest buildings, including adobes like the simple but majestic Mission San Francisco Solano. Surrounding the Sonoma Plaza are a number of historic buildings, including the fading but still regal Sebastiani Theatre, built in 1933.

High Plateau.   Photographed by Lisa Kristine of Lisa Kristine Gallery in Sonoma

• *See a flick*

Sonoma Film Institute, housed at Sonoma State University but open to the public, is low on atmosphere but high on quality. Screenings cover a wide range, from art house to classics to foreign films. Sonoma and Napa are home to many top-name stars, and the two counties' landscapes are cinema stars in their own right: both are favorite locations for Hollywood feature films.

Sebastiani Theatre (707-996-2020, 476 1st St. E., Sonoma, CA 95476) is a delightful old restored theater showing first-run films.

• *Buff up on history*

Mission San Francisco Solano (707-938-9560 938-1519 (mission); contact: Parks & Recreation Dept., 20 114 E. Spain St., Sonoma, CA 95476, Corner of Spain St. & 1st St. E., Sonoma Plaza, Sonoma CA 95476) The Sonoma mission was the last to be established, and the mission system was dissolved in 1833. It became a center of religion and culture under General Mariano Vallejo's rule, but it was sold by the Catholic Church in 1881. Used over the years as a blacksmith's shop and

Insider Secret:
While traveling the world with her camera, **Lisa Kristine** has run out of food and water and contracted diseases, but she's taken it all in stride. Why? It began when, as a child, she was fascinated by her mother's anthropology books. Kristine goes to the ends of the earth to get her amazing shots because she's "fascinated by people everywhere." (www.lisakristine.com)

The historic Sebastiani Theatre shows first-run films. Tim Fish

hay barn, the mission was nearly lost until the state intervened in 1906; restoration began three years later.

General Vallejo Home (707-939-6188, contact: Parks & Recreation Dept., Third St. and W. Spain St., Sonoma, CA 95476, 0.5 mi. west of Sonoma Plaza) General Mariano Vallejo may have been the most powerful man in Northern California in the 1850s, but he had a sense of poetry about him when he named his house Lachryma Montis. Latin for "tears of the mountain," the name was derived from a mountain spring on the property. Vallejo's home, finished in 1852, reflects his embrace of North American culture. Instead of an adobe house, he built a two-story Gothic Victorian. The house was prefabricated—designed and built on the

East Coast and shipped around Cape Horn. Vallejo and his family lived in the house for 35 years; the state bought the property in 1933.

RECREATIONAL FUN

• *Bike, hike, fly, play; then spa*
Sonoma Valley Cyclery (www.sonomavalleycyclery.com, 707-935-3377, 20091 Broadway, Sonoma, CA 95476) helps you slow your pace and explore Wine Country by bicycle.

Sugarloaf Ridge State Park (707-833-5712, 2605 Adobe Canyon Rd., Kenwood, CA 95452; 7 miles east of Santa Rosa on Highway 12, north on Adobe Canyon Road) This 2,500-acre park offers 50 developed campsites, an observatory,

Especially for the art lover in Sonoma County

Sonoma's many art galleries and open artists' studios offer work from the sublime to the comic(s)—sure to delight the art enthusiasts in your party.

Lisa Kristine (p. 182)

Artifax International Gallery & Gifts (p. 181)

Charles M. Schulz Museum (p. 225)

Sonoma Film Institute, Sonoma State University (p. 183)

Tigers Guardian. Photographed by Lisa Kristine of Lisa Kristine Gallery in Sonoma

TrainTown holds great allure for kids.   Tim Fish

25 miles of nature trails, hiking, horseback-riding trails, and exhibits. Trailers and campers up to 28 feet long are permitted.

TrainTown (www.traintown.com, 707-938-3912, 20264 Broadway, Sonoma, CA 95476; 1 mile south of Sonoma Plaza) Take a 20-minute ride on a scale-model steam train around 10 acres of beautifully landscaped park, through a 140-foot tunnel, over bridges, and past historic replica structures. Also offered: a petting zoo, exhibits, and amusement rides. TrainTown is open daily June to September, and Friday to Sunday the rest of the year. Admission: general admission and parking is free; amusement rides additional.

Vintage Aircraft (707-938-2444, www.vintageaircraft.com, Sonoma Valley Airport, 23982 Arnold Dr., Sonoma, CA 95476) Red Baron, move over. These scenic tours of Napa Valley and Sonoma County are in vintage biplanes that have been meticulously restored. Aerobatic flights are also available, offering loops, rolls, and "kamikaze" flights. Not for the faint of heart.

Sonoma Golf Club (707-996-0300, 707-939-4100, www.sonomagolfclub.com, 17700 Arnold Dr., Sonoma, CA 95476) This is a private course—an individual can play only if he or she is a guest at the Fairmont Sonoma Mission Inn. It offers 18 championship holes, par 72; a driving range; a putting green; and a restaurant. Price: moderate to expensive.

Jack London State Historic Park.

Jack London State Historic Park (707-938-5216, 707-939-6191 (kiosk), 2400 London Ranch Rd., Glen Ellen CA; off Arnold Drive) Writer Jack London fell in love with the Valley of the Moon and began buying land there in 1905. By the time he died in 1916, he was immersed in the innovative projects of his Beauty Ranch. Visitors can traverse these 800 acres, seeing the remains of the Londons' Wolf House mansion, hiking 7 miles of trails, and taking in a scenic three-and-a-half-mile climb with breathtaking views of the Valley of the Moon.

Fairmont Sonoma Mission Inn and Spa (www.fairmont.com/sonoma, 707-938-9000, 800-862-4945, 100 Boyes Blvd., Hot Springs, CA 95416) Who's that lounging in the mineral pool? Billy Crystal? The waters at this Wine Country favorite for the rich and famous have made this site a destination since Native Americans first considered it a healing ground. It's also Wine Country's most expensive spa. The inn has recently tapped into a new source of mineral water, and the soft and lightly green liquid warms the pool and Jacuzzi. The spa house is a stylish combo of mission and art deco, and the pool area is in a peaceful grove of trees. The array of treatments is mind-boggling, from Swedish and sports massage to seaweed body wraps, hair and foot care, waxing, color analysis, and nearly a dozen different facials. There's also a fitness center. Spa products include Sonoma Lavender Kur, a bubble bath, a body wrap.

8

Bodega Bay & West County

BODEGA BAY IS BEST KNOWN as the backdrop of Alfred Hitchcock's thriller *The Birds*. The filming began in 1961, and for three years the cameras rolled in this foggy coastal town. Tippy Hedren shared the screen with hundreds of avian costars, both mechanical and live.

One of the most dramatic scenes of the film takes place at the 150-year-old Potter Schoolhouse behind St. Theresa's Church in Bodega. The building, five miles south of Bodega Bay, is still standing, one of the town's most popular tourist attractions. Fans of the Hitchcock film often stop by for a photo out front. It's a private home now, but it's occasionally open for private tours.

Insider Secret:
One of the most stunning (and undiscovered) drives in Wine Country is the stretch from Occidental to Bodega Bay on **Coleman Valley Road.** (The locals would prefer to keep this hush hush, so don't tell them we sent you.) This route is the most scenic approach to the bay; you'll see sheep, cows, and the occasional llama. (Take Coleman Valley Road from Occidental to Bodega Bay.)

Once you secure a snapshot, be sure to sample some clam chowder on the piers and, by all means, don't leave town without catching a glimpse of Bodega Head with the thrashing waters of the Pacific ocean below. (See details in the entry for Sonoma Coast State Beach under Recreational Fun)

The beauty of Bodega Bay is in its calm: the fishing boats in the quiet waters, the docks, and yes, the birds.

Checking In

Best places to stay in and around Bodega Bay and West County.

There's nothing like being lulled to sleep by the surf, and that's what many of the places in this lodging section offer. From bed & breakfasts to small resorts, pampering is at a premium, so

LEFT: A fishing boat in Bodega Bay. Tim Fish

Travel Like an Insider:

Our Top 10 Picks for Bodega Bay and West County

1. Iron Horse (www.ironhorsevineyards.com) This winery amid the undulating hills of Green Valley is one of Sonoma County's most respected producers of sparkling wine. Barry and Audrey Sterling bought the estate, a former railroad stop, in 1976. The tour here reveals the classic *méthode champenoise* process used in making French-style bubbly.

2. Inn at Occidental (www.innatoccidental.com) Perched on a hill overlooking the quiet village of Occidental, this comfortable three-story Victorian inn is a jewel, one of Wine Country's best. It is well off the beaten path and delightfully so. Guarded by fruit trees and a lush courtyard garden with a fountain, the inn was built in 1876.

3. Tides Wharf Fish Market One of the joys of living on the Pacific Ocean is fresh seafood. Most prized locally are Dungeness crab and salmon. Crab season runs from mid-November to the end of May, and the local salmon season runs from mid-May to September.

4. Sonoma Coast State Beach This is one of a string of beaches along 18 miles of coastline stretching from Goat Rock to Bodega Head. Each has its own personality and invites different activities, whether it's tidepooling or a serious game of volleyball. Wildflowers brighten the cliffs in the spring. The coast is always cool in the summer, supplying an escape from inland heat.

5. Underwood Bar & Bistro (www.underwoodgraton.com) If you like to eat where the winemakers hang out, this restaurant is practically a private club for the West County wine industry. The interior is a masculine blend of urban and country, and there's a long bar that's always hopping. Service is a little too laid back at times, but the food is appealing and hearty.

6. Korbel Champagne Cellars (www.korbel.com) As you drive through the gorgeous redwood forests of the Russian River area, you'll see this century-old ivy-covered stone wine cellar rising nobly from a hillside. Korbel is one of Wine Country's most popular destinations, offering romance, history, and beauty.

7. Mom's Apple Pie (www.momsapplepieusa.com) This roadhouse makes fat pies even better than most moms', served in tin pans or by the slice. The coconut cream and the fresh Gravenstein apple are to die for. Mom's also serves lunch, offering sandwiches and salads.

check out the amenities and, naturally, the surf access.

APPLEWOOD INN (www.applewood inn.com, 707-869-9093, 800-555-8509, 13555 Hwy. 116, Guerneville, CA 95446; Price: Expensive to Very Expensive) This mission-style inn hidden in a stand of redwoods is one of Sonoma County's finest. It's romantic and formal yet familiar, like a wealthy grandmother's house. The site was originally an apple orchard and now harbors a circa-1922 mansion with nine rooms and Piccola Casa, a matching house added in 1995, with seven rooms.

Rare finds at Sophie's Cellars.

8. Sophie's Cellars (www.sophiescellars.com) This savvy shop amid the redwoods has great finds and highbrow artisan cheeses to boot. The owners have an in with vintners producing the best of the boutiques. Consider yourself lucky to be tipped off to this place. It has wines from Sonoma, Napa, and beyond, including imports from France and Italy, among other countries.

9. Merry Edwards (www.merryedwards.com) Food was Merry's gateway to wine, and she makes a hell of a blackberry pie. But it's her pinot noir and her sauvignon blanc that makes the greatest impression on your palate. Her winery is, for the most part, a house of pinot. Stop by here and you won't regret it.

10. Osmosis (www.osmosis.com) A truly unique experience, Osmosis is the only place in the Western world to offer Japanese-style enzyme baths. The baths are similar to mud baths in only one way: you're covered from neck to toe. In this case, though, it's not mud but a sawdust-like mix of fragrant cedar, rice bran, and more than six hundred active enzymes.

Three new suites and an additional building called The Gatehouse were added in 1999. The common area is centered on a huge double-sided stone fireplace. Breakfast is served in the inn's freestanding restaurant, Applewood (see listing under Restaurants), and the inn also has a cooking school.

BODEGA BAY LODGE AND SPA (www.bodegabaylodge.com, 707-875-3525, 888-875-2250, 103 Hwy. 1, Bodega Bay, CA 94923; Price: Expensive to Very Expensive) This wood-shingled seaside lodge—well appointed and intimate—is sheltered from coastal winds but close enough for the sound

A sweeping view of the Bodega Coast. Tim Fish

In the great outdoors of Sonoma County

The **Bodega Headlands** stretch like a curved arm out to sea. Dramatic cliffs provide a spectacular vista of the Pacific coast. This is the best area to watch for whales in winter and early spring.

Goat Rock Beach extends from the sandbars along the mouth of the Russian River, where sea lions and their young can be seen at certain times of year.

of the surf. All rooms have ocean or bay views and private balconies, and many feature fireplaces, vaulted ceilings, spa baths, refrigerators, wet bars, and coffeemakers. Even the pool and whirlpool offer breathtaking views. The Duck Club restaurant is expensive, but it's one of the best on the Sonoma coast.

FARMHOUSE INN RESTAURANT & SPA (www.farmhouseinn.com, 707-887-3300, 800-464-6642, 7871 River Rd., Forestville, CA 95436; Price: Expensive to Very Expensive) Built as a farmhouse in 1878, this inn later became a horse ranch and later still, a roadhouse lodge. Today, not only is it one of the most stylish inns in Sonoma

County, but it's also home to one of the finest restaurants in Wine Country. The interior of the main house sets a distinct New England tone, with a long, Shaker-style dining room where a rich breakfast feast is spread. The din of traffic on River Road may jangle some nerves, but noise drops considerably at night. The innkeeper and staff are exceptionally friendly.

INN AT OCCIDENTAL (www.innat occidental.com, 707-874-1047, 800-522-6324, 3657 Church St., Occidental, CA 95465; Price: Expensive to Very Expensive) Perched on a hill overlooking the quiet village of Occidental, this comfortable, three-story Victorian inn is a jewel, one of Wine Country's best.

It is well off the beaten path and delightfully so. Guarded by fruit trees and a lush courtyard garden with a fountain, the inn was built in 1876. The Wolsborns are exceptional hosts, offering wine, cheese, and homemade cookies by the living room hearth each evening. A superb gourmet breakfast is served in the dining room or on the porch.

INN AT THE TIDES (www.innatthe tides.com, 707-875-2751, 800-541-7788, 800 Hwy. 1, P.O. Box 640, Bodega Bay, CA 94923; Price: Moderate to Very Expensive) Six coastal acres with natural landscaping surround this inn—actually 12 separate lodges scattered over a hillside. The 86 guest rooms are agreeably designed, and each has a bay or ocean view, with a refrigerator, coffeemaker, and a hide-a-bed. The inn is home to Sonoma County's leading winemaker dinner; if interested, inquire when making your reservations. Continental breakfast is served across Highway 1 at The Tides.

RAFORD HOUSE INN (www.raford house.com, 707-887-9573, 800-887-9503, 10630 Wohler Rd., Healdsburg, CA 95448; Price: Moderate to Expensive) In the heart of rural Sonoma County, this inn is ideally located for touring the wineries of Russian River and Dry Creek valleys. An 1880 Victorian, it sits like a jewel on a gentle slope overlooking vineyards and tall redwoods. Stately palm trees stand as sentinels on the front lawn, and at the end of a tall staircase is a wide porch, an ideal place to kick off your shoes and watch the hummingbirds flitter by.

SONOMA ORCHID INN (www.sono maorchidinn.com, 707-869-4466, 888-877-4466, 12850 River Rd., Guerneville, CA 95446; Price: Moderate to Expensive) Within walking distance of Korbel Champagne Cellars and the Russian River, this circa-1906 inn is built of redwood and has 10 guest rooms, each with a private bath. Hawthorn Cottage has a king-sized bed, a fireplace, and a cozy window

Typical breakfast fare for guests of the Inn at Occidental.

seat. Madrone has a king-sized bed, a sitting area with a sofa, and a private brick patio. The inn serves decadent "skip-lunch breakfasts," replete with caloric dishes such as stuffed French toast soufflé.

SANTA NELLA HOUSE (www .santanellahouse.com, 707-869-9488, 887-869-9488, 12130 Hwy. 116, Guerneville, CA 95446; Price: Moderate to Expensive) Nestled in a quiet redwood forest, this inn is an 1870 Victorian with a grand wraparound veranda. There are four guest rooms, all with private baths and furnished with functional antiques and queen-sized beds. All have wood-burning fireplaces. A full breakfast—artichoke soufflé with basil-chive roasted potatoes is just one of many specialties—is served in the kitchen by the wood-burning stove. The parlor/music room is a favorite gathering place.

SEA RANCH LODGE (www.sea ranchlodge.com, 707-785-2371, 800-732-7262, 60 Sea Walk Dr., Sea Ranch, CA 95497; Price: Expensive to Very Expensive) On bluffs above the Pacific Ocean, this lodge has one of the best vistas in Wine Country. All but one of the 20 rooms face the sea—cozy window seats offer front-row viewing for spectacular sunsets—and some of the rooms have fireplaces. The location is remote, but if you're in need of a peaceful getaway, this is it. Outside, the weathered wood recalls New England, and the interior feels like a rustic cabin, with knotty pine, cathedral ceilings, and quilted bedspreads. Some rooms have fireplaces and hot tubs. Three caveats: The lodge is historic, so the walls are a bit thin; locate your room's flashlight immediately because lighting is poor outside at night; and bring a sweater because fog keeps the locale cool even in summer. The restaurant is adequate

but pricey—but, oh, that view! Hiking trails are well marked along the bluffs, and the inn is dog friendly.

SONOMA COAST VILLA & SPA (www.scvilla.com, 707-876-9818, 888-404-2255, 16702 Hwy. 1, Bodega, CA 94922; Price: Expensive to Very Expensive) This Mediterranean-style resort on 60 acres is great for roaming. The pastoral hillsides are lovely, and there are plenty of meandering gardens. The inn's 18 rooms are furnished with modern Mediterranean decor, including Italian slate floors; all the rooms have fireplaces, and many have whirlpool tubs and private patios. A continental breakfast is served in the dining room.

Other Accommodations
Bodega Coast Inn (707-875-2217, 800-346-6999, www.bodegacoastinn.com, 521 Hwy. 1, Bodega Bay, CA 94923; Moderate to Very Expensive; AE, D, DC, MC, V) Once a Holiday Inn, this inn has 45 attractively appointed rooms and suites, with balconies offering lovely views of Bodega Bay harbor. A few rooms have fireplaces, whirlpool tubs, and vaulted ceilings. Some rooms have two-person whirlpools.

Bodega Harbor Inn (707-875-3594, www.bodegaharborinn.com, 1345 Bodega Ave. at Coast Hwy. 1, Bodega Bay, CA 94923; Inexpensive; MC, V) This offers 14 rooms, 2 suites, cottages, and vacation homes. Some rooms have bay views, decks, fireplaces, and kitchens. It's a bit funky, but comfortable.

Fairfield Inn & Suites (707-829-6677, 866-388-4979, 1101 Gravenstein Hwy. S., Sebastopol, CA 95472; Inexpensive to Expensive; AE, D, DC, MC, V) Completed in late 1998, this pleasant, 82-room inn is just one of two hotels Sebastopol offers. Included are

Spa Heaven in Sonoma Valley

Fairmont Sonoma Mission Inn and Spa (www.fairmont.com). Who's that lounging in the mineral pool? The array of treatments offered is mind-boggling . . .

Osmosis (www.osmosis.com) is the only place in the Western world to offer Japanese-style enzyme baths.

The perfect touch after a day of wine tasting.

a pool, spa, gym, and continental breakfast. Each room has a refrigerator and coffeemaker. Wi-fi Internet access is available.

Santa Rosa Courtyard by Marriott (707-573-9000, 175 Railroad St., Santa Rosa, CA 95401; Moderate to Expensive; AE, D, DC, MC, V) It has 138 nonsmoking rooms—plus a swimming pool, spa, café, lounge, and room service. It's handicapped accessible and is close to downtown and historic Railroad Square shopping area.

Timber Cove Inn (707-847-3231, 800-987-8319, www.timbercoveinn .com, 21780 N. Coast Hwy. 1, Jenner, CA 95450; Moderate to Very Expensive; AE, MC, V) This inn is charming but funky, with a breathtaking location perched on a rocky cliff overlooking the ocean. Many of the 50 rooms have ocean views; some have fireplaces and private hot tubs. Included are a restaurant and lounge.

Local Flavors

Taste of the town—local restaurants, cafés, bars, bistros, etc.

RESTAURANTS

Good eats are plentiful in Bodega Bay and West County. There's great seafood—including some of the best clam chowder on the West Coast. Go ahead, indulge. If you gain a few pounds, call it research.

APPLEWOOD INN AND RESTAURANT (www.applewoodinn .com, 707-869-9093, 800-555-8509, 13555 Hwy. 116, Guerneville, CA 95446; Price: Expensive; Cuisine: California) If you can't spend the night— Applewood is one of the best inns in Wine Country (see listing under Lodging)—then dinner is the next best thing. The main house, built in 1922, is an architectural gem done in the Mediterranean style. The restaurant is styled to be the estate's barn. Long and narrow with cathedral ceilings and a stone fireplace, it's handsome and masculine. The food is excellent, and specialties include seared wild king salmon and herbs de Provence-crusted rack of lamb. Desserts often include fruit from the inn's own orchard. The wine list is impressive, highlighting Russian River Valley selections, and is generally well priced. The service is sharp and intelligent, well paced, courteous, and professional.

BAY VIEW RESTAURANT AT THE INN AT THE TIDES (www.innatthe tides.com/dining.asp, 707-875-2751, 800-541-7788, 800 Hwy. 1, Bodega Bay, CA 94923; Price: Expensive; Cuisine: Seafood, California) If the hectic hum of The Tides or Lucas Wharf is too much, and if you seek something more than basic fish, the Bay View might be an alternative. Though the food is simply on par with those two popular restaurants—good, but not great—the presentation has more flair, and the view is more impressive. If these factors are important, you might not mind the added cost. The menu is dominated by local seafood, and two interesting entrées are the Bodega Bay bouillabaisse and the cioppino. If you prefer meat, the filet mignon Hitchcock is a tasty pick. The wine list is superbly selected, with a credible list by the glass. The decor is elegant if a bit generic, with a beamed cathedral ceiling and Scandinavian furnishings. Servers are polite and efficient.

DUCK CLUB (www.bodegabay lodge.com, 707-875-3525, 103 Hwy. 1, Bodega Bay, CA 94923, at Bodega Bay Lodge; Price: Moderate to Very Expensive; Cuisine: Seafood, California) This out-of-the-way restaurant—hidden amid the lush landscaping of Bodega Bay Lodge—is worth a search. It offers the best food on the Sonoma coast. The decor is strictly country club, but the views over the harbor and wetlands are gorgeous, and a blazing fire warms the room. The menu may be too broad, with the kitchen seemingly stretched at times. Offerings range from seafood to pork chops to steaks and chicken. Good picks include the Dungeness crab cakes, crisp roast half Liberty duck with blackberry ginger sauce, and the pistachio-crusted halibut. Service is solid, and the restaurant now has a full bar.

FARMHOUSE INN & RESTAURANT (www.farmhouseinn.com, 707-887-3300, 800-464-6642, 7871 River Rd., Forestville, CA 95436; Price: Moderate to Expensive) With a kitchen that delivers one of the best food and wine experiences in Sonoma, this is one country inn that offers more than just charm. The setting is a 135-year-old farmhouse painted a pale yellow and trimmed in black and white and situated in the heart of Russian River Valley vineyards. Guests feel as though they're at a chic dinner party, not a restaurant. The food blends modern French with vibrant California cuisine. Specialties include something called Rabbit, Rabbit, Rabbit—rabbit done three ways: confit, bacon-wrapped loin, and roasted rack. It's delightful, as are fascinating creations such as farmhouse cassoulet with house-made rabbit sausage and duck confit. The impressive wine list takes a worldly view, with excellent selections from France, Germany, and, of course, California. Wine service is superb, thanks to master sommelier Geoff Kruth.

K & L BISTRO (707-823-6614, 119 S. Main St., Sebastopol, CA 95472; Price: Expensive; Cuisine: French, California) A small space with exposed brick walls, this casual bistro draws a crowd of locals every night. It's hard to deny the appeal of the place—the food is decent in a hearty, comforting way, with a menu that includes crab cakes, mussels in white wine, a tasty hamburger, and steak frites. The wine list has some good finds and the price is right.

LUCAS WHARF (707-875-3522, 595 Hwy. 1, Bodega Bay, CA 94923; Price: Moderate to Expensive; Cuisine: Seafood) Built on piers overlooking Bodega Bay harbor, Lucas Wharf is cozy and romantic, with a fireplace and cathedral ceiling. From your table, you'll see great sunsets and fishing boats unloading the catch of the day. Choose what's fresh off the boat, and you won't go wrong—particularly salmon when it's in season (May through September) and Dungeness crab in season (from November to May). There's also a hearty fisherman's stew in a tomato broth. The wine list is weighted to local wines, with savvy picks in the line-up. Lucas Wharf is popular with locals and tourists alike, so be prepared to wait for a table on weekends.

MIREPOIX (www.restaurantmirepoix .com, 707-838-0162, 275 Windsor River Rd., Windsor, CA 95492; Price: Moderate to Very Expensive; Cuisine: French) After you've been in Wine Country a few days, it's easy to get your fill of California cuisine. That's why this French-style brasserie is so appealing. The dining room is a cozy den of 24 seats with an open kitchen. The menu is the same all day, and though it evolves with the season, it's basically French comfort food: mussels in white wine, *steak au poivre*, and coq au vin. The wine list is on the short side but it hits all the right notes and the prices are good.

PIZZAVINO 707 (www.pizzavino707 .com, 707-829-9500, 6948 Sebastopol Ave., Sebastopol, CA 95472; Price: Expensive to Very Expensive; Cuisine: American, Mediterranean) This is a big restaurant—130 seats and 30 outside— with a warehouse feel: exposed brick walls, an open kitchen with a wood-fired oven, an open floor plan that soars two levels high, and rustic wood and metal highlights that somehow lend an overall atmosphere of warmth. There's an energy to the place that's palpable. There's also a similar hearty passion and zest in the food. The seasonal menu focuses on local ingredients, and standouts include pizzas, grilled hanger steak, grilled paprika chicken and rib-eye. The service seems casual at first, but it's attentive and sharp. The wine list, though generally focused on Sonoma, has an eclectic selection from around the world and a good range of prices.

TIDES WHARF AND RESTAURANT (www.innatthetides .com, 707-875-3652, 800-541-7788, 835 Hwy. 1, Bodega Bay, CA 94923; Price: Expensive; Cuisine: Seafood) The Tides was immortalized by Alfred Hitchcock in *The Birds,* but you wouldn't recognize it now. The current dining room has a high-raftered ceiling and stunning views of the harbor from every seat. The food is competent at best, but the catch of the day is usually a good bet: a voluminous list including red snapper, swordfish, lingcod, and Pacific oysters. Local specialties include salmon, in season May through September, and Dungeness crab, in season from November to May. A delicious local classic is the crab cioppino: crab, prawns, scallops, mussels, and clams swimming in a shallow pool of zesty Italian sauce. The lunch menu is almost identical to dinner, but it's a few dollars cheaper. The wine list is sound; ditto the service.

UNDERWOOD BAR & BISTRO (www.underwoodgraton.com, 707-823-7023, 9113 Graton Rd., Graton, CA 95444; Price: Moderate to Expensive; Cuisine: Eclectic) If you like to eat where the winemakers hang out, this restaurant is practically a private club for the West County wine industry. The interior is a masculine blend of urban and country, and there's a long bar that's always hopping. Service is a little too laid back at times, but the food is appealing and hearty. The kitchen takes influences from all over the globe, with a menu that ranges from an eclectic selection of small plates such as crab cakes and roasted beets to hamburgers, and Catalan fish stew. The wine list is modest but offers lots of value; it's devoted largely to California but with a handful of selections from around the world.

WINERIES

Wine lovers have plenty to choose from in the West County, from big wineries like Korbel to the smaller boutiques like Merry Edwards. Prime your palate for a great tasting tour.

HARTFORD FAMILY WINERY (www.hartfordwines.com, 707-887-8010, 707-877-8030, 800-588-0234 ext. 8011 or 8022, 8075 Martinelli Rd., Forestville CA 95436; Tasting: Daily 10–4:30) If you've ever dreamed of retiring to some grand estate in wine country, Hartford is the sort of place you might have in mind. Hidden amid the lush canyons of West County, this stately mansion produces pinot noir, zinfandel, and chardonnay that are deeply flavored and intense. The winery is part of the Jess Jackson family of wineries, which means it has access to top vineyards in Sonoma County. Inside, the tasting room has the venerable atmosphere of a private club.

IRON HORSE VINEYARDS (www.swanwinery.com, 707-887-1507, 9786 Ross Station Rd., Sebastopol, CA 95472; Tasting: Daily 10–3:30) This winery amid the undulating hills of Green Valley is one of Sonoma County's most respected producers of sparkling wine. Barry and Audrey Sterling bought the estate, a former railroad stop, in 1976. Elegant in its sheer simplicity, the winery stretches throughout a series of wooden barns and is surrounded by vineyards and gardens. The tour reveals the classic *méthode champenoise* process used in making French-style bubbly. In addition to its line of opulent sparkling wine, Iron Horse produces chardonnay and pinot noir, both fine examples.

JOSEPH SWAN VINEYARDS (www.swanwinery.com, 707-573-3747, 2916 Laguna Rd, Forestville, CA 95436; Tasting: By appointment) Hardly more than a bungalow, this modest structure belies Joseph Swan's near-legendary status in Wine Country. Beginning in 1969, Swan was a pioneer of zinfandel, crafting heroically ripe and long-lived wines. Pinot noir became Swan's star in the 1980s. Swan died in 1989, and son-in-law Rod Berglund is now winemaker. Although the zins are no longer legendary, they remain fine and authentic creations.

KORBEL CHAMPAGNE CELLARS (www.korbel.com, 707-824-7000, 707-824-7316, 13250 River Rd., Guerneville, CA 95446; Tasting: Daily 10–5) As you drive through the gorgeous redwood forests of the Russian River area, you'll see this century—old, ivy-covered stone wine cellar rising nobly from a hillside. Korbel is one of Wine Country's most popular destinations, offering romance, history, and beauty. To avoid the crowds in summer, arrive early in the morning or late in the afternoon. The half-hour tour is great fun.The Korbel brothers from Czechoslovakia came to Guerneville for the trees, which were perfect for cigar boxes. When the trees were cleared, they planted grapes and made

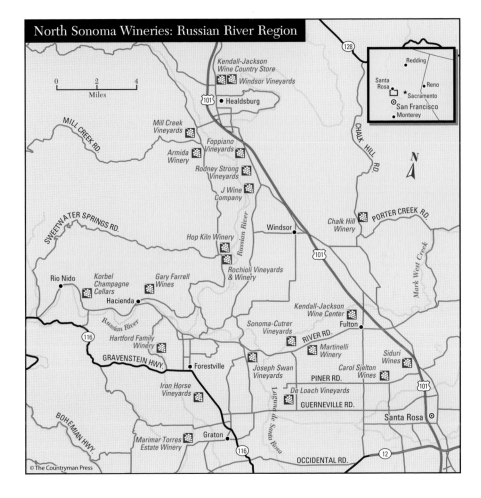

wine using *méthode champenoise,* the traditional French method of making champagne. You'll poke your nose in large wood aging tanks and learn the mystery of the riddling room, where sediment is slowly tapped from each bottle. The tasting room is one of the friendliest, and any or all of the winery's dependable sparklers are offered. During the summer, Korbel's prized antique garden is also available for touring.

MARIMAR TORRES ESTATE
(www.marimarestate.com, 707-823-4365, 11400 Graton Rd, Sebastopol,

CA 95472; Tasting: Daily 11–4) Marimar Torres's family in Spain has been making wine for generations, so when she came to Sonoma County in the mid-1970s, she was beginning her own wine legacy. In 1992 she built this Catalan farmhouse-inspired winery amid the isolated, rolling hills of West Sonoma, and planted 60 acres of pinot noir and chardonnay vineyards. The wines reflect a European passion for refinement and elegant complexity. The tasting room hardly seems like one. It's more like you've stopped in for a glass of wine at a neighbor's place down the road. Offerings include a Tapas and Wine Pairing for $35, which includes five different wines and four tapas. Drop-ins are welcome, but reservations are greatly appreciated.

MARTINELLI WINERY (www.martinelliwinery.com, 707-525-0570, 3360 River Rd., Windsor, CA 95492; Tasting: Daily 10–5) This historic hop barn painted a vivid red is home to a prized zinfandel called Jackass Hill. The wine comes from the steepest hillside vineyards in Sonoma County, planted in 1905. Like many old-vine zins, it grabs your taste buds like a two-horse team. The winery also makes a tasty chardonnay and pinot noir, and they're all lush and complex. This a family winery, through and through, having four generations of Martinellis farming.

MERRY EDWARDS WINERY (www.merryedwards.com, 707-823-7466, 2959 Gravenstein Highway N., Sebastopol, CA 95472; Tasting: Mon.–Sat. 9:30–4:30) Merry Edwards is best known for producing cult pinot noirs, jammy, full-bodied beauties from the Russian River Valley. But Edwards is also making noise with a striking sauvignon blanc. In addition, she dab-

Winemaker Merry Edwards at her house of pinot noir. Ben Miller

bles in chardonnay and sparkling wine on a less regular basis. Edwards is well respected as one of California's first woman winemakers, drawing plenty of attention in the early 1970s for her determination to show she had the muscle to make wine along with the guys. She ultimately decided to be her own boss, founding her winery in 1997. Edwards and her crew are proponents of sustainability, and among the concoctions you might see in her vineyards are organic mushroom composts.

SONOMA-CUTRER VINEYARDS (www.sonomacutrer.com, 707-237-3489, 877-797-3489, 4401 Slusser Rd., Windsor, CA 95492; Tasting and Tours: By appointment) Harvest is called "crush," yet crush is a crude way to describe how Sonoma-Cutrer makes chardonnay. Pampering is more like it. Grapes arrive in small boxes and are then chilled to 40 degrees in a specially designed cooling tunnel. Then they are hand sorted and, left in whole clusters, are put through a gentle, membrane press. A tour reveals the entire process as well as an underground aging cellar. Once the leader in California chardonnay, Sonoma-Cutrer now has keen competition. Brice Cutrer Jones, a jet fighter pilot in the Vietnam War, founded the winery in 1981 and built an ultramodern facility that blends into the hills. (Sonoma-Cutrer also has two world-class croquet courts.) In 1999 the winery was purchased by conglomerate Brown-Forman, which owns Fetzer Vineyards and other well-known consumer brands such as Jack Daniels and Southern Comfort.

Palate Adventures

Offerings in Bodega Bay and West County.

Offerings in Bodega Bay and West County reflect the region's proximity to the coast. You'll find delectable crab cakes and chowder as well as ice cream shops and, you guessed it, wine.

• *Sample the fresh seafood*
One of the joys of living on the Pacific Ocean is fresh seafood. Most prized locally are Dungeness crab and salmon. Crab season runs from mid-November to June, and the local salmon season runs from mid-May to September.

Spud Point Crab Company (www.spudpointcrab.com, 707-875-9472, 1910 Westshore Rd., Bodega Bay, CA) People come from as far away as Europe to taste Carol Anello's clam chowder and crab cakes, thanks to Yelp reviews on the Net.

Tides Wharf Fish Market (707-875-3554, 835 Hwy. 1, Bodega Bay, CA 94923) This cozy, down-home spot on the Bay offers tasty clam chowder and seafood of all stripes.

• *Snag a prized bottle*
Sophie's Cellars (www.sophiescellars .com, 707-865-1122, 20293 Hwy. 116, Monte Rio, CA., 95462) This shop is a real find, a place where you can score the best of the boutiques, and the cheeses are an adventure as well. Expect the top names in wine; while there are offerings from all over the world, the bottlings are weighted to California.

• *Stop in for some good eats and tasty treats*
Mom's Apple Pie (www.momsapple pieusa.com, 707-823-8330, 4550

Insider Secrets:

Spud Point's Carol Anello makes only 80 crab cakes on Saturdays and another batch of 80 on Sundays. They're ready at 1 PM each day, first come, first serve, and it's a mad dash. (www.spudpoint crab.com)

A cadre of America's wealthiest movers and shakers gather each summer at the Bohemian Grove, and a Grove member once shocked the owners of **Sophie's Cellars** by purchasing $20,000 worth of wine in one day.

There are two secret ingredients that make **Mom's Apple Pies** so delectable: the Gravenstein apples and the pampering. Mom (aka Betty Carr) says it's all about keeping a focused eye on the oven. "You must baby-sit this pie," she jokes.

Gravenstein Hwy. N., Sebastopol, CA 95472) This roadhouse makes fat pies better than most moms, served in tin pans or by the slice. The coconut cream and the fresh Gravenstein apple are to die for. Not just pies are made here; Mom's also serves lunch, offering sandwiches and salads.

Korbel Delicatessen (707-824-7313, 13250 River Rd., Guerneville, CA 95446) Under a cathedral ceiling on an acid-washed floor, five or six tables offer shady views through tall windows. Outside are plenty of additional tables. Here you can get muffins, salads, sandwiches, beer on tap, champagne and wine by the glass, and ales of all kinds (amber, pale, port, golden wheat). There are breads, jams and jellies, and vinegars, too.

Screamin' Mimi's (www.screaminmimisicecream.com, 707-823-5902, 6902 Sebastopol Ave., Sebastopol, CA 95472) They make their own ice cream and sorbets here, and it's all wonderful. Put your diet on hold to free yourself up for these delectable treats.

• Get it fresh from the farm
Sonoma County Farm Trails (www.farmtrails.org, 707-837-8896) is an informal collective of farms. Also worth seeking out is Twin Hill Ranch (707-823-2815, 1689 Pleasant Hill Rd., Sebastopol, CA 95472), which specializes in apples, nuts, and dried fruit. Enjoy a roaring fire on chilly days. Kozlowski Farms (707-887-1587, 5566 Gravenstein Hwy. N., Forestville, CA 95436) is an orchard turned down-home gourmet enterprise. This Sonoma County treasure specializes in jams and jellies, apple butter, and raspberry and other flavored vinegars as well as apples and other fresh produce.

• Take part in a Wine Country seasonal tradition
Bodega Bay Fish Fest (www.bbfishfest.org, 707-875-3866, Bodega Bay, CA 94923) This is a decades-old tradition for this coastal town made famous by Alfred Hitchcock's *The Birds*. This spring (typically April, early May) celebration includes bathtub races, harbor tours, kite flying, a golf tournament, and a boat parade. The high point of the weekend is the annual blessing of the fleet.

Gravenstein Apple Fair (www.gravensteinapplefair.com, 707-824-1765, Ragle Ranch Park, Sebastopol, CA 95472) Sebastopol, once the apple capital of the world, today specializes in the distinctive Gravenstein variety. There's a potpourri at this mid-August event: arts and crafts, music, hay rides, storytelling, and, of course, apple treats of all kinds.

Sebastopol Apple Blossom Festival (www.sebastopol.org, 707-823-3032, 877-828-4748, downtown Sebastopol, CA 95472) When the apple trees are in striking form in April, you won't find a more beautiful place than Sebastopol. Apples rule, of course. Partake of the apple fritters, cobbler, and pies, plus enjoy music, games, parade, and arts and crafts.

To Do
Check out these great attractions and activities . . .

SHOPPING

The town of Sebastopol offers the best shopping in the West County, and it's worth spending time (and money) here, even though it's a pretzel of a town. Our favorites: Global Village (707-829-4765, 172 N. Main St., Sebastopol, CA 95472) is truly an international affair, featuring women's clothes come from Bali, Peru, and India—to name just a few countries—and there's also jewelry and some men's and unisex clothing, too. East of Eden (707-829-1968, 103 Main St., Sebastopol, CA 95472) carries new fashions, wedding gowns, and accessories, with a few vintage items. Country Home (707-829-1793, 195 N. Main St., Sebastopol, CA 95472) provides the accessories—candles, cookie jars, bath lotions, and baskets. Stepping inside this shop is like walking through a Country Living magazine. Wild Things (707-829-3371, 130 S. Main St., Suite 102, Sebastopol, CA 95472) is one of the most hip nature shops you'll ever come across with finger puppets, screen-painted T-shirts, and beautiful cards. At Toyworks (707-829-2003, 6940 Sebastopol Ave., Sebastopol, CA 95472) peruse the goodies: globes, kites, puzzles, and even kits for building your own volcano. Copperfield's Used & Rare Books (707-829-0429, 176 N. Main St., Sebastopol, CA 95472) is a bookstore that seems to have a New Age state of mind with shelves are lined with secondhand volumes with entire walls filed with art and fiction. Rosemary's Garden (707-829-2539, 132 N. Main St., Sebastopol, CA 95472) is an herbal apothecary and gift store that's well stocked with products to soothe the soul, including Chinese herbs, tea blends, and massage oils. Antique Society (707-829-1733, 2661 Gravenstein Hwy. S., Sebastopol, CA 95472) is Sonoma County's largest antiques collective, with more than one hundred dealers. Ray's Trading Co. (707-829-9726, 3570 Gravenstein Hwy. S., Sebastopol, CA 95472) is a salvage company recognized as an important resource for Bay Area people restoring Victorian homes with bins full of antique doorknobs and drawer pulls, and the company is even a source for windows and doors.

CULTURAL OUTINGS

• *Step out into film history*
Perhaps Sonoma County's most famous edifice was popularized by Alfred Hitchcock: the Potter Schoolhouse, featured prominently as Bodega Bay School in the 1963 movie *The Birds*, is located in the small burg of Bodega in West County. Movie buffs are constantly stopping by for a photo out front. It's a private home now, but it's occasionally open for private tours.

• *See a movie*
Sebastopol Cinemas (707-829-3456, McKinley St. & Petaluma Ave., Sebastopol, CA 95472) This five-theater cinema is inside a refurbished brandy distillery. It shows first-run films.

• *Tour the galleries*
Bodega Landmark Studio (707-876-3477, www.artbodega.com, 17255 Bodega Hwy., Bodega, CA 94923) West County artists are the specialty here, with a focus on oils, watercolors, ceramics, blown glass, fine art photography, and jewelry.
   Ren Brown Collection (www.renbrown.com, 707-875-2922, 1781 Hwy. 1, Bodega Bay, CA 94923) Modern Japanese prints are the focus of this gallery, and famous Japanese artists exhibiting include Shinoda Toko and Tanaka Ryohei.

• Visit a historical treasure

Fort Ross (www.fortrossstatepark.com, 707-847-3286, 19005 Coast Hwy. 1, Jenner, CA., 95450) A quick history quiz: who were Sonoma's first settlers (besides the Indians, of course)? If you said the Spanish, you're wrong. It was actually the Russians, who established Fort Ross, which predated the Sonoma Mission by 11 years. The Russian-American Trading Company, a firm controlled largely by the Imperial Russian government, came to California to escape the cruel winters of Alaska and to hunt for valuable sea otters. Its workers landed south in Bodega Bay, which they called Rumiantsev, and explored to the north. On a windy bluff overlooking the Pacific, they built their fort and community, now the centerpiece of Fort Ross State Historic Park.

• Ring out the summer with a river festival

Russian River Jazz and Blues Festival (www.omegaevents.com, 707-869-1595, Johnson Beach, Guerneville, CA 95446) For two days following Labor Day, music

The Potter Schoolhouse, featured in Hitchcock's *The Birds,* is still a popular tourist stop even though it's a private home now. Tim Fish

lovers sun on the beach or listen from floating inner tubes. Saturday features jazz, while Sunday focuses on blues. The lineup in the past has included Grover Washington and David Benoit.

• *Check out the pub scene*
Dempsey's Ale House (www.dempseys.com, 707-765-9694, 50 E. Washington St., Petaluma, CA 94952) This is Wine Country's best brewpub—period. From the outside, Dempsey's doesn't look like much—it's in a generic shopping center—but it offers a handsome interior plus outdoor seating right along the Petaluma River. Peter Burrell brews superior ales, particularly his Red Rooster, and the food is better than you'll find at any pub. Chef Bernadette Burrell worked in the kitchen at Mustards Grill, so expect pork chops, wood-fired pizzas, and roasted half chickens.

Jasper O'Farrell's (707-829-2062, 6957 Sebastopol Ave., Sebastopol, CA 95472) This is a full-service pub that serves wine, beer, and spirits. A DJ is the entertainment on Wednesdays, Fridays, and Saturdays. Most Thursdays are Karaoke night, and Tight Wad Tuesdays serve bargains starting at $2.50.

• *Enjoy serious theater*
Sonoma County Repertory Theatre (www.the-rep.com, 707-823-0177, 104 N. Main St., Sebastopol, CA 95472) Since its inception in 1995, this company has quickly become the area's leading theater, staging a mix of classics and cutting-edge dramas, comedies, and occasionally a musical. Performances are in a small Sebastopol theater. Scott Phillips is the artistic director. Top productions have included Shakespeare's *The Tempest* and *Hamlet* as well as *The Glass Menagerie, A Streetcar Named Desire, Tuesdays with Morrie,* and *Assassin.*

RECREATIONAL FUN

• *Head for the coast*
Sonoma County's 62-mile coastline has a rustic beauty that's scarcely changed from the days when the Miwok and Pomo Indians were the only inhabitants in the area. Visitors flock to the Sonoma coast to enjoy some of the most spectacular views in all of California. The rugged cliffs, continually battered by the wild Pacific Ocean, afford a setting of breathtaking beauty. Thanks to the foresight of those who fought to preserve public access to the coast, there are many outlets from which to view the ocean along Highway 1. Particularly popular is the stretch between Bodega Bay and Jenner, where several beaches offer a variety of topography and vistas for hiking, picnicking, wetsuit diving, surfing, or just relaxing.

Whatever your activity, it's important to remember at all times that the Pacific Ocean can be dangerous. Every year, deaths are caused by unpredictable waves and the strong undertow. Be cautious.

Bodega Bay harbor offers protection from the rough Pacific surf and serves as the homeport for many commercial fishing boats. After gaining fame as the setting of Alfred Hitchcock's *The Birds*, the town of Bodega Bay has now become a well-known stopover and destination spot for California residents and visitors alike. Sport fishing, harbor cruises, and whale-watching trips can be arranged from Porto Bodega Marina, off Highway 1 on Bay Flat Road. The gentle beaches on the west side of the harbor afford a perfect spot for windsurfing or sea kayaking.

• Be a beach bum

Here are some of the beaches along the coast, listed from north to south. For detailed information, call the Sonoma County Tourism Program (800-576-6662). Some of the beaches have a day-use fee.

Bodega Headlands (707-875-3483, at the end of Bay Flat Road, off Highway 1, Bodega Bay, CA 94923) Originally part of the Sierra Nevadas, the headlands stretch like a curved arm out to sea. For 40 million years, they have ridden the Pacific Plate northward, out of step with the land on the other side of the San Andreas Fault. The cliffs of the headlands provide a spectacular vista of the Pacific Ocean coast. They provide the best spots to watch for whales in the winter and early spring. It's not a bad idea to bring binoculars and a jacket. Also of interest at the headlands is the Bodega Marine Lab (www.blm.ucdavis.edu, 707-875-2211, 2099 Westside Rd., Bodega Bay, CA 94923), open to the public on Friday from 2 to 4 PM. It's educational, and kids will love it.

Doran Regional Park (707-875-3540, Doran Beach Rd., off Highway 1, south of Bodega Bay, CA 94923) This is a popular family spot because of its level, sandy beach and overnight camping facilities. An annual sand castle competition is held every August. Salt Point State Park (707-847-3221, 800-444-7275, 25050 Hwy. 1, 95450, north of Timber Cove) Here you'll find 4,114 acres along 5 miles of shore, offering picnicking, horseback riding, fishing, skin diving, and hiking. More than

Kids play on a beach at Bodega Bay.   Tim Fish

20 miles of trails wind through tall forests, windswept headlands, a stunted Pygmy forest, and grassy valleys along the San Andreas Fault. Camping is available. Adjacent to the park is Kruse Rhododendron State Reserve. In May and June the brilliant pink blossoms of native rhododendrons brighten the forest along the path.

Goat Rock Beach (707-875-3483, 3905 Bodega Bay, CA 94923, off Highway 1, south of Jenner) Named for the huge beach rock that bears a resemblance to the hunched back of a grazing goat, the beach extends from the sandbars along the mouth of the Russian River, where sea lions and their young exit the waters of the river at certain times of the year. They're fun to watch, but please don't disturb them.

Sonoma Coast State Beach (707-875-3483, Salmon Creek, Bodega Bay, CA 94923) This is actually a chain of many beaches along 18 miles of coastline, from Goat Rock to Bodega Head. Each has its own personality and invites different activities, whether it's tidepooling or a serious game of volleyball. Wildflowers brighten the cliffs in the spring. The coast is always cool in the summer, supplying an escape from inland heat.

Bodega Dunes (707-875-3483; 2485 Hwy. 1, Bodega Bay, CA 94923) Here you'll find a boardwalk and 5 miles of trails through the dunes. No dogs are allowed on the beach, trails, or dunes because of endangered western snowy plover in these areas, but dogs are allowed in the campground, which has 98 sites for tents and RVs up to 31 feet long.

• Get in the water

The Sonoma coast is Wine Country's busiest recreational spot. Whatever water sport you prefer—scuba diving, abalone diving, surfboarding, kayaking—there's plenty to do on the coast. The water temperatures range from 40 to 55 degrees, making a full wetsuit a minimum requirement, with many divers preferring drysuits for added comfort. Diving is a year-round activity, as long as the sea is calm. Divers must respect the power of the ocean.

Abalone can be harvested from April to December (excluding July). Scuba equipment is not allowed while hunting these succulent creatures, and there's a limit of four abalone per person. You'll also need a license to harvest them.

Pinnacles Dive Center (www.pinnacledive.com, 707-542-3100, 2112 Armory Dr., Santa Rosa, CA 95401) Offers diving courses, rentals, equipment sales, and diving trips.

Bodega Bay Surf Shack (www.bodegabaysurf.com, 707-875-3944, 1400 Hwy. 1, Bodega Bay, CA 94923) Here you'll find instruction and tips, and rentals and sales, including kayaks.

Bodega Bay Kayak (www.bodegabaykayak.com, 707-875-3955,) Offers rentals, sales, and tours at $45 for four hours.

• Try tidepooling

The Sonoma coastline is as productive as a tropical rain forest. When the tide goes out twice daily, life from the sea—starfish, snails, and sea anemones, among others—takes refuge in the rocks.

Be patient and discover the magic. A hermit crab may creep out of its turban shell; a sea anemone's green tentacles may entwine a mussel. Track the sculpins as they scurry through the water, and keep an eye out for starfish playing dead. These oases of sea life are full of old-timers. Starfish may be 10 years old and snails may be 20 to 30 years old.

Remember: Please don't remove anything from the pools; even an empty shell might be a hermit crab's mobile home. Tidepoolers are advised to wear waterproof boots for the best exploration. Be cautious. Crabs pinch, octopuses bite, and sea urchin spines are prickly. Also, beware of sleeper waves—those unexpectedly large waves that sneak up and sweep away beachcombers.

For additional insight into the world of the tidepool, visit the Bodega Marine Laboratory (www.bml.ucdavis.edu/index/html, 707-875-2211, 2099 Westside Rd., P.O. Box 247, Bodega Bay, CA 94923). The laboratory is open to the public on Friday from 2 to 4 PM.

Where are the best places to tidepool? Nearly any rocky place along Sonoma Coast State Beach, which stretches between Bodega Bay and Jenner. The Bodega Marine Lab recommends two: Try the north end of Salmon Beach, which is accessible from any Highway 1 pulloff north of the Salmon Creek Bridge. Shell Beach, a few miles south of Jenner on Highway 1, is more remote, requiring a trip down steep stairs, but it's worth it.

• Go whalewatching

One of the great attractions in California is the opportunity to watch gray whales in their annual round-trip migration between summer feeding grounds in the Bering Sea and their breeding and birthing waters off Baja California. From late May to October, the gray whales feed in the cold Pacific waters to build up fat for their 12,000-mile pilgrimage. Then, beginning in late November, they head south, passing close enough to shore to navigate by sight as well as to avoid killer whales in the deeper waters. Their return usually starts in late February and lasts until early June.

The Point Reyes Lighthouse (415-669-1534) at the tip of the Point Reyes National Seashore in Marin County—about a 1.5-hour drive from Santa Rosa—offers one of the best vantage points in the state for whalewatching. The lighthouse is open from 10 to 4:30 daily except Tuesday and Wednesday, but parking is limited and extremely crowded on weekends. Call ahead to check on visibility, because the lighthouse sits on the windiest and rainiest spot on the entire Pacific Coast.

Sonoma County offers good whalewatching sites, including Gualala Point, Stillwater Cove, Fort Ross, and Bodega Head. On a clear day, you'll have plenty of company to share sightings—everyone bundled against the sea breezes, toting binoculars and picnic lunches, and ready to spend several hours searching for the telltale white spouts shooting above the blue Pacific waters.

For a close-up view, reserve a place on a whalewatching boat out of Bodega Bay. Remember that it's typically 15 degrees colder on the water, so wear plenty of warm clothes. Law prohibits boaters from harassing whales, but the large mammals have little fear of man and often approach boats at sea. All boats leave from Porto Bodega Marina on Bay Flat Road, off Highway 1. The boating season is January through April, and boats run weather-permitting. Contact Bodega Bay Sport Fishing Center (707-875-3344, 1410 Bay Flat Rd., Bodega Bay, CA 94923) or The Boathouse (707-875-3495, 1445 Hwy. 1, Bodega Bay, CA 94923)

Insider Secret:

A Japanese enzyme bath at **Osmosis** is a relaxing treatment, although you may feel as though you're in a petri dish, with all those enzymes working on you.

• *Indulge in a one-of-a-kind spa* Osmosis (www.osmosis.com, 707-823-8231, 209 Bohemian Hwy., Freestone, CA 95472) A truly unique experience, Osmosis is the only place in the Western world to offer Japanese-style enzyme baths. The baths are similar to mud baths in only one way: You're covered from neck to toe. In this case, though, it's not mud but a sawdust-like mix of fragrant cedar, rice bran, and more than six hundred active enzymes. The concoction ferments and generates gentle and natural heat. Guests don kimonos and begin their treatment in a Japanese sitting room, sipping enzyme tea as they gaze through shoji doors into the Japanese garden. Baths can be taken solo or with a friend. The treatment concludes with a shower and a 30-minute blanket wrap or Swedish massage. Enzyme bath with 75-minute massage: $170.

9

Santa Rosa

SANTA ROSA is the "chosen spot of all this Earth as far as Nature is concerned"—that's according to the late Luther Burbank, the town's favorite son. The genteel plant genius courted Mother Nature as he developed more than 800 strains and varieties of plants over his 55-year career.

Burbank's "chosen spot" has grown to be the largest city in California Wine Country and the fifth-largest city in the San Francisco Bay Area. It's 50 miles north of the Golden Gate Bridge and 30 miles east of the Pacific Ocean, with Mediterranean weather.

Others who have left their indelible mark on the city are the late Charles Schulz, creator of the comic strip *Peanuts,* and John Ash, the celebrity chef who has been called the father of Wine Country cuisine. As you roam throughout the city, you'll spy small-framed sculptures of the Peanuts characters, a tribute to Schulz. You'll also hear good things about the John Ash Restaurant; the raves are well deserved, even though Ash no longer has ownership ties to it.

Santa Rosa may be the largest city in Sonoma County, but when it comes to tourists, it's often trumped by Healdsburg and Sonoma, which are even more immersed in wine culture. That said, Santa Rosa still manages to be the chosen spot for many tourists, because it has its share of boutique wineries and good eats, as well as a more energetic nightlife than any other city in Wine Country. For instance, Monti's, Rendez-Vous Bistro, and Franco's are all hot spots on the weekends. Franco's, which offers Sangria Fridays, is making the biggest play for the late-night crowd by serving pizza by the slice from 11 PM until 2:30 AM on Fridays and Saturdays (see listings under Restaurants).

LEFT: Giraffes are among the wild things at Safari West.

Travel Like an Insider:

Our Top 10 Picks for Santa Rosa

1. Siduri (www.siduri.com) The name *Siduri* comes from the Babylonian goddess of wine. The lush pinot noirs you'll find at this winery can be pricey but they're well worth the *dinero*.

The artful Siduri label.

2. Flamingo Resort Hotel (www.flamingo resort.com) French country furnishings and mature landscaping make this 170-room resort hotel friendly and comfortable in an unfussy way. Guests have access to an adjacent fitness center, and the 25-meter outdoor pool is heated year-round.

3. Vintners Inn (www.vintnersinn.com) Surrounded by a 92-acre vineyard, Vintners Inn is one of Sonoma County's finest establishments. It's a European-style hotel with an old world atmosphere, from its French country decor to the central plaza with a fountain. The inn is convenient to both Sonoma and Napa Valley wineries. Next door is the superb **John Ash & Co.** restaurant.

4. Safari West Wildlife Preserve and Tent Camp (www.safariwest.com) This is no Jurassic Park—no danger lurks—but it's based on the same idea: making the wild accessible. View wildlife like wildebeest and giraffe as you tour the preserve in a rugged, open-air vehicle, then spend the night here in an authentic African tent (luxuriously appointed) and go to sleep listening to the sounds of the savannah.

5. Luther Burbank Home and Gardens (www.lutherburbank.org) Plant genius Luther Burbank remains Santa Rosa's favorite son eighty-five years after his death. The half-hour tour of the Luther Burbank house is full of facts and artifacts and includes a glimpse inside one of Burbank's original greenhouses. The garden, as you might expect, abounds in Burbank creations, particularly the Paradox Walnut Tree and the Burbank Rose.

Checking In

Best places to stay in and around Santa Rosa.

In Santa Rosa there are plenty of lodging options to choose from, whether you opt for flat-out pampering or a budget-savvy getaway.

FLAMINGO RESORT HOTEL (www.flamingoresort.com, 707-545-8530, 800-848-8300, 2777 4th St., Santa Rosa, CA 95405; Price: Inexpensive to Very Expensive) French country furnishings and mature landscaping make this 170-room resort hotel friendly and comfortable in an unfussy way. Sonoma Valley's premium wineries are just minutes east on Highway 12. Guests have access to an adjacent fitness center, and the 25-meter outdoor pool is heated year-round. Specialty shops and excellent restaurants are just blocks away on Farmers Lane. It's popular with both business travelers and tourists.

6. **Charles M. Schulz Museum** (www.schulzmuseum.com) The late Charles Schulz was a Santa Rosa native, and the town continues to celebrate him with sculptures of comic strip characters throughout the city. Schulz is an icon who created a sophisticated cast of characters, taking their angst and pure-hearted faith to the TV screen for millions to see. This spot in Santa Rosa is a designated place to honor Schulz. It's actually more of a museum and gift shop than a gallery, but it's worth checking out if you're a *Peanuts* fan because many of Schulz's originals are on display.

7. **McDonald Avenue** Many of Santa Rosa's great buildings were lost in the 1906 earthquake, though McDonald Avenue on the west edge of downtown survived. Alfred Hitchcock filmed *Shadow of a Doubt* in Santa Rosa, which is shown extensively in the film. The McDonald Mansion, also known as **Mableton,** inspired by the plantation homes of Mississippi, was built in 1878 and remains the city's architectural prize.

8. **Petite Syrah** (www.syrahbistro.com) This restaurant will delight serious Syrah drinkers who spend as much time lingering over the wine list as they do the menu. Of course, the wine list has a fine selection of Syrahs, with key French Rhone wines, even though it's weighted to California. The food, on the whole, is impressive, and the service couldn't be better—prompt and intelligent.

9. **Zazu** (www.zazurestaurant.com) Zazu might as well post a sign out front: "Upscale Comfort Food." From this funky little roadhouse in the heart of the Russian River Valley, chef-owners John Stewart and Duskie Estes, who describe Zazu as "playful Americana and rustic Northern Italian inspired," produce hearty yet sophisticated fare.

10. **Rosso** (www.rossopizzeria.com) The food here has more than an Italian accent. It's fluent. The pizza is true Neapolitan style, crisp and yeasty. And other dishes are equally impressive, like the smoked and braised beef short ribs with soft polenta and the seasonal whole oven-roasted Dungeness crab.

FOUNTAINGROVE INN HOTEL (www.fountaingroveinn.com, 707-578-6101, 800-222-6101, 101 Fountaingrove Pkwy., Santa Rosa, CA 95403; Price: Inexpensive to Very Expensive) The redwood-and-stone exterior of this luxury hotel is modern but blends harmoniously with the landscape, and the deliberately low sweep of the architecture affords an unobstructed view of the Round Barn historical landmark just up the hill. The 124 rooms are elegantly simple and decorated with tasteful furnishings. Continental buffet breakfast is included for business travelers, and standard hotel services are available. The hotel offers wine-touring packages as well as golf packages.

GABLES (www.thegablesinn.com, 707-585-7777, 800-GABLESN, 4257 Petaluma Hill Rd., Santa Rosa, CA 95404; Price: Expensive) The 15 gables over keyhole-shaped windows lend the name to this 1877 high-Victorian Gothic Revival inn. Other features include ceilings that soar to 25 feet, a mahogany staircase, and three Italian marble fireplaces. The seven spacious guest rooms at the Gables (all with private bath, featuring a clawfoot tub) include four suites. The inn is air-conditioned throughout. A full gourmet breakfast and afternoon snacks are included.

HILTON (www.winecountryhilton .com, 707-523-7555, 3555 Round Barn Blvd., Santa Rosa, CA 95403; Price: Moderate to Expensive) This pleasant hotel, with views of Santa Rosa and easy access to Highway 101 and the local wineries, had a $6 million facelift in 2004. The 250 spacious guest rooms and suites are scattered over 7 acres, and though the rooms aren't lavish, they are quite comfortable. The hotel caters to business travelers; all rooms have telephone-equipped desks. There are full hotel services, and the pool area is refreshing and upscale. Ask for

a room with a view when making your reservation.

HOTEL LA ROSE (www.hotellarose .com, 707-284-2879, 800-527-6738, 308 Wilson St., Santa Rosa, CA 95404; Price: Moderate to Very Expensive) This historic hotel—built in 1907 from stone extracted from the mountain ridges east of Santa Rosa—is in Railroad Square, once the hub of commerce in Sonoma County. Now, the square is an eclectic urban area busy with bohemian coffeehouses, nightclubs, and a few street folks. Reconstructed in 1985, the hotel and adjacent carriage house have a total of 49 A European breakfast is included. Josef's Restaurant in the hotel is recommended.

HYATT VINEYARD CREEK (www.hyatt.com, 707-284-1234, 170 Railroad St., Santa Rosa, CA 95401;

Hotel La Rose is a historic inn in Santa Rosa's Railroad Square. Tim Fish

Price: Moderate to Expensive) A recent addition to downtown Santa Rosa, this hotel appeals to conventioneers more than tourists. Still, it's a pleasing if somewhat generic hotel, with 155 rooms on three floors. The decor is standard, but many rooms overlook courtyards and the pool area, which is situated along a bucolic creek. Highway 101 is nearby, making it easily accessible to Wine Country touring, but traffic can be noisy, even at night. Many of Santa Rosa's best restaurants are within walking distance.

SAFARI WEST WILDLIFE PRESERVE AND TENT CAMP (www.safariwest.com, 707-579-2551, 800-616-2695, 3115 Porter Creek Rd., Santa Rosa, CA 95404; Price: Expensive to Very Expensive) Billed as "The spirit of Africa in the heart of the Wine Country," at Safari West you can now stay overnight in authentic, canvas African safari tents with hardwood floors, in close proximity to but separated from exotic wildlife. Each tent has a king-sized bed or two doubles and a bathroom with a shower. A three-hour tour, scheduled separately, will take you through the 400 acres of wilderness, revealing some of the three hundred exotic mammals and birds. (The tour is not included in the price for an overnight stay.)

VINTNERS INN (www.vintnersinn .com, 707-575-7350, 800-421-2584, 4350 Barnes Rd., Santa Rosa, CA 95403, Price: Expensive to Very Expensive) Surrounded by a 92-acre vineyard, Vintners Inn is one of Sonoma County's finest establishments. It's a European-style hotel with an Old World atmosphere, from its French country decor to the central plaza with a fountain. The 44 guest rooms are separated into three buildings that ring the courtyard. Climbing the staircase in each building is akin to going upstairs to bedrooms in an elegant farmhouse. The oversized rooms in this Provençal-influenced inn have beamed ceilings and pine furniture, some dating back to the turn of the previous century. Continental breakfast is included; room service is also available. The inn is convenient to both Sonoma and Napa Valley wineries. Next door is the superb John Ash & Company restaurant.

Best Bests for Kids in Sonoma Valley

Charles M. Schulz Museum (p. 225) and **Snoopy's Gallery** (p. 229) Kids will love to learn more about the man who created Charlie Brown and the gang—Charles Schulz was a Santa Rosa native.
TrainTown (p. 186) Take a ride on a scale-model steam train, visit the petting zoo, and enjoy a variety of train-themed amusement rides.
Doran Regional Park (p. 206) This is a popular family spot because of its sandy beach, overnight camping facilities, and annual sand castle competition every August.

Local Flavors

Taste of the town—local restaurants, cafés, bars, bistros, etc.

RESTAURANTS

The city of Santa Rosa has its share of creative chefs who know how to unearth the best Mother Nature has to offer and then put their signature on it. California cuisine is showcased in these restaurants, playing up local, fresh produce.

FRANCO'S (www.francosristorante .com, 707-523-4800, 505 Mendocino Ave., Santa Rosa, CA 95401; Price: Inexpensive; Cuisine: Italian) This is a family-styled joint right in the heart of downtown Santa Rosa. It serves wood-fired pizzas and rustic Italian food. Frankly, it's not the best Italian food around—Rosso puts it to shame—but it's a great venue for families and for the late-night crowd. Sangria Fridays and pizza by the slice on Fridays and Saturdays from 11 PM to 2:30 AM are a hit.

FLAVOR BISTRO (www.flavorbistro .com, 707-573-9600, 96 Old Court-house Square, Santa Rosa, CA 95404; Price: Moderate to Expensive; Cuisine: California) If you're exploring down-town Santa Rosa, this easygoing bistro is a good choice, particularly if you have kids. The dining room is big and roomy, and there are plenty of tables right out front to watch the tykes play on the lawn of Courthouse Square. The menu is family-friendly, offering a little of everything: salads, sandwiches, pastas, and pizzas, using only organic ingredients. The meats are hormone-free and the fish of the day is always wild, never farmed. Many items are homemade in-house every day, from the breads to the pastas to desserts. Flavor's award-winning wine list offers more than 50 wines by the glass and emphasizes local wines. The service is generally sharp and attentive.

JACK & TONY'S RESTAURANT & WHISKY BAR (www.jackandtonys .com, 707-526-4347, 115 4th St. #B, Santa Rosa, CA; Price: Moderate to Expensive; Cuisine: Modern American Regional Cooking) Whisky lovers congregate here for good eats and serious drinking. There are more than 170 different expressions of scotch, bourbon, and Irish, American, and Japanese whiskies, ranging from $5 to $100. But there's also plenty of regional bottlings for wine lovers. The cuisine here is hearty, classic comfort food. Dishes include red-wine-marinated hangar steak, cornmeal-crusted rainbow trout, and homemade soup.

JACKSON'S BAR AND BISTRO (www.jacksonbarandoven.com, 707-545-6900, 135 4th St., Railroad Square, Santa Rosa, CA; Price: Moderate to Expensive; Cuisine: California Comfort) This savvy restaurant plays to the sophisticated family in Wine Country with great eats and smart prices. The decor is warm and inviting and the comfort food is irresistible. Popular entrées include wood-fired pizza, the grilled pork chop, and the wood-oven-roasted mac & cheese. Chef Josh Silvers and wife Regina are ingenious business partners who named this bistro after their son. It's not surprising it's a hit in Wine Country.

JOHN ASH & CO. (www.vintnersinn .com/dining.asp, 707-527-7687, 4330 Barnes Rd., Santa Rosa, CA 95403; Price: Very Expensive) Chef John Ash continues to pioneer Wine Country cuisine, but today, he has nothing to do with the daily operation of the restau-

The ingenious chef Josh Silvers, of Jackson's Bar and Bistro.

Expensive; Cuisine: California) This restaurant, tucked in Montgomery Village shopping center, manages to have a hopping night life, with people elbowing for a spot at the bar. The food is also great, which is a draw. Specialties revolve around a rotisserie and include prime rib for two, sweet-and-sour roasted duck, and Tuscan-styled baby-back ribs.

MOMBO'S PIZZA (www.mombospizza.com, 707-528-3278 & 707-823-7492, 1880 Mendocino Ave. Santa Rosa, CA & 560 Gravenstein Hwy N. Sebastopol, CA; Price: Inexpensive; Cuisine: Italian) Great pizza here. Thin crust. Divine. If you're worried about calories, there's even an offer to "lighten up" your pizza" and tone down your pie with less cheese and fewer toppings at a 20 percent discount. Mombo's also has tasty sandwiches, including hot meatball and hot Italian sausage. This recently won a contest of local bests, which means something because the locals bring to the table discerning pizza palates.

RENDEZ-VOUS BISTRO (707-526-7700, 614 4th St., Santa Rosa, CA 95401; Price: Moderate to Expensive; Cuisine: French) This is a hot spot in downtown Santa Rosa; a lively crowd makes it sometimes hard to snag a table. The bistro is no match for Thomas Keller's Bouchon in Yountville, which makes you feel like you're in Paris. While Rendez-Vous Bistro is more like Disney World's Epcot Center, it still has its place. The restaurant plays up local artisans and produce from farms, making French classics like coq au vin, cassoulet, and crepes.

rant. His protégé, Jeff Madura, lacks Ash's brilliance, but the restaurant remains a destination. Madura emphasizes local ingredients and strives to make each entrée visually beautiful. The menu is ever changing but offers imaginative salads and pastas, lighter seafood dishes, and hearty steak and pork chops. The wine list is one of the best in Wine Country, and the by-the-glass selection is excellent. The service is attentive and pampering. The setting is a bucolic site next to Vintners Inn, with vineyard views through French windows and plenty of outdoor dining when weather permits.

MONTI'S (www.starksrestaurants.com, 707-568-4404, 714 Village Ct., Santa Rosa, CA 95405; Price: Moderate to

ROSSO (www.rossopizzeria.com, 707-544-3221, Creekside Center, 53 Montgomery Dr., Santa Rosa, CA 95401; Price: Moderate to Expensive; Cuisine:

Wood-fired pizza is a house specialty at Rosso. Dan Delgado

Italian.) If you want to travel to Italy without a passport, this is the place to be. The food here has more than an Italian accent. It's fluent. The pizza is true Neapolitan style, crisp and yeasty. And other dishes are equally impressive, like the smoked and braised beef short ribs with soft polenta and the whole over-roasted Dungeness crab. The brick oven is productive and a great visual. The wine list has a good supply of imports and local favorites offering over 100 wines at reasonable prices.

SANTI RESTAURANT (www.santi restaurant.com, 707-528-1549, 2097 Stagecoach Rd., Santa Rosa, CA; Price: Moderate to Expensive; Cuisine: Italian) This is a crossroads for people who love all things Italian. With Traverso's Gourmet Foods & Liquors as its next-door neighbor, Santi's and surrounds could be Santa Rosa's Little Italy. Foodies will relish the authentic Italian dishes at Santi, which include Ligurian seafood stew, pasta, and *piatti*. The food is exceptional, and while the service lags on occasion, we have faith it will correct itself over time. The decor is bright and airy, but in nice weather, nothing beats the patio dining. This is a smart Santa Rosa pick.

STARK'S STEAKHOUSE (www .starkssteakhouse.com, 707-546-5100, 521 Adams St., Santa Rosa, CA; Price: Moderate to Expensive; Cuisine: Steakhouse) Stark's is playing to the millennials, the offspring of the baby boomers, a young urban population that love the classics and cocktails in equal measure. Here prime and dry aged steaks are the rage. The owners— Mark and Terri Stark—have a restaurant empire in Sonoma County. There's a page on their website devoted to it. They include Willi's Wine Bar and Monti's Rotisserie & Bar in Santa Rosa, and Willi's Seafood & Raw Bar in Healdsburg. These entrepreneurs have it figured out, pairing clever entrées with top-rate service.

PETITE SYRAH BISTRO (www .syrahbistro.com, 707-568-4002, 205 5th St., Santa Rosa, CA 95401; Price:

Expensive; Cuisine: French and American) Syrah will delight serious Syrah drinkers, who spend as much time lingering over the wine list as they do the menu. Of course, the wine list has a fine selection of Syrahs, with key French Rhone wines, even though it's weighted to California. The prices are fair, but there could be a better selection by the glass. Situated in the historic City 205 Building, the restaurant is rustic-chic, with a peaked ceiling, wooden beams, modern art, and an open kitchen. The food, on the whole, is impressive. Good picks include the pan-roasted Petaluma chicken breast and the grilled lamb sirloin. There's always a good selection of local artisanal cheeses, and desserts are well executed. Service couldn't be better—prompt and intelligent. Syrah is a fine addition to the dining scene in Wine Country, particularly with the addition

Diners indulge at Syrah Bistro.

of its new Petite Syrah Wine Shop attached to the restaurant. It's fun to order and then shop while you're waiting for dinner.

WILLI'S WINE BAR (www.willis winebar.net, 707-526-3096, 4404 Old Redwood Hwy. Santa Rosa, CA 95403; Price: Expensive; Cuisine: Eclectic) This roadhouse-style restaurant is always packed with locals and tourists alike. The interior, done in dark wood and warm colors, fits like a pair of jeans, and there's a soothing patio out back when the weather cooperates. The kitchen offers a large menu of small plates and takes its influence from Asia and the Mediterranean. There's always something intriguing and intensely flavored on the table, whether it's Tuscan pork riblets, Dungeness crab tacos, or foie gras "poppers." There's a fine wine list, which also has an international point of view, and many wines are available by the glass.

ZAZU (www.zazurestaurant.com, 707-523-4814, 3535 Guerneville Rd., Santa Rosa, CA 95401; Price: Expensive; Cuisine: Northern Italian, California) Zazu blends delicious American classics such as buttermilk mashed potatoes and grilled sweet corn with creative variations on lamb, seafood, pork, and duck. Be sure to try the flat iron steak with blue cheese ravioli and sautéed chard. Chef-owners John Stewart and Duskie Estes, who also run the equally good Bovolo in Healdsburg, are passionate about rustic Italian food, making *sopressata* and *coppa* by hand, for example. There are about 150 wines on the list, and local producers are featured extensively. Prices range from moderate to expensive. The decor of Zazu is country chic with eclectic furnishings, and the service is warm but crisply attentive.

North Sonoma Wineries: Russian River Region

See page 199 to view this map.

WINERIES

Santa Rosa offers a range of tasting opportunities, from giant Kendall-Jackson to boutique Siduri, with many in between. Our list is heavy on the boutiques, where you can enjoy hand-crafted wines and get a peek at how they're produced. Your Santa Rosa sipping escapade begins here.

CAROL SHELTON WINES (www .carolshelton.com, 707-575-3441, 3354-B Coffey Lane, Santa Rosa, CA 95403; Tasting and Tours: Daily by appointment 11–4) Carol Shelton was assistant winemaker of Healdsburg's Rodney Strong when she decided she wanted to be her own boss. In 2000 Carol and her husband, Mitch Mackenzie, a former software engineer, launched the brand Carol Shelton Wines, specializing in powerhouse zinfandel. Their bottlings have whimsical names like Wild Thing, which is produced using only wild yeasts found on organic grapes. Another bottling, Karma Zin, refers to the good luck Shelton had in finding a 100-plus-year-old vineyard in the Russian River Valley. Shelton produces roughly 5,000 cases a year, making her operation decidedly boutique. Call for same-day appointments. You won't be disappointed.

DE LOACH VINEYARDS (www .deloachvineyards.com, 707-526-9111, 800-441-9298, 1791 Olivet Rd., Santa Rosa, CA 95401; Tasting: Daily 10–4:30) After the French wine company Boisset bought this winery from Cecil De Loach in 2003, people didn't know what to expect. The De Loach

Duskie Estes and John Stewart of Zazu and Bovolo fame.

family had been making wines since the mid-1970s but fell on hard financial times and the wines began to suffer. In just a few years, Boisset has turned things around dramatically. The chardonnays and pinot noirs are classic Russian River: supple, rich, and elegant. All of the De Loach wines are available in the tasting room located in the handsome and grand redwood building at the end of a long drive embraced by vineyards.

KENDALL-JACKSON WINE CENTER (www.kj.com, 707-571-8100, 5007 Fulton Rd., Fulton, CA 95439; Tasting: Daily 10–5) Kendall-Jackson is a major force in California wine, particularly in its home base of Sonoma County. K-J, as it's known, operates several wineries in the area and uses this faux chateau as a visitors' center. It's rather Disney-like in its notion of grandeur, but the garden is lovely. Inside, you can taste a wide range of

K-J wines. Be sure to try the fleshy yet crisp sauvignon blanc.

SIDURI (www.siduri.com, 707-578-3882, 980 Airway Court, Suite C, Santa Rosa CA 95403; Tasting and Tours: Daily by appointment 10–3) The name *Siduri* comes from the Babylonian goddess of wine. Adam and Dianna Lee, two wine lovers, thought it was a fitting name for their house of pinot noir. They began modestly, with a small quantity of pinot from the 1994 vintage, and now produce pinot from vineyards as far north as Oregon's Willamette Valley and as far south as Santa Barbara County. These lush pinots are pricey but well worth the *dinero.* Siduri is a gravity-flow winery

Dianna and Adam Lee are the duo behind Siduri.

that operates out of a no-frills warehouse, and it's interesting to tour. A footnote: Siduri also produces a label called Novy, a nonpinot family venture. Varietals include Syrahs, zins, and grenache.

Palate Adventures

Santa Rosa has much to offer the epicurious.

• *Treasure hunt for boutique wine*
Bottle Barn (www.bottlebarn.com, 707-528-1161, 3331 A. Industrial Dr., Santa Rosa, CA 95403) This warehouse in Santa Rosa has a huge selection, with a few hard-to-find wines and generally bargain prices.

Traverso's Gourmet Foods (www.traverso.com, 707-542-2530, 877-456-7616, 2097 Stagecoach Road, Santa Rosa, CA 95403) This Italian deli doesn't carry a huge selection of wine, but it offers only the best quality in all price ranges. Bill Traverso knows wine but is so unpretentious about it that you don't have to pretend you do. Traverso's has the best stock of Italian wines in the region.

• *Explore good eats at highbrow markets and cafés*
Oliver's Markets (www.olivermarkets.com, 707-537-7123, 560 Montecito Center, Santa Rosa, CA 95409; other locations include: 707-284-3530, 461 Stony Point Rd., Santa Rosa, CA. 95401; Oliver's in Cotati: 707-795-9501, 546 E. Cotati Ave.) These upscale grocery stores may be bigger than others listed, but they're just as food and wine savvy. They carry high-quality food and well-chosen wines. The Cotati store has an ever-popular wine bar where people taste wines, with winemakers often there to provide running commentary. Winemaker Gina Gallo of Gallo of Sonoma is a frequent guest.

Pacific Market (707-546-3663, 1465 Town and Country Drive, Santa Rosa, CA., 95404) These stores are meccas for those who crave sophisticated cuisine. There's fresh produce, fish, meat, and a great assortment of pastas, sushi, and baked goods, with wine sections touting regional wines. Just order dinner—

chicken Marsala, scalloped and baked veggies—warm it up, and impress your family and friends.

Traverso's Gourmet Foods (www.traversos.com, 707-542-2530, 877-456-7616, 2097 Stagecoach Road, Santa Rosa, CA 95403) Traverso's has evolved into the county's best gourmet deli and wine shop, never losing touch with its Italian roots. Dangling from the ceiling are prosciutto and flags of Italy. The deli case is a painting of salads, ravioli, and hearty meats. Sandwiches are marvelous.

> **Insider Secret:**
> Shop like a local at the Saturday- and Wednesday-morning **Santa Rosa Farmers Market,** where you'll find fresh everything— coffee, fruit, vegetables, fish, and baked goods. (Wed. & Sat. 8:30 AM to noon. Veterans Bldg East Parking Lot, 1351 Maple Avenue)

Village Bakery (707-527-7654, 1445 Town & Country Dr., Santa Rosa, CA) Tasty quiches and savory pastries, pear and ginger muffins, and Swedish cardamom rolls. Caloric, but good.

Michelle Marie's Patisserie (www.michellemaries.com, 707-575-1214, 2404 Magowan Dr., Santa Rosa, CA 95405) This upscale café serves tasty sandwiches, salads, and soups, and offers inventive desserts and highbrow wedding cakes.

• Have a cup of joe

A'Roma Roasters (www.aromaroasters.com, 707-576-7765, 95 5th St., Santa Rosa, CA 95401) Facing historic Railroad Square, A'Roma is a touch bohemian, with exposed rafters, a copper countertop, and a coffee-bean roaster as a centerpiece. There are lots of tables, and you'll find yourself ogling goodies such as the chocolate decadent torte.

Flying Goat Coffee (www.flyinggoatcoffee.com, 707-575-1202, 10 4th Street, Santa Rosa, CA 95401) This cozy coffee shop in Santa Rosa's historic Railroad Square has great lattes and impressive French pressed coffee. It's a good place to meet up with friends or go solo to get some work done.

• Sample what's on tap

Russian River Brewing Company (www.russianriverbrewing.com, 707-545-2337, 725 4th St., Santa Rosa, CA 95404) The Russian River Brewing Company has 10 specialty brews on tap, ranging from Damnation, a Belgian-style ale, to Pliny the Elder, a double IPA. Brewmaster Vinnie Cilurzo is passionate about what he does. Cilurzo is experimenting with aging beer in wine barrels to make his brews more complex. Eats include thin-crusted pizza, calzones, and salads, and the atmosphere of the pub is big, roomy, and energetic.

Third Street Aleworks (www.thirdstreetaleworks.com, 707-523-3060, 610 3rd St., Santa Rosa, CA 95404) A popular downtown hangout, this brewpub has a stylish, almost industrial atmosphere, with polished-metal highlights and an open balcony. Third Street makes some great beer, including the Annadel pale ale. The food is better than most pubs, particularly the pizza and the spicy Cajun selections. If the weather is good, there's plenty of room on the patio, and in the balcony there are two pool tables and large communal tables.

• Take your appetite around the world

ASIAN

The best Chinese in Wine Country is found at Gary Chu's (707-526-5840, www
.garychus.com, 611 5th St., Santa Rosa, CA). The room is an elegant blend of Chinese and art deco, and the food is stylishly gourmet. Impeccable ingredients are
cooked with light sautés instead of oppressive sauces. Try the spicy plum sauce
pork. An amazing Japanese food restaurant, owned by Gary Chu, is Osake (www
.garychus.com, 707-542-8282, 2446 Patio Ct., Santa Rosa, CA), which is just off
busy Farmers Lane. It has a sleek, upscale decor and innovative cuisine. Another
great stop is Sushi To Dai For (707-576-9309, 110 4th Street, Santa Rosa, CA).
Tasty sushi. Clever presentations.

MEXICAN

In Sonoma County, chains dominate, and the results are less than impressive. The
Cantina (707-523-3663, 500 4th St., Santa Rosa, CA 95401) is a slick, brick palace
with an active bar and a heated patio. A better chain experience is at Chevys (www
.chevys.com, 707-571-1082, 24 4th St., Santa Rosa, CA 95401). The food isn't
authentic, but it's fresh and nicely done, especially the fajitas. Taqueria Santa Rosa
(www.taqueriasantarosa.com, 707-575-5793, 711 Stonypoint Rd., Suite 5, Santa
Rosa, CA. 95403; another location: 707-538-2642, 791 Montiecito Ave., Santa
Rosa, CA. 95409) uses whole beans, not canned refried beans, and grilled meat.

• Satisfy your urge for New York pizza

La Vera (707-575-1113, www.laverapizza.com, 629 4th St., Santa Rosa, CA 95404)
For those who demand New York–style pizza, there's La Vera. The cheese stretches for a city block, and the meats are explosions of pepperoni and sausage. The
crust is that perfect unison of crunchy and chewy. The atmosphere is more formal
than most pizzerias, with polished brass and wood.

• Make the seasonal scene

If there's one thing they know how to do in Wine Country, it's throw a party. There
are enough festivals and fairs to keep you busy all year. Here, we list some of the
most popular seasonal attractions.

Sonoma Valley Harvest Fair (www.harvestfair.org, 707-545-4200, Sonoma
County Fairgrounds, 1350 Bennett Valley Rd., Santa Rosa, CA 95401) The fair
brings in top wine experts from around the country. Then local wine buffs gather
to compare their taste buds to those of the judges. This is great fun in October.
There's also plenty of food, and the annual grape stomping contest is a crazy
attraction. Admission.

Harmony Festival (www.harmonyfestival.com, 707-542-4200, Sonoma County
Fairgrounds, 1350 Bennett Valley Rd., Santa Rosa, CA 95401) An only-in-Califor-
nia type of event, this celebration of food, music, and "lifestyle"—an annual June
fair—includes everything from puppet theater to psychic palm readers. Admission.

Sonoma County Fair (www.sonomacountyfair.com, 707-545-4200, Sonoma
County Fairgrounds, 1350 Bennett Valley Rd., Santa Rosa, CA 95401) Sonoma
County practically shuts down for two weeks every July as thousands pour in from
the countryside for food, music, rides, blue-ribbon animals, and produce. You can
even bet on horse races.

To Do

Check out these great attractions and activities . . .

SHOPPING

Santa Rosa's downtown is on the cusp of a revival, with the action revolving around the Barnes & Noble bookstore in the old Rosenberg department.

What was once just a cozy mix of bookstores and coffeehouses is now filling in with interesting gift shops and clothing stores—stores that appear to have staying power. Our favorites: Barnes & Noble (707-576-7494, 700 4th St., Santa Rosa, CA 95404) appeals to the tourist, with expanded sections on local authors, local travel, and local wineries. The Pottery Studio (707-576-7102, 632 4th St., Santa Rosa, CA 95404) allows you to play artist: select a ceramic piece, paint it, and fire it in the kiln. Corrick's (707-546-2423, 637 4th St., Santa Rosa, CA 95404) features upscale gift items and office supplies in one shop. E. R. Sawyer (707-546-0372, 638 4th St., Santa Rosa, CA 95404) sells fine jewelry and watches—even waterproof watches. Snoopy's Gallery & Gift Shop (www.snoopygift.com, 707-546-3385,1665 West Steele Lane, Santa Rosa, CA 95403) offers a wide selection of *Peanuts* memorabilia, attire, comforters, prints, and novelty items. If you're a fan of Charles M. Schulz and the *Peanuts* strip, you won't want to miss this shop. Hampton Court Essential Luxuries (707-578-9416, 631 4th St., Santa Rosa, CA 95404) carries obscure European fragrances, bath and body lotions, and even romantic clothing. California Luggage Co. (707-528-8600, 609 4th St., Santa Rosa, CA 95404) carries a broad range of luggage plus convenient travel necessities. It also does repairs for travelers passing through. The Last Record Store (707-525-1963, 1899-A Mendocino Ave., Santa Rosa, CA 95401) sells CDs, cassettes, and records, and its eclectic inventory includes rock, jazz, classical, world music, blues, and Celtic music. Whistle Stop Antiques (707-542-9474, 130 4th St., Santa Rosa, CA 95401) is a collective with some 35 dealers offering collectibles and general line of furniture. Sonoma Outfitter (707-528-1920, 145 3rd St., Santa Rosa, CA 95401) features clothing for men and women, with lines such as Patagonia and Sigrid Olsen. Outdoor gear includes kayaks and camping equipment. Hot Couture (707-528-7247, 101 3rd St., Santa Rosa, CA 95401) has vintage clothing that dates back to the early 1900s up through the 1960s. Disguise the Limit (707-575-1477, 100 4th St., Santa Rosa, CA 95401) carries theatrical goods, gag gifts, and clothing for the avant garde. While few tourists find their way there, Montgomery Village in Santa Rosa has become a popular place for locals to shop for clothing, home and garden accessories, and gifts. The outdoor shopping center encompasses about four blocks, so the best way to shop it is to stroll through it. Upbeat shops include Ireko, an upscale home and garden shop; and clothing stores such as J. Jill and Chico's for the hip yet professional woman.

CULTURAL OUTINGS

• *Take an architectural tour*

Many of Santa Rosa's great buildings were lost in the 1906 earthquake, though many historic structures on McDonald Avenue on the west edge of downtown survived. Alfred Hitchcock filmed *Shadow of a Doubt* in Santa Rosa. Downtown has changed considerably since then, but the McDonald Avenue residential area, shown extensively in the film, remains the city's architectural prize. Just west of downtown is a lovely neighborhood of large homes, wide streets, and tall trees. The centerpiece is Mableton, at 1015 McDonald. Built in 1878, it was inspired by the plantation homes of Mississippi.

• See it on the big screen

Airport Cinemas, Stadium 12 (707-522-0330, 409 Aviation Blvd., Santa Rosa, CA 95403) This 12-screen complex has stadium seating and is one of the best in Wine Country. It even has a café.

Roxy, Stadium 14 (707-522-0330, 85 Santa Rosa Ave., Santa Rosa, CA 95404) This state-of-the art cinema has it all: great sound and projection plus stadium seating with rocking chairs. The place to see the latest action blockbuster and it has a café to boot.

Rialto Cinemas (707-525-4840, www.rialtocinemas.com, 551 Summerfield Rd., Santa Rosa, CA. 95405) It's a venue for independent, foreign, classic and popular movies.

• Take in a local exhibit

Santa Rosa Junior College Gallery (707-527-4298, www.santarosa.edu-art-gallery, 1501 Mendocino Ave., Santa Rosa, CA 94503) Here you'll find group shows by faculty and students.

Charles M. Schulz Museum (www.schulzmuseum.org, 707-579-4452, 2301 Hardies Lane, Santa Rosa, CA 95403) This museum gives you a peek at where the late Charles Schulz actually created the *Peanuts* cast of characters. It also has galleries of comic strips and even a video nook to watch the *Peanuts* television specials. If you're a comic strip buff, you won't want to miss this museum.

> **Insider Secret:**
> Charles Schulz witnessed the heated debate over *Running Fence,* a 24-mile-long installation in Sonoma by the environmental artist Christo, and ultimately created a comic strip in 1978 with the final panel showing Snoopy's house wrapped in the white nylon fabric used in the Christo project. Here's the upshot: copies of a Christo-wrapped Snoopy house are for sale in the **Charles M. Schulz Museum**'s gift shop.

The Charles M. Schultz Museum pays homage to the creator of *Peanuts,* a Santa Rosa native. Photo by Stephanie Shea courtesy of the Charles M. Schulz Museum and Research Center

• Dig the history

Luther Burbank Home and Gardens (www.lutherburbank.org, 707-524-5224, 204 Santa Rosa Ave., CA 95404) Plant genius Luther Burbank remains Santa Rosa's favorite son. Seventy-five years after his death, buildings and businesses bear his name. At the turn of the 20th century his fame was international. Burbank arrived from his native Massachusetts in 1877. In a letter home he wrote—and Santa Rosans love to quote this: "I firmly believe . . . this is the chosen spot of all this earth as far as nature is concerned."

Sonoma County Museum (www.sonomacountymuseum.org, 707-579-1500, 425 7th St., Santa Rosa, CA 95401) On the National Register of Historic Places, the structure is a mix of Spanish and Roman influences, and it's considered one of the few remaining examples of classic Federal-style architecture in California. Lobby displays detail the history of the building and its laborious

The Luther Burbank Home and Gardens is a Santa Rosa standout.

move two blocks north. The main exhibit room offers rotating displays keyed to Sonoma history. This building also houses the Museum of Contemporary Art, formerly housed in the Wells Fargo Center of the Arts.

California Indian Museum & Cultural Center (www.cimcc.org, 707-527-4479, Santa Rosa Junior College, 5250 Aero Dr., Santa Rosa, CA 95403) Holdings here include artifacts and current works by Native American artisans.

• Go symphonic

Santa Rosa Symphony (www.santarosasymphony.com, 707-546-8742, Wells Fargo Center for the Arts, 50 Santa Rosa Ave., Santa Rosa, CA 95404) Bruno Ferrandis is the conductor. Musicians—all of respectable talent—come from around the Bay Area. All are professionals with day jobs; others keep busy roaming from one orchestra to another. Famed soloists are featured in each concert. Recent soloists have included guitarist David Tanenbaum, pianist Andre Watts, and famed cellist Yo-Yo Ma. The Wells Fargo Center for the Arts, a former church, is a large hall of about fifteen hundred seats. The acoustics aren't what they might be, but the symphony strives to overcome the limitations.

• Paint the town red

There's plenty to do after 10 PM in Santa Rosa. The Friday edition of the *Santa Rosa Press Democrat* is a good source for what's happening.

> **Insider Secret:**
> Imagine yourself in the company of Who's Who in 1915. Now take a glimpse of a photo at the **Luther Burbank Home and Gardens** that chronicles a visit paid to the plant genius by inventor extraordinaire Thomas Edison and industrialists Henry Ford and Harvey S. Firestone.

Santa Rosa is the center of Sonoma County's nightlife, although the outlying areas have a number of fine night spots. Sonoma County's premier stage is the Wells Fargo Center for the Arts (www.wellsfargocenterarts.org, 707-546-3600, 50 Mark West Springs Rd., Santa Rosa, CA 95403). Once a sprawling church complex, the center's main stage is the largest hall in the area, seating about 1,500 people. Recent headliners have included k.d. lang, Collective Soul, Tori Amos, Bonnie Raitt, and B.B. King.

Try the Last Day Saloon (www.lastdaysaloon.com, 707-545-5876, 120 Fifth St., Santa Rosa, CA 95401), which has the best Bay Area rock and blues bands. The Vine (www.vinesantarosa.com, 707-527-6600, 707-393-7104, 528 7th St., Santa Rosa, CA 95401) draws a college crowd with its entertainment, music, cocktails, beer, and wine.

Santa Rosa's hotels are another good source for late-night fun. Try the Flamingo Lounge (www.flamingoresort.com, 707-545-8530, 2777 4th St., Santa Rosa, CA 95405) and Equus Lounge Bar of Fountain Grove Inn (707-566-3169, 101 Fountain Grove Pkwy., Santa Rosa, CA 95403) There are happening pubs in Santa Rosa. Try Third Street Aleworks (707-523-3060, 610 Third St., Santa Rosa, CA 95404). Check out the second floor of The Cantina (707-523-3663, 500 4th St., Santa Rosa, CA 95404) if you like to dance to DJs spinning 1970s tunes and modern R&B. The crowd is young.

• *See a play*

Summer Repertory Theatre (www.summerrep.com, 707-527-4418, 1501 Mendocino Ave., Santa Rosa, CA 95401) No one has a bigger local following than SRT. Every summer, the Santa Rosa Junior College organizes this three-ring circus of theater, bringing in talented student actors and technical staff from around the country. Opening several major productions in four weeks and performing them in a repertory format packs a year's experience into two months.

6th Street Playhouse (www.6thstreetplayhouse.com, 707-523-4185, 52 West 6th St., Santa Rosa, CA, 95401) This is a relatively new addition to the Sonoma theater scene but many of the players involved are veterans. Recent productions include *The Grapes of Wrath*.

RECREATIONAL FUN

• *Roam Wine Country aloft . . .*

Soaring silently above the vineyards and rolling hills of Wine Country in a hot-air balloon is an experience you won't quickly forget. Up & Away Hot Air Ballooning (www.up-away.com, 707-836-0171, 800-711-2998) offers daily flights for small groups. Balloons typically fly through the Russian River Valley.

• *. . . Or on a bike*

Want to slow the pace of your Wine Country tour? Try a bike. Annadel State Park (707-939-3911) at times has more mountain bikers than runners on its trails. Many local parks have extensive bike trails, including Spring Lake County Park in Santa Rosa (707-539-8092). Two excellent guides for specific trails are *Sonoma County Bike Trails* and *Rides In and Around the Napa Valley*.

Many inns offer bikes for casual day trips, and most bike shops rent two-wheelers for the day. Also, Getaway Adventures (www.getawayadventures.com, 707-942-0332, 800-499-2453, 2228 Northpoint Pkwy., Santa Rosa, CA 95407) organizes tours through Napa and Sonoma counties, suggests routes, and includes helmets and the like. It offers wine tours called "Sip and Cycle," and hiking, kayaking, and other theme tours. Another option for bike rental is Rincon Cyclery (www.rinconcyclery.com, 707-538-0868, 800-965-BIKE, 4927 Sonoma Hwy., Suite H, Santa Rosa, CA 95409)

• Splash around

Lake Ralphine (707-543-3424, Howarth Park, 630 Summerfield Rd., Santa Rosa, CA 95409) This is a popular spot for water activities, from boating to feeding ducks. Stocked with fish, this small man-made lake has a city-run boat rental where rowboats, canoes, and paddleboats are available for a minimal fee. Powerboats are not permitted.

Spring Lake (707-539-8092, off Montgomery Dr., Santa Rosa, CA 95409) This lovely 75-acre lake is open only to canoes, rowboats, and kayaks—all of which can be rented during the summer. Windsurfing and rafting are also allowed. There's a separate lagoon for swimming. For boat rentals, call 707-543-3424.

• Grab the kids and go

Kids and kids at heart can find all sorts of fun, from pony rides and water slides to a planetarium show guaranteed to stretch the imagination.

Howarth Park (707-543-3425, Montgomery and Summerfield Rds., Santa Rosa, CA 95409) This popular, city-run park offers a merry-go-round; pony rides; a petting zoo; a small railroad; play and picnic areas; paddleboats, canoes, and rowboats to rent; and ducks to feed on Lake Ralphine. Activities are open on the weekends in the winter.

Planetarium (707-527-4465, Santa Rosa Junior College, Room 2001 Lark Hall, 1501 Mendocino Ave., Santa Rosa, CA 95401) This excellent planetarium is open to the public on weekends during the school year. Shows are offered at 7 and 8:30 PM Friday and Saturday, and 1:30 and 3 PM Sunday during the fall and spring academic year. There are no reservations, so arrive early to park. Admission: $4 general, $2 students and seniors, no children under 5 admitted.

Safari West (www.safariwest.com, 707-579-2551, 3115 Porter Creek Rd., Santa Rosa, CA 95404) This 400-plus acre park features 150 species, including 400 rare and endangered animals. Not a drive-through animal park, this is a 2.5-hour tour that's comparable to a real African safari.

Scandia Family Fun Center (www.scandiafunland.com, 707-584-1361, 5301 Redwood Dr., Rohnert Park, CA 94920) Here you'll find little Indy racers, miniature golf, baseball batting cages, bumper boats, spin bumper cars, and a game arcade. This is a favorite recreation center for kids and families and is packed on summer weekends. There's even a Viking Pizza vendor inside. Separate fees for each activity; hours vary.

• Tee off

Golf courses cover the rich valleys and rolling hills of Wine Country as eagerly as vineyards. One of the region's favorite recreational activities, golf can be played year-round in this mild climate.

Bennett Valley Golf Course (707-528-3673, 3330 Yulupa Ave., Santa Rosa, CA 94505) This municipal course offers 18 holes, par 72; three pros; a shop; a driving range; a putting green; and a restaurant and lounge. Reserve one week ahead.

Oakmont Golf Club (707-539-0415, 7025 Oakmont Dr., Santa Rosa, CA 95409) This club comprises two private and public 18-hole championship courses, par 72, designed by Ted Robinson; four pros; two shops; a driving range; and lessons. Reservations are suggested.

Sonoma County adamantly maintains its rural flavor, despite its growing population and worldwide tourist appeal. There is plenty of interest in horse breeding, competition, and riding.

Armstrong Woods Pack Station (www.redwoodhorses.com, 707-887-2939, Armstrong Redwoods State Natural Reserve, 17000 Armstrong Woods Rd., P.O. Box 287, Guerneville, CA 95446) Offers rentals for trail rides through Armstrong Redwoods State Reserve and Austin Creek State Recreation Area. Also offers trail rides.

Armstrong Redwoods State Reserve.

Horse-racing fans converge each summer at the Sonoma County Fair (707-545-4200, www.sonomacounty fair.com, 1350 Bennett Valley Rd., Santa Rosa, CA 95404) to watch California's fastest horses vying for a purse of nearly $2 million. During the rest of the year, the fairgrounds offer The Jockey Club (707-524-6340), with simultaneous broadcasting of races at Golden Gate Fields, Bay Meadows, and Hollywood Park.

• *Strap on your skates*

The late famed cartoonist and ice-skating buff Charles Schulz built the Redwood Empire Ice Arena (707-546-7147, www.snoopyhomeice.com, 1667 W. Steel Ln., Santa Rosa, CA 95403) in 1969, and it's one of Sonoma County's most popular spots. The rink, surrounded by walls painted with Alpine scenes, is the site for recreational and would-be Olympic skaters, birthday parties, and holiday ice shows with professional figure skaters. Next door is Snoopy's Gallery & Gift Shop (707-546-3385), filled with every conceivable item relating to Snoopy and the Peanuts gang as well as skating gear, including high-tech in-line skates.

• *Hit the tennis court*

La Cantera Racquet and Swim Club (www.lacanteraraquetclub.com, 707-544-9494, 3737 Montgomery Dr., Santa Rosa, CA 95405) Courts are open to members and guests. Altogether, there are 12 courts, four of them lit. There's an on-site pro, leagues, and tournaments.

Montecito Heights Health and Racquet Club (707-526-0529, www.monte citoheights.com, 2777 4th St., Santa Rosa, CA 95405) Courts are open to members and guests. There are five unlit courts, an on-site pro, leagues, and tournaments.

Santa Rosa Public Courts (707-543-3282, Santa Rosa, CA 94928) are available at Howarth, Finley, and Galvin parks, Burbank Playground, Santa Rosa Junior College, and Santa Rosa and Montgomery high schools.

PART III

Transportation & Climate

GETTING HERE & GETTING AROUND

GRIDLOCK IS NOT the rarity it used to be in Wine Country, so it pays to know your way around. Highways 101 and 29, the main thoroughfares through Napa and Sonoma counties, are always hectic, especially on weekends. In addition, the terrain conspires against smooth travel—any approach requires a minor mountain expedition.

Perhaps that's why in the late 1700s the earliest explorers came by water. The Sonoma coast was the area's first highway marker, and as sailing ships from around the globe made for the New World, the Napa and Petaluma rivers, which connect with San Pablo Bay, allowed early settlers a fast way inland.

By the mid-1800s, trails from the Central Valley took travelers along Clear Lake to Bodega Bay as well as south and east along the bay to Benicia. Carts and stagecoaches brought folks along primitive roads, stirring up dust in the summer and churning up mud in the winter. By the 1860s, steamships were chugging up and down the Napa and Petaluma rivers, but soon railroads steamed onto the scene, with names like Southern Pacific and San Francisco North Pacific, connecting the towns of the two budding counties to the East Bay.

The automobile changed everything, for better and for worse. Sonoma County remained somewhat innocently isolated from San Francisco—it's a long loop around that bay—until the big day in May 1937, when the Golden Gate Bridge opened a speedier route north, and Napa and Sonoma counties became one of the travel destinations for San Francisco and for the world. Today, in fact, 50 percent of the people who visit Wine Country each year originate their getaway in San Francisco.

There are numerous ways to get to and get around Wine Country. Let us be your guide.

Getting to Napa & Sonoma
By Air
Air travelers bound for Wine Country can arrive at and depart from one of three major airports handling numerous domestic and international airlines, and there's

LEFT: Drink in this wine culture.

also a regional airport serving the area.

San Francisco International (SFO), Oakland International (OAK), and Sacramento International (SMF) are all within easy driving distance of Napa and Sonoma counties. Charles M. Schulz Sonoma County Airport is a regional airport located just a few miles northwest of Santa Rosa: 707-546-7740. It's home to Horizon Air, which makes two daily flights to LAX in Los Angeles and a daily flight to Las Vegas, Portland, and Seattle/Tacoma. The regional airport is named after the famed cartoonist of the *Peanuts* comic strip, who lived and worked in Santa Rosa for more than 30 years.

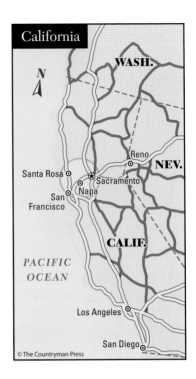

By Car

Although planes and trains will bring you to the threshold of Wine Country, a car is a necessity in Wine Country proper. Public transportation is limited, and the landscape is so vast that you'll need your own wheels. Traffic is common on Saturday and Sunday and during peak summer months, so an ambitious itinerary can be cut short by the weekend tourist crush.

Renting a Car

Because a car is almost a requirement in Wine Country, visitors arriving by air inevitably rent a vehicle. Most major rental companies, of course, work out of the metro airports, and they're typically helpful in plotting routes and will often supply drivers with basic maps to reach their destinations. Just in case, here are a few directions:

San Francisco International Airport: To find your way to Wine Country from the Bay Area's largest airport, take Highway 101 north into San Francisco. The highway empties onto the streets, so watch the signs carefully. Continue through the city across the Golden Gate Bridge, and you'll soon find yourself in central Sonoma County. To reach the town of Sonoma or the Napa Valley, take Highway 37 in Novato, and connect with Highway 121.

Miles: 72 to central Sonoma County; 82 to Napa Valley.

Time: 90 minutes.

Oakland International Airport: To reach Napa County and the city of Sonoma, take I-80 north through Oakland, and connect with Highway 29 north. For Napa, stay on Highway 29, and for the city of Sonoma, take Highway 12/121. To reach central Sonoma County, take I-80 north through Oakland, exit on I-580, and then connect with Highway 101 north, which takes you into the heart of Sonoma County.

Miles: 82 to central Sonoma County; 46 to Napa Valley.

Time: 1 hour to Sonoma; 45 minutes to Napa.

Sacramento International Airport: Take I-5 south, and connect with

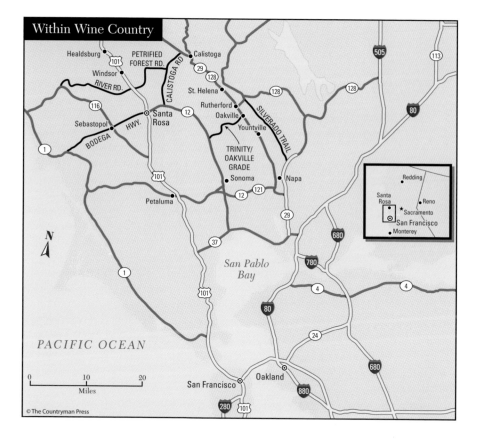

the I-80 west bypass. Follow the signs to San Francisco. Take Highway 12 to Napa, continuing west to the cities of Sonoma and Santa Rosa.

Miles: 61 to Napa; 97 to central Sonoma County.

Time: 90 minutes to Napa; 2 to 2.5 hours to central Sonoma County.

You can also rent a car after arriving in Napa and Sonoma counties. Local information and reservation numbers are listed below. Reservations up to a week in advance are recommended.

Napa County
Budget Rent-A-Car (800-527-0700)
Enterprise Rent-A-Car (707-253-8000)
Hertz (707-265-7575)

Sonoma County
Avis (800-331-1212)
Budget Rent-A-Car (800-527-0700)
Enterprise Rent-A-Car (800-261-7331)
Hertz (707-528-0834 or 800-654-3131)

Airport Shuttle
Here's an alternative to renting a car at the airport: reasonably priced express shuttle buses and vans operate to and from the San Francisco, Oakland, and Sacramento airports. These comfortable vehicles operate 16 to 20 hours a day, seven days a week. Shuttles depart from airports about every one to two hours, depending on the operator, and deliver passengers to selected drop-off points in Wine Country.

One-way fares (cash only) range

from $18 to $35, depending on the operator, the drop-off point, and any excess luggage requirements. Reservations are not usually required, but on weekends and in peak seasons buses fill up, and you may be forced to stand in the aisle. Schedules fluctuate, so it's smart to reserve shuttle services in advance.

Airport Express, SFO to Santa Rosa (707-837-8700, 800-327-2024)

Evans Airport Service, SFO and OAK (Oakland) to Napa (707-255-1559, 707-944-2025, 800-294-6386)

Gateway Express Shuttle (Napa), SMF to Napa 1-800-253-3826, Sacramento International Airport to Napa, scheduled shuttle service on 22-passenger buses to Napa.

California Wine Tours, SFO to the city of Sonoma (707-938-4246)

By Bus

Greyhound bus service to Sonoma and Napa counties is very limited. It's also possible to ride Greyhound to San Francisco, and then make connections on Golden Gate Transit to reach Wine Country. A travel agent will have the most up-to-date information on Greyhound schedules and connections.

Greyhound in San Francisco (1-800-231-2222)

Golden Gate Transit (415-923-2000, 414-455-2000 or 707-541-2000) For travel between San Francisco and Sonoma County; one-way fare from San Francisco to Santa Rosa is $9.70 for Adults and $4.85 for Senior, Disabled, and Youth.

Once inside Wine Country, public bus service is available through Sonoma County Transit and Napa Valley

Bouchon is a little bit of Paris in Yountville.

Plan ahead by making reservations. Tim Fish

Transit. This method of travel could be indispensable for the Wine Country visitor on a tight budget. One drawback: bus stops, which can be few and far between, are usually not close to wineries and other tourist attractions.

One-way fares average between $1 and $2.50, and weekend service is limited. If buses will be your primary form of transportation, it may be essential to gather the most current timetables and route maps, which are updated frequently. The cities of Santa Rosa, Napa, Healdsburg, and Petaluma also offer bus service within their city boundaries.

Napa County
The VINE (800-696-6443, 707-251-2800) The Napa city bus travels mainly along Highway 29 between Calistoga and Vallejo, with bus and ferry connections to and from San Francisco.
VineGo (707-251-2800) Offers limited service between most Napa Valley towns.

Sonoma County
Sonoma County Transit (707-576-7433, 800-345-7433) For travel within Sonoma County.

Santa Rosa Transit (707-543-3333) City bus.
Petaluma Transit (707-778-4460) City bus.
Healdsburg In-City Transit (707-431-3324) City bus.

By Train
Amtrak's westbound *California Zephyr* and north-to-south *Coastal Starlight* trains drop off Napa County–bound passengers in the city of Martinez, about 40 miles south of Napa. Amtrak has continuing ground transportation that delivers passengers directly to Napa but not Sonoma.

For Amtrak information and reservations, call 800-872-7245 (or 800-USA-RAIL) or check the Web site at www.amtrak.com. It's advisable to consult a travel agent for assistance in booking Amtrak, 1151 Pearl St., Napa.

Just for the record, the Napa Valley Wine Train is actually a gourmet restaurant on rails and not a true form of transportation. (See p. 54 for listing.)

By Limousine
The ultimate in personal transportation is the limousine, and for many visitors to Wine Country, chauffeured travel goes hand in hand with wine tasting. For others, the pricey, three-hour ride to the Sonoma coast can be a romantic and unforgettable luxury.

Both Napa Valley and Sonoma County have an abundance of professional limousine services that will map out wine-tasting itineraries for the novice or deliver connoisseurs to wineries of their choosing. Most also offer daylong, fixed-rate touring packages with extras, such as gourmet picnic lunches or evening dining, included in the price. Per-hour rates range from $45 to $165, depending on the limo and the tour. That doesn't include taxes, driver gratuities, parking fees, or bridge tolls. A three- or four-hour minimum is standard, and complimentary champagne is often served. Reservations are required at least two or three days in advance and as much as a week in advance during peak vacationing months. Some recommend booking at least a month ahead of time.

For your added safety, the limousine service you engage should be both licensed and insured. Ask your hotel concierge to recommend a service or talk to your travel agent. Listed below are some of Wine Country's most popular limousine services. Companies may be based in one county, but they frequently take passengers all over Wine Country and beyond.

Napa County
Antique Tours (707-226-9227)
Evans Inc. (707-255-1559)
Executive Limousine Service (707-257-2949)

Sonoma County
California Wine Tours (800-294-6386)
Style N Comfort (707-578-3001, 800-ITS-LIMO)
Ultimate Limousine Service (707-542-5466)
Pure Luxury Limousine Service (707-795-1615)

By Taxi
When buses are too inconvenient and limousines too expensive, call for an old standby: a taxicab. The cab companies below are on duty 24 hours a day, seven days a week. Per-mile fares average $3.

Napa County
Napa Valley Cab (707-257-6444)
Black Tie Taxi (707-259-1000)
Yellow Cab Napa (707-226-3731)

Sonoma County
Bill's Taxi Service (707-869-2177)
Vern's Taxi Service (707-938-8885)
George's Yellow and Checker Taxi's (707-544-4444)
Santa Rosa Taxi (707-579-1212 or 707-206-2006)

Tip: You can contact Bay Area 511 by dialing 511 from your cell or landline to get direct access to traffic info, public transportation, freeway aid, Clipper, Rideshare, bicycling, and Fast-track information. You may also go to 511.org for updated transportation information and advisories.

CLIMATE

The late Luther Burbank, known as the plant wizard, called Napa and Sonoma counties "the chosen spot of all the earth as far as nature is concerned." The moderate weather is a blessing for those who have suffered midwestern and northeastern blizzards. In Napa and Sonoma the winter is cool, with temperatures dipping down to the 40s. The rainy season begins in late December and lingers until April. Of course, the droughts in recent years have made the season somewhat unpredictable, and the locals count raindrops with good cheer. Rain makes for a lush countryside and hillsides ribbed with green vineyards.

Temperature and Precipitation

Average Temperatures

	Napa	Sonoma
October	62.0	62.2
January	47.6	47.2
April	56.6	56.6
July	67.4	70.0

Average Annual Total Precipitation

	Napa	Sonoma
Rain	24.64	29.94
Snow	0	0

Napa County

www.wunderground.com/auto/sfgate/CA/Napa.html

Sonoma County

www.westernwx.com/sonoma
www.sonomawinegrape.org/weather

Information
& Travel Resources

A LITTLE PEACE OF MIND goes a long way in Wine Country. The information compiled in this chapter covers emergencies as well as everyday practical matters. The travel resources will help you get the most out of your Wine Country rambles.

INFORMATION

Hospitals

Healdsburg District General Hospital (707-431-6500, 1375 University Ave., Healdsburg) 24-hour emergency care, with a physician on duty. Call the general number and ask for the Emergency Room.

Petaluma Valley Hospital (707-778-1111, emergency room: 707-778-2634, 400 N. McDowell Blvd., Petaluma) 24-hour emergency care.

Queen of the Valley Hospital (707-252-4411, emergency room: 707-257-4038, 1000 Trancas St., Napa) 24-hour emergency care, with a physician on duty.

Santa Rosa Memorial Hospital (707-546-3210, emergency room: 707-525-5207, 1165 Montgomery Dr., Santa Rosa) 24-hour emergency care, with a physician on duty.

Sonoma Valley Hospital (707-935-5000, emergency room: 707-935-5100, 347 Andrieux St., Sonoma) 24-hour emergency care.

St. Helena Hospital (707-963-3611, emergency room: 707-963-6425, 10 Woodland Road, St. Helena, CA 94574)

Sutter Medical Center of Santa Rosa (707-576-4000, emergency room: 707-576-4040, 3325 Chanate Rd., Santa Rosa) 24-hour emergency care.

Late-Night Food & Fuel

Insomnia after too much gourmet food or wine? Or perhaps you're just a weary traveler looking for a place to gas up. Whatever the case, here are some options for night birds.

LEFT: The winning chardonnay that jolted the wine world at the Paris Tasting of 1976.

Napa County

Lucky Supermarkets (707-255-7767, 1312 Trancas St., Napa, CA 94558)

Bel Aire Shell Service (707-226-1720, 1491 Trancas St., Napa, CA 94558)

Sonoma County

Flamingo Shell (707-542-4456, 2799 4th St., Santa Rosa, CA 95405)

Safeway (707-528-3062, 1799 Marlow Rd., Santa Rosa, CA 95401)

Safeway (707-522-1455, 2751 4th St., Santa Rosa, CA 95405)

Safeway (707-996-0633, 477 W. Napa St., Sonoma, CA 95476)

Radio Stations

KRCB 90.9 FM (707-585-8522, Rohnert Park) National Public Radio and classical and eclectic music

KFGY 92.9 (707-543-0100, Santa Rosa) Country

KJZY 93.7 FM (707-528-9393, Santa Rosa) Light jazz

KRSH 95.5 and 95.9 FM (707-588-0707, Healdsburg) Adult alternative

KNOB 96.7 FM (707-588-0707, Santa Rosa) Adult hits from the 1960s to the present

KVRV 97.7 FM (707-543-0100, Santa Rosa) Classic rock

KXTS 98.7 FM (707-588-0707, Santa Rosa) Hispanic

KVYN 99.3 FM (707-258-1111, Napa) Adult contemporary

KSXY 100.9 (707-588-0707, Middletown/Santa Rosa) Top 40

KZST/100.1 FM (707-528-4434, Santa Rosa) Adult contemporary

KXFX 101.7 FM (707-543-0100, Santa Rosa) Heavy metal/rock

KMHX 104.1 FM (707-543-0100, Santa Rosa) Today's mix

KSRO 1350 AM (707-543-0100, Santa Rosa) News and talk

KVON 1440 AM (707-258-1111, Napa) News, talk, sports

Road Service

Puncture your tire on a broken bottle of 1995 Rafanelli zinfandel? Stranger things have happened. For emergency road service from AAA anywhere in Napa or Sonoma counties, call 800-222-4357. Listed below are other 24-hour emergency road services.

Napa County

Calistoga Towing (707-942-4445)

Vine Towing (707-226-3780)

Sonoma County

ABC Towing (707-433-1700, Healdsburg)

Sebastopol Tow (707-823-1061)

Santa Rosa Towing (707-542-1600)

TRAVEL RESOURCES

Chambers of Commerce and Visitor Bureaus

Napa County

Calistoga Chamber of Commerce (www.calistogachamber.com, 707-942-6333, 1133 Washington St., Calistoga, CA 94515)

Napa Valley Conference and Visitors Bureau (www.napavalley.com, info@napavalley.org, 707-226-5813 ext. 106, 1310 Napa Town Center, Napa, CA 94559

St. Helena Chamber of Commerce (www.sthelena.com, 707-800-799-6456, 1010 Main St., Suite A, St., Helena, CA 94574)

Yountville Chamber of Commerce (www.yountville.com, 707-944-0904, 6484 Washington St., Suite F, Yountville, CA 94599)

Sonoma County

Bodega Bay Area Visitors Center (www.bodegabay.com, 707-875-3866, 850 Hwy. 1, Bodega Bay, CA, 94923)

Healdsburg Chamber of Commerce and Visitors Bureau (www.healdsburg.com, info@healdsburg.com, 707-433-6935 and 800-648-9922, 217 Healdsburg Ave., Healdsburg, CA 95448)

Petaluma Area Chamber of Commerce (www.petalumachamber.com, pacc@petalumachamber.com, 707-762-2785, 6 Petaluma Blvd. North, Suite A2, Petaluma, CA 94952)

Russian River Chamber of Commerce and Visitors Center (www.russianriver.com, news@russianriver.com, 707-869-9000, 16209 1st St., Guerneville, CA 95446)

Korbel Visitor Center (www.russianriver.com, news@russianriver.com, 707-869-9000, 13250 River Rd. (in the Railroad Station), Guerneville, CA 95466)

Santa Rosa Chamber of Commerce (www.santarosachamber.com, chamber@santarosachamber.com, 707-545-1414, 637 1st St., Santa Rosa, CA 95404)

Santa Rosa Convention and Visitor Bureau (visitsantarosa.com, 707-577-8674 and 800-404-7673, 9 4th St., Santa Rosa, CA 95401)

Sebastopol Chamber of Commerce (www.sebastopol.org, info@sebastopol.org, 707-823-3032 and 877-828-4748, 265 S. Main St., Sebastopol, CA 95472)

Sonoma County Tourism Bureau (www.sonomacounty.com, info@sonomacounty.com, 707-522-5800 and 800-576-6662, 3637 Westwind Blvd., Santa Rosa, CA 95403)

Sonoma Valley Visitors Bureau (www.sonomavalley.com, info@sonomavalley.com, 707-996-1090 and 866-966-1090, 453 1st St. E., Sonoma, CA 95476. A second office is now open below Cornerstone Sonoma, 707-933-3010, 23570 Arnold Dr. (Hwy 121), Sonoma, CA 95476)

Guided Tours

Looking for some packaged fun? Consult the tour companies listed here. A wide range of options are available, from bicycle rambles to helicopter tours of Wine Country.

Getaway Adventures (www.getawayadventures.com, 707-568-3040 and 800-499-2453, 2228 Northpoint Pkwy., CA 95407) Day trips priced at $149 per person have bikers pedaling to five or six wineries, with a gourmet lunch to boot. The company also books weekend and four- to six-day bike and multisport trips (biking, hiking, kayaking). Adventurers will find the Pedal 'N Paddle Tour invigorating. It features a half day of kayaking and a half day of bicycling. Rentals are available.

Viviani, Inc. (www.viviani.com, 707-265-1940 or 800-658-9997, 2800 Jefferson St., Napa, CA 94558) This is highbrow travel at its best. Viviani specializes in corporate, incentive, and exclusive events in California' s Wine Country, offering private, customized tours that bestow special access. You'll meet winemakers, hike in private vineyards, and learn the art of *méthode champenoise* that monks perfected so long ago in Champagne. Among its many offerings are half-day winery tours, full-day tours with lunch, and a tour of Napa for those departing from San Francisco.

Wine & Dine Tours (www.wineanddinetour.com, 707-963-8930, 800-946-3868, P.O. Box 204, St. Helena, CA 94574) This tour is for the discriminating traveler who would like to stop in at small boutique wineries in Napa Valley and Sonoma Valley. Most of the wineries are private or by appointment only.

Index